AMERICAN LIGHTHOUSES

HELP US KEEP THIS GUIDE UP TO DATE

Every effort has been made by the authors and editors to make this guide as accurate and useful as possible. However, many things can change after a guide is published—establishments close, phone numbers change, facilities come under new management, etc.

We would love to hear from you concerning your experiences with this guide and how you feel it could be improved and kept up to date. While we may not be able to respond to all comments and suggestions, we'll take them to heart and we'll also make certain to share them with the authors. Please send your comments and suggestions to the following address:

The Globe Pequot Press
Reader Response/Editorial Department
P.O. Box 480
Guilford, CT 06437

Or you may e-mail us at:

editorial@globe-pequot.com

Thanks for your input, and happy travels!

AMERICAN LIGHTHOUSES

A Definitive Guide

Second Edition

PHOTOGRAPHS BY BRUCE ROBERTS

TEXT BY RAY JONES

The
Globe
Pequot
Press

Guilford, Connecticut

Cover photos: (front) Pointe aux Barques, Michigan; (back—from top to bottom) Nobska Point Light, Massachusetts; Ponce de Leon Inlet Light, Florida; Split Rock Light, Minnesota; Alki Point Light, Washington; (back—screen) Whitefish Point, Michigan.

Photo on title page: Eagle Harbor Light, Michigan

All photographs, unless otherwise credited, are by Bruce Roberts.

Page design by Lisa Reneson

Library of Congress Cataloging-in-Publication Data
Roberts, Bruce, date
      American lighthouses: a definitive guide/photographs by Bruce Roberts; text by Ray Jones.—2nd ed.
         p. cm.
      Includes index.
      ISBN 0-7627-2269-X
      1. Lighthouses—United States—Guidebooks. I. Jones, Ray, 1948- II. Title.
VK1023.R63 2002
387.1'55'0973—dc21   2002021551

Manufactured in the United States of America
Second Edition / First Printing

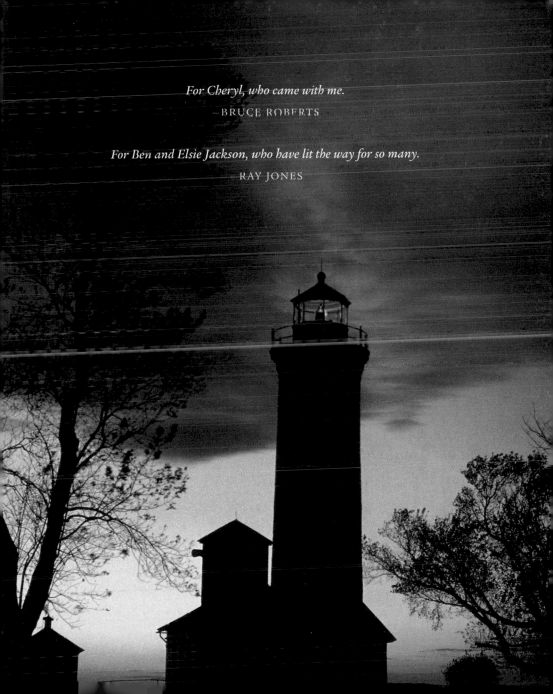

For Cheryl, who came with me.
—BRUCE ROBERTS

For Ben and Elsie Jackson, who have lit the way for so many.
RAY JONES

Acknowledgments

Many thanks to those who supplied photography and other help:
Nancy A. Pizzo; Rick Polad; H. Kent Edwards; Kim Andrews of Harbour Lights; Mark Riddick, New Light Photography; William G. Kaufhold; Bob and Sandra Shanklin, The Lighthouse People; Ben Russell; John W. (Jack) Weil; Frank Parks; Daniel J. Gruszka; Dave Kramer; Lamar C. Bevil, Jr.; Lee Radzak at Split Rock Lighthouse, who was the perfect lighthouse keeper for Bruce's picture; Dick Moehl, president of the Great Lakes Lighthouse Keepers Association; Don Terras of the Grosse Point Lighthouse; Ken Black of the Shore Village Museum in Rockland, Maine; James W. Claflin of Kenrick A. Claflin & Son; Cullen Chambers at Tybee Island Light Station; Dave Snyder, former park historian, Apostle Islands National Lakeshore; Jeanne and George Couglar of the Tibbetts Point Lighthouse; Steve Harrison, historian, Cape Hatteras National Seashore; Tim Harrison of *Lighthouse Digest* magazine and Lighthouse Depot, for supplying photographs of isolated Maine lights that supplemented Bruce's photography; Candace Clifford of the Maritime Initiative; Dane and Judy Alden and Henry Gonzalez for their advice.

A special thanks to Dr. Robert Browning, U.S. Coast Guard Historian, for all his assistance in locating old photos and helping with identification of the lights and many other considerations.

We are especially grateful to Grace McEntee for her invaluable editorial assistance and advice on style.

CONTENTS

The information in this guidebook was confirmed at press time.
We recommend, however, that you call establishments before
traveling to obtain current information.

INTRODUCTION

The Romance of Lighthouses

Very likely tucked away among your most pleasant memories is an evening stroll along a beach, an experience perhaps warmed by the companionship of a friend or a child. Probably you remember the feeling of moist sand under your bare feet, the kiss of a light breeze in your face, or the roar of the sea—in the dark it sounds less like waves striking sand and more like those eternal oceans you hear in a shell. But if there was a lighthouse beacon flashing in the distance, calling to you from the horizon, that part of the memory is especially bright.

Lighthouses and their beacons appeal to our sense of wonder, and as with the ocean itself, we attach a mythological importance to them. Even when we are far inland and away from the shore, the mere image of a lighthouse on a postcard, a stamp, or a company logo will remind us of the sea and of our powerful connection to it.

Nearly everyone, young or old, male or female, sailor or landlubber, is fascinated by lighthouses. And why not? Lighthouses are fun. Lighthouses are filled with meaning and mystery. Among our most historic and romantic structures, they are often located in beautiful places—on spectacular promontories or pristine barrier islands. Many, with their soaring brick walls, intricate steel skeletons, or cozy dwellings covered with Victorian gingerbread, are architectural treasures. Nearly all are more than a century old and some more than two centuries. Most are associated with drama—tragic shipwrecks, heroic rescues, self-sacrifice, and loves lost or found.

Of course, lighthouses have a very practical value for mariners, who still make good use of them. Even nowadays, when radar and satellites make pinpoint navigation possible, seamen are likely to put more faith in what they can see with their own eyes. To understand why this is so, consider that whenever the power goes out at home, we immediately go groping through drawers searching for candles and matches. We need light; otherwise, we'll start bumping into things.

Anyone who has ever experienced total darkness, as sailors do on a moonless, starless night, will know what it's like to feel utterly lost and cut off from the solid earth. The blackness is tangible. It swirls around you like a liquid, making it impossible to tell up from down, let alone north from south or east from west. So it is very easy to imagine the joy a hundred generations of mariners have felt at the sight of a lighthouse beacon on the horizon.

It has been said that men have always made better navigators than they have brothers. The carnage of a thousand sea battles would seem to prove the point. But lighthouses stand as a powerful argument against that view. They save lives, provide direction, and welcome travelers to safe harbor. The people who build or maintain them ask nothing in return.

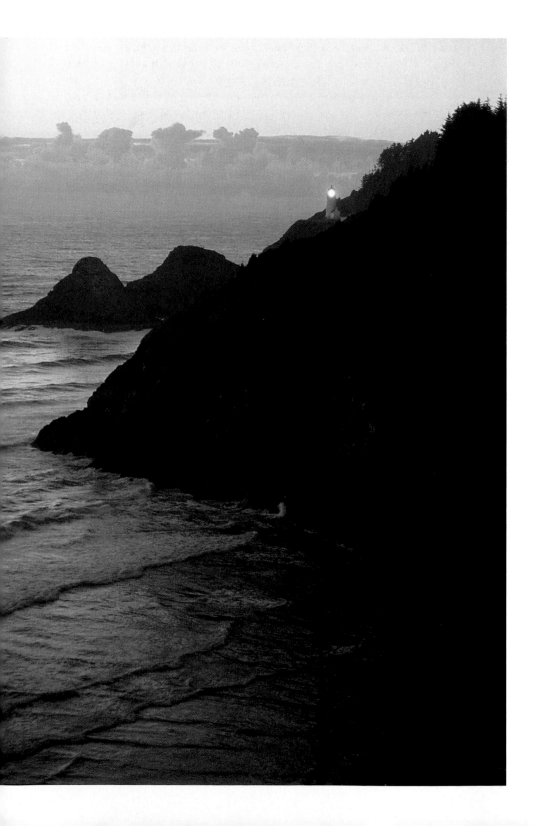

In this sense the hundreds of lights that extend in a sparkling chain along our coasts represent our very best instincts as Americans. They mark us as an open society, a hospitable people more than happy to welcome others to our shores. For countless thousands of immigrants, the very first glimpse of America was the flash of a navigational beacon—perhaps the Point Bonita Light near the Golden Gate, the Montauk Light at the far eastern end of Long Island, or even of Lady Liberty herself—the Statue of Liberty was, in fact, once a lighthouse.

Ironically, the tall sentinels that have welcomed so many to America and have saved so many ships and lives are themselves now in danger of extinction. Over the last half a century, technical advances in navigation and budgetary concerns have led to the abandonment and destruction of one lighthouse after another. Some have been torn down, others have been permanently scarred by vandals, and a few have collapsed into the sea. But the story of America's lighthouses may yet have a happy ending.

The magnificent first-order Fresnel lens warms the night sky over Currituck Beach on the Carolina Outer Banks—just as it has since 1875.

Civic-minded individuals and organizations all over the country are working tirelessly to save our remaining historic lighthouses, and as you'll discover in the pages that follow, they are succeeding. Lighthouses have been guiding ships and sailors for at least three thousand years. Perhaps now they are guiding all of us to a better understanding of our past and of ourselves as Americans.

This guidebook is your invitation to take part in the ongoing lighthouse adventure. This introductory section provides a look at the history of America's light

Perched on a cliff far above the Pacific, Oregon's Heceta Head Light warns mariners away from this beautiful but extraordinarily dangerous coast.

towers, the engineers who built them, and the keepers who, along with their families, lived at the lighthouses and lit their lamps each night.

Following the introduction we'll take you on an imaginary journey beginning in far Downeast Maine, travel down the eastern seaboard, along the Gulf of Mexico, up the Pacific coast from Southern California to the remote Aleutian Islands in Alaska, west to the Hawaiian Island of Kauai, and finally through the Great Lakes, from Ontario to the far shores of Superior. Through words and breathtaking photography, you'll visit more than five hundred lighthouses, learn their dramatic histories, and see how they work. Ample travel information is included so that you can experience and photograph the old towers yourself and, if you like, walk the nearby beaches to watch the lights flashing in the night.

Lighthouses Through History

The ancient Greeks were a seafaring people, so it should come as no surprise that they included a lighthouse among their Seven Wonders of the World. Along with the Pyramids of Egypt, the Hanging Gardens of Babylon, the Colossus of Rhodes, and the other wonders, they ranked the Pharos, history's first great lighthouse, among the most important and spectacular man-made structures of any age. Rising 450 feet into the blue Mediterranean skies, Pharos was the tallest lighthouse of all time. With almost twelve centuries of nearly continuous operation, it was also the one with the longest service record.

Built about 280 B.C. on an island in the bustling harbor of the Greco-Egyptian city of Alexandria, Pharos guided ships to the world's busiest seaport. The light, produced by a fire blazing on the tower's roof, could be seen from nearly thirty miles away. Ancient mariners needed the Pharos light because Alexandria stood on the flat Nile Delta and there were no mountains or other natural features to help them locate the city.

Peoples had long made a practice of banking fires on hills and mountainsides to bring their sailors home from the sea. With Pharos, its artificial mountain, Alexandria pulled in ships from the entire known world. The sight of the Pharos light blazing far up near the dome of the sky must have charged the breasts of countless sea captains with awe. In time, the delta city became the busiest and most prosperous city on Earth, and it remained so for nearly a thousand years, or about as long as its lighthouse stood—it was eventually destroyed by an earthquake.

Trading ships from Greece, Carthage, and Rome flocked to the city's wharves to load up on the grain that grew in such wondrous abundance along the banks of the Nile. It was for possession of Alexandria and her grain markets that Julius Caesar invaded Egypt and, later, Octavius fought and defeated Antony and Cleopatra. Without Egypt's grain to feed the empire's teeming masses, Rome's conquests would have been meaningless. And without the Pharos light, the lumbering Roman grain ships might never have found Alexandria. Thus, in a very real sense, the Roman empire was dependent on a lighthouse.

Like Rome, the United States of America is a highly commercial nation, part industrial and part agrarian. As with Rome, the growth and prosperity of our country has depended on safe navigation of the waters leading to our busy port cities.

A fanciful depiction of the Pharos Lighthouse in Alexandria, Egypt. Built by Ptolemaic kings about 280 B.C., it stood until destroyed by an earthquake more than a thousand years later. (From an eighteenth-century engraving provided courtesy Department of Rare Books, William R. Perkins Library, Duke University.)

Thus, lighthouses have been a major concern for Americans right from the nation's beginning.

Early U.S. Lighthouses

America's oldest light station was located on Little Brewster Island at the outer entrance of Boston Harbor. Built in 1716, the Boston Lighthouse was a cylindrical stone structure with a lantern room at the top. Its design set the pattern for hundreds of lighthouses that would come afterward. Destroyed during the Revolutionary War raids by both Continental and British forces, it was rebuilt in 1783.

Marking the entrance to Nantucket Harbor in Massachusetts, Brant Point Light (1746) was the second lighthouse built in the original thirteen colonies. A rather flimsy wooden structure, it burned or was blown over several times, only to be rebuilt by the island's tenacious whalers and fishermen.

America's third lighthouse, Beavertail Light (1749), marked the passage into Rhode Island's Narragansett Bay. Its square rubble-stone tower anchored the southern tip of sandy Conanicut Island, which the pirate Captain Kidd had used as a hideout during the 1600s. Like the Boston Light, this one was knocked out of operation during the Revolutionary War. By 1790, however, it was repaired and back in service.

Built with the proceeds of a public lottery, New London Light (1760) in Connecticut survived the Revolution intact. During the Revolutionary War continental privateers often used the light to help find refuge from pursuing British warships.

An octagonal brick structure, Sandy Hook Light (1764) stood near the mouth of the Hudson and showed the way to New York City's harbor. New Yorkers had financed and built this strategic tower, but since it was actually located in New Jersey, the legislature of the Garden State laid claim to the facility during the Revolution. This precipitated a protracted legal squabble that was settled only when the federal government took control of this and other light stations in 1789.

Guiding ships into Delaware Bay and the river beyond, Cape Henlopen Light (1765) was one of the most important navigational markers in America. For sea captains caught in a storm, this Delaware light was a particularly welcome sight, as it marked one of the few harbors of refuge along the entire eastern coast. Even in the worst weather, the waters behind the cape were nearly always calm. Burned by British sailors and marines in 1777, Cape Henlopen Lighthouse was repaired and relit in 1784.

Charleston Light (1767), located on a low sandy South Carolina island frequently inundated by tides, pointed the way to the harbor of one of America's oldest and most gracious cities. For decades it was the only significant navigational light south of the Virginia capes.

The oldest standing light tower in the United States, the Sandy Hook Lighthouse remains in operation after more than 235 years. Although built by New Yorkers, the station is located in New Jersey.
© William G. Kaufhold

Serving the famed Massachusetts community founded by the Pilgrims, Plymouth Light (1768) was unique in that it displayed not one but two lights from the same building. The twin beacons set the light apart from ordinary lanterns that marked nearby harbors.

During its early years Portsmouth Light (1771) consisted of little more than a lantern hoisted up the flagpole of Fort William and Mary, on the banks of New Hampshire's Piscataqua River. In 1775 the keeper felt free to temporarily set aside his duties and take a wagon-load of gunpowder to the embattled Massachusetts Minutemen dug in on Bunker Hill outside Boston. A proper wood-frame lighthouse was eventually built at Portland. During the 1780s it received a pair of famous visitors: Revolutionary War hero General Marquis de Lafayette and his old commander, George Washington himself.

Built to warn mariners away from Thatcher Island, a ship-killing rock off the north coast of Massachusetts, Cape Ann Light (1771) consisted of two separate towers. The island was named for a colonial clergyman and his family who had been shipwrecked here in 1635. The station's first keeper was a notorious Tory. When the Revolution broke out, a party of Massachusetts militiamen hustled him off the island, plunging the twin lights into darkness until after the war.

Though some large American cities such as Baltimore had no lighthouses during the colonial and early post-colonial period, tiny Nantucket Island had two. The Brant Point Light got a neighbor in 1784, when the Great Point Lighthouse was built on the southern end of the island.

Intended to guide ships safely over the treacherous sandbar at the harbor entrance, the Newburyport Light (1788) in Massachusetts made the first known use of a range-light system. Two lights were displayed, one higher and some distance behind the other. Ships sailing in safe water saw the lights in perfect perpendicular alignment. To mariners straying out of the main channel, the upper light appeared to tilt in one direction or the other.

For most sailors at this time, however, finding a safe channel as they approached the American coastline was a matter of risky guesswork. The lights listed above were the only worthy navigational guideposts along the entire American coast, that is, until the nation's first president took the oath of office in 1789.

The Lighthouse President

A farmer and lifelong landlubber, George Washington had little interest in ships or the sea, but he was always an enthusiastic promoter of lighthouses. The consummate American, Washington had an abiding interest in money and the making of it, and he could see the commercial potential in a well-conceived system of navigational markers. Even before the Revolution, he took note of ports and headlands that might someday need light towers.

In 1789, as president, he urged Congress to make lighthouses a national priority. The Congress responded by passing a "Lighthouse Bill," only the ninth piece of legislation enacted by the nation's fledgling government. This bill placed all existing coastal lighthouses under federal control. It also created the "Lighthouse Establishment," which would come to be known as the United States Lighthouse Service. In one form or another, the service would survive for more than 150 years, right up until 1939, when the U.S. Coast Guard took full responsibility for the nation's navigational aids. By that time nearly one thousand fine lighthouses marked the Atlantic and Gulf coasts in the East, the Pacific and Bering Sea coasts in the West, and the shores of the Great Lakes in the Midwest.

A century and a half earlier, however, when the Lighthouse Service was in its infancy, the number of operational lights was pitifully small. Ships and lives were being lost with grim regularity. To remedy this the service undertook a major construction program that added a dozen major lights during the 1790s, the nation's first full decade of independence. Lighthouses either completed or under construction by the end of the eighteenth century included those at Cape Henry, Virginia (completed in 1791); Portland Head, Maine (1791); Tybee, Georgia (1791); Seguin, Maine (1795); Bald Head Island, North Carolina (1796); Montauk Point, New York (1797); Baker's Island, Massachusetts (1798); Cape Cod, Massachusetts (1798); Cape Hatteras, North Carolina (begun in 1798); Ocracoke, North Carolina (begun in 1798); Gay Head, Massachusetts (1799); and Eaton's Neck, New York (1799).

Appropriately, this initial burst of lighthouse construction was nearly complete when George Washington died during the final weeks of 1799. The old general missed witnessing, by only two weeks, the beginning of the nineteenth century and, with it, the opening of a whole new era of expansion and prosperity. Washington had done more than most people to make this new and optimistic age possible. Among his most important contributions, however, was one that is not frequently recognized: his insistence on an efficient system of lights for America's coasts and navigable inland waters.

Lighthouse Engineers

By the mid-1800s the United States had more lighthouses than any other nation on Earth. More than two hundred major or minor lights shone from one place or another along its coasts. But though America's light towers outnumbered those of other maritime powers such as Britain, France, and Spain, they lagged far behind in the quality of their construction and the reliability of their beacons. Improvements, such as the use of the advanced, though expensive, Fresnel lenses, designed in France during the early nineteenth century, were delayed by the tight budgets imposed by Congress and by the bureaucratic monovision of treasury auditor Stephen Pleasonton. For more than thirty years, beginning in 1820, Pleasonton lorded over the Lighthouse Service in an imperious—and parsimonious—manner. By 1850, however, Pleasonton's influence began to wane, unleashing a revolution in American lighthouse technology.

In 1852 the Lighthouse Board, composed of experienced military officers, engineers, and seamen, took charge of the Lighthouse Service. Almost immediately, the board embarked on an ambitious program aimed at expanding and upgrading navigational aids along America's coasts. With the U.S. economy booming and coastal trade on the increase, Congress was willing to foot the huge bill for these improvements. To accomplish its task the board would rely on the skills, energy, and fresh ideas of young military engineers such as George Gordon Meade and Danville Leadbetter.

A Sea Captain's Lamp

Winslow Lewis had epitomized the old way of building lighthouses. A former New England sea captain, he represented the age of wooden sailing ships, stone forts, and, naturally enough, stone light towers. About 1810, while suffering through a long stretch of unemployment, Lewis invented a lamp and parabolic reflector system that he said would make America's navigational beacons more powerful. The Lewis system was quickly adopted, and the U.S. government paid him $60,000 to place his devices in all of the nation's lighthouses, a process that would take him seven years. No doubt, Lewis's reflectors were a considerable improvement over earlier systems, but they would prove vastly inferior to the Fresnel lens soon developed by the French. Even so, the Lighthouse Service would keep most of its Lewis reflectors in place until after 1850.

Having found an advocate in Pleasonton, who admired his knack for thrift, Lewis was soon being hired not just to equip lighthouses but to build them. He preferred towers of a conventional, conical design with stout walls of stone or brick, and he built them well. Many of the dozens of light towers Lewis built on sites from Maine to Louisiana still stand to this day.

Perhaps Lewis's best known success—and failure—came at Frank's Island, Louisiana, where he was hired in 1818 to build an ornate lighthouse and customs office near the primary entrance to the Mississippi. Designed by a government architect who had never visited the site, the absurdly inappropriate structure was far too heavy for the river's delta marshlands and collapsed into a pile of useless rubble only a few days after it was finished. Lewis then contracted to build a sensibly modest tower of his own design, completing it, as we would say nowadays, under budget and ahead of schedule. Although the tower has sunk more than twenty feet into the Mississippi mud, it still stands today, a testament to the workmanship of Lewis's construction crews. But Lewis's outmoded reflectors and stone towers were no match for the challenges that would face the Lighthouse Service in the 1850s.

Two Lighthouse Generals

George Meade could hardly have presented a sharper contrast to Winslow Lewis. Part of a younger, better-educated generation of American lighthouse experts, Meade was a trained engineer. In 1835 Meade graduated from West Point at the age of only twenty. After fighting in the Seminole War in Florida, he became a surveyor for the Army Corps of Topographical Engineers, helping to set the boundary between the United States and the then Republic of Texas. In time he developed an interest in marine engineering and lighthouses. His innovative work on light towers in the Delaware Bay convinced his superiors that Lieutenant Meade could help with the seemingly impossible task of marking the Florida Keys.

Arriving at Carysfort Reef in 1850, Meade supervised construction of an iron-skeleton lighthouse designed by I.W.P. Lewis, who happened to be the nephew—and harshest critic—of Winslow Lewis. The revolutionary screw-pile technology and open structure of the Carysfort tower appealed to the modern instincts of Meade, the engineer. It was an approach Meade would take—and improve on—again and again over the next several years as he built towers at Sand Key, Sombrero Key, and many other sites. One essential Meade innovation was the use of large metal disks to help anchor screw piles to an unstable sand or coral base. Of course, Meade always sought to match methods to the designs of the site. For Seahorse Key, located well to the north of Tampa and off the track followed by most hurricanes, he designed a classic brick and wood-frame combination tower and dwelling much like those later built in the Northwest.

Another U.S. Army engineer building Gulf lighthouses at about this same time was Captain Danville Leadbetter. Although a few years older than Meade, Leadbetter had graduated from West Point one year later, in 1836.

Instead of iron and steel, Leadbetter pre-ferred to use brick, but his often octagonal towers proved as stable and durable as any of the skeleton structures built by Meade. Completed in 1858, his tower at Sand Island off Alabama's Mobile Bay stood more than two hundred feet tall. Leadbetter's brick tower at Port Pont-chartrain was stabilized by a submerged concrete pad. But his most unusual design may have been that of the Sabine Pass Lighthouse, with its extraordinary finlike buttresses. Spreading the weight of the tower over the damp, yielding ground, the buttresses have held the tower in rock-solid plumb for more than 140 years. A Leadbetter design for the Cape San Blas Lighthouse in the Florida Panhandle region was never built but might have been a wonder to behold. His creative plan called for a ninety-foot brick tower set atop screw-pile stilts.

Danville Leadbetter Courtesy Massachusetts Commandery Military Order of the Loyal Legion of the U.S. Army Military History Institute.

The Architecture of Victory

The outbreak of the Civil War in 1861 changed the professional status and destiny of millions. The same was true of Meade, who quickly rose to the rank of general in the Union Army, and of Leadbetter, who did the same on the Confederate side. But the war had very different fates in store for the two men.

Highly valued for his engineering skills, General Leadbetter was put in charge of Gulf coast fortifications and, not coincidentally, its lighthouses. With a navy vastly inferior to that of the Union, however, the Confederates had little use for coastal lights, likely only to benefit their enemies. Under Leadbetter's direction Southern troops often removed and carefully hid Fresnel lenses and other useful equipment to keep them out of the hands of the enemy. But some lighthouses thought to be of particular use to Union blockade fleets were marked for destruc-tion. In a moment of supreme and poignant irony, Leadbetter sent out a raiding

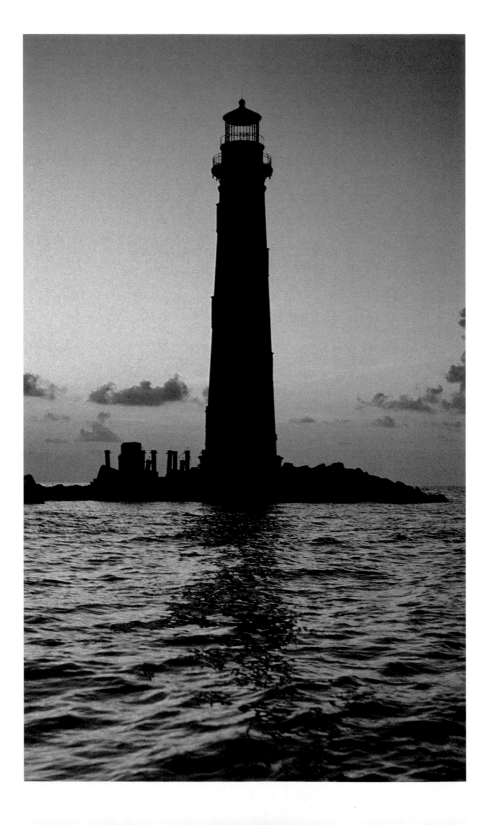

party to blow up the Sand Island Lighthouse, which he himself had so proudly built only a few years earlier.

As the war progressed and began to go badly for the South, Leadbetter was recruited to design defensive positions for Confederate infantry. As it turned out, the general had far less skill in creating structures meant to take lives than he had earlier with light towers intended to save them. His entrenchments and other defensive arrangements were thought by some to have been partly responsible for Confederate defeats at Knoxville and Chattanooga.

Drawing from *Harpers Weekly*, from private collection of Jim Cobb

George Meade

Following the war, there were few opportunities in the United States for a former Confederate general to work as a lighthouse engineer. To support himself and his family, Leadbetter sought work in Mexico and Canada. Exhausted, he died in Canada in 1866, little more than a year after he returned to civilian life.

Meade, on the other hand, fought in several important engagements while working his way up to the rank of major general. A string of early defeats suffered by the Union Army of the Potomac had led President Lincoln to fire one general after another. Meade inherited this revolving-door command on the eve of the critical battle of Gettysburg. Had Robert E. Lee's Confederates won this battle and surged on toward Washington, the South would likely have won the war. But Meade had learned in Florida how to build a structure capable of weathering a storm. On a series of hills overlooking Gettysburg, he erected his defense, and on the third and final day of the battle, when Lee let loose the thirteen-thousand-man hurricane of Pickett's charge, its foundations held fast.

(Opposite page) *The Gulf of Mexico has swallowed up Alabama's Sand Island, but its abandoned 1872 lighthouse still stands. An earlier Sand Island tower, designed by Danville Leadbetter, was blown up by Confederate forces under his command.*

Lighthouse Keepers

"No man is an island." So said John Donne, the often-quoted British poet and clergyman. But Donne, who died in 1631, never knew any of the lighthouse keepers who for more than two centuries helped make America's coasts safe for navigation. For these brave men and women, life was indeed an island. Surviving on low government salaries, they lived mostly on wild headlands and treeless ledges very far from what most of us would call civilization. Often the closest town was itself a backwater, a remote outpost. In bad weather, even the nearest rural church might seem impossibly distant.

When storms rushed in from the ocean, as they often did, lighthouse keepers could not follow the example of the mariners they served and run for some calm harbor. Since their ships had stone foundations and no engines, sails, rudders, or helms, they had to stay and take whatever the sea threw at them. To fight back against gale and gloom, they had only their lights and their wits. The lamps, which more often than not stood at the top of winding staircases with hundreds of steps, were in constant need of attention. But whatever the conditions or the health of the keeper, they had to be kept burning. As a result, keepers always worked nights and rarely had a day off.

Lighthouse keepers endured this sort of existence, not necessarily for any high-minded or romantic reason—for instance, because they loved the sea, the wind, or the isolation—but for the same reason most people work: It rewarded them with a place to live and a smattering of pay. It was also a job worth doing, a job that had to be done.

Growing Up on a Rock

The keepers were not the only ones who faced hardship, danger, and punishing weather. Their families usually shared in the heavy work of keeping the lights burning, often displaying the same heroic resolve as the keepers themselves.

On a stormy night in 1856, young Abbie Burgess drew a chair to the kitchen table of the battered keeper's residence on isolated Matinicus Rock off the coast of Maine and dipped her pen into ink. A lonely seventeen-year-old, separated by at least twenty-five miles of turbulent ocean from the nearest country store, barn dance, or church social, she had decided to write a letter to a pen pal on the mainland.

You have often expressed a desire to view the sea out in the ocean when it is angry. Had you been here on 19 January [1856], *I surmise you would have been satisfied. Father was away* [Keeper Sam Burgess had gone to Rockland to purchase supplies and was trapped there by a sudden nor'easter, leaving his bedridden wife and daughter to weather the storm alone.] *early in the day, as the tide rose, the sea made a complete breach over the rock, washing every movable thing away, and of the old dwelling not one stone was left upon another. The new dwelling was flooded, and the windows had to be secured to prevent the violence of the spray from breaking them in. As the tide came, the sea rose higher and*

*higher, till the only endurable places were the light towers. If they stood, we were
saved, otherwise our fate was only too certain. But for some reason, I know not
why, I had no misgivings, and went on with my work as usual. For four weeks,
owing to the rough weather, no landing could be effected on the rock. During this
time, we were without the assistance of any male member of our family. Though at
times greatly exhausted with my labors, not once did the lights fail. I was able to
perform all my accustomed duties as well as my father's.*

*You know the hens are our only companions. Becoming convinced, as the gale
increased, that unless they were brought into the house they would be lost, I said to
mother, "I must try to save them." She advised me not to attempt it. The thought,
however, of parting with them without an effort was not to be endured, so seizing
a basket, I ran out a few yards after the rollers had passed and the sea fell off a little, with the water knee deep, to the coop, and rescued all but one. It was the work
of a moment, and I was back in the house with the door fastened, but I was none
too quick, for at that instant my little sister, standing at the window, exclaimed,
"Oh, look! Look there! The worst sea is coming." That wave destroyed the old
dwelling and swept the rock. I cannot think you would enjoy remaining here any
great length of time for the sea is never still and, when agitated, its roar shuts out
every other sound, even drowning our voices.*

A few months after the extraordinary month-long Atlantic storm described in
her letter, Abbie Burgess married a young assistant lighthouse keeper. She and her
husband eventually became keepers of the Matinicus Rock Lighthouse.

Redcoats, Indians, and Leaky Boats

The wind and weather were not the only dangers faced by lighthouse keepers.
Getting to their duty station, especially those on remote points or rugged islands,
could place keepers at considerable risk to life and limb. America's very first lighthouse keeper was George Worthylake, a part-time shepherd who tended the Boston
Harbor Lighthouse on Brewster Island. Little more than a year after he was
appointed keeper, Worthylake's small boat capsized, and he drowned while return-
ing from Boston, where he had gone to collect his pay. Many later keepers would
suffer similar fates.

Some keepers kept firearms handy, and for good reason. In 1777 the keeper of
the Cape Henlopen Lighthouse was attacked by a landing party of redcoat marines
from the British warship *Roebuck*. As it turned out, the *Roebuck* was low on supplies,
and the famished marines were far more interested in a nearby herd of cattle than
in the lighthouse or its keeper. A burst of gunfire stampeded the animals, however,
and as the keeper later boasted to his friends, he gave the British "bullets instead of
beef."

In 1836 Cape Florida keeper John Thomas found himself under attack by a war
party of Seminoles. Thomas barricaded himself inside the tower, which had
fortresslike brick walls five feet thick. Soon a flaming arrow set fire to the station's
oil supplies, forcing Thomas to climb the tower steps, which burned away behind

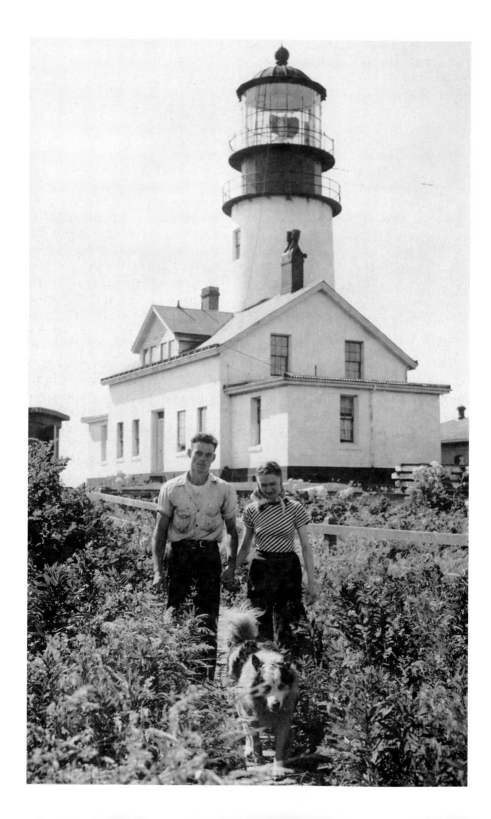

him. In the metal lantern room, Thomas managed to keep just beyond the reach of the flames, but even so, he was nearly roasted alive. Later Thomas was rescued by sailors from the U.S. warship *Concord*. Although the tower steps were now gone, they managed to fire a line to him with a musket and then lower him to ground in a basket. After his burns had healed, Thomas returned to his duties as a lighthouse keeper.

Keepers often loved their work, and many remained at it for a lifetime. More than a few ended their days at home in their lighthouses. Like many keepers before him, Emil Mueller, keeper of the splendidly isolated Rock of Ages Lighthouse in Lake Superior, was on duty when he died in 1930. As a storm raged outside, Mueller had climbed the steps of the thirteen-story steel-plated tower to check the station lamps. His assistant, C. A. Mickey, who was asleep far below, was understandably terrified when Mueller came crashing down onto the bunk beside him. Mickey was uninjured, but Mueller lay dead of a heart attack. Mickey's explanation for the tragic incident was a simple one. "Too many steps," he said. "His old heart just gave out."

Ida Lewis, perhaps America's most famous keeper, lived practically her entire life at the Lime Rock Lighthouse in Newport, Rhode Island. Born in 1842, Ida was still a very small girl when she arrived at Lime Rock with her father, Captain Hosea Lewis. A former revenue cutter pilot, Captain Lewis had been forced into semiretirement by illness. Lewis had thought that, despite his failing health, he could handle the duties of lighthouse keeper. As it turned out he could not, and by the time his daughter reached her early teens, she had largely taken over running the lighthouse. In addition to keeping the lamps burning and the Fresnel lens polished and sparkling, young Ida raised two younger sisters and a brother and looked after her father and mother who, in time, both became invalids. Upon her father's death in 1872, she was named official keeper of the Lime Rock Lighthouse.

Ida Lewis might have lived out her life in relatively peaceful obscurity had it not been for her penchant for effecting daring rescues. Whenever anyone fell overboard in Newport Harbor, Ida rushed off to the rescue in the light station skiff. Over the years she single-handedly pulled more than a dozen drunken sailors and careless boys and at least one sheep from the harbor's chilling waters. News of her exploits reached the ears of journalists, and Ida Lewis became the subject of feature articles in newspapers all across the country. Eventually Ida's story was told in *Harper's Weekly Magazine*, for which she became a sort of nineteenth-century cover girl. Some said that for a time Ida Lewis was the most famous woman in America. As such, she received visits—always at Lime Rock, for she never left her station—from some of the country's most famous people. At one time or another, the Astors, Belmonts, and even President Ulysses S. Grant had tea with her in the lighthouse parlor.

Despite her fame, though, Ida remained keeper of Lime Rock to the end of her days. In all, she tended the light for more than half a century. When the sad news came that Ida Lewis had died at her post on October 24, 1911, the bells of vessels in Newport Harbor tolled throughout the night.

Although lighthouse keepers faced loneliness and many hardships, some considered their lives idyllic. Surrounded by lush summer growth, a 1940s-era keeper enjoys the company of his wife and family dog at the isolated Cape Flattery Lighthouse in Washington. Courtesy U.S. Coast Guard

Lighthouse Lenses

Fresnels: Man-made Stars that Brighten the Night

The business end of a lighthouse is, of course, at the top. The lighting apparatus is kept in the lantern room as high above sea level as the tower and the elevation of the site can make possible. Height adds to the beacon's range, or distance from which it can be seen. But equally important to the beacon's effectiveness is the strength of the light itself. Usually a lens, mirror, or other optical device is used to concentrate the light, often into a single brilliant flash. For many years the most efficient way of doing this was with a Fresnel lens.

Invented in 1822 by French physicist Augustin Fresnel, these big prismatic glass lenses were designed to snatch every flicker of light from even the smallest lamp and concentrate it into a powerful beam that could be seen from dozens of miles away. Fresnel's elegant lenses did their job so well that they soon became standard equipment in lighthouses throughout much of the world.

The new Fresnel technology, however, was virtually ignored for several decades in the United States, where Winslow Lewis's far less effective parabolic reflectors were employed right up until the middle of the nineteenth century. One reason the United States was slow to adopt the Fresnel system was the considerable expense of the highly polished lenses, which had to be imported from France. Another was the bureaucratic fussiness of Stephen Pleasonton, the U.S. Treasury auditor who served for many years as head of the so-called Lighthouse Establishment. Displaying undisguised favoritism for Lewis, a personal friend, Pleasonton continued to equip U.S. lighthouses with his outdated reflectors even though they were demonstrably inferior to Fresnel lenses. Following the release of a highly critical report written by Lewis's own nephew, Pleasonton was forced into retirement.

In 1852 stewardship of America's navigational lights passed to a Lighthouse Board, which consisted of military officers, engineers, harbor masters, and experienced seamen. The board immediately undertook a complete over-

The glass prisms of a Fresnel lens concentrate light into a power beam that can be seen from dozens of miles away.

At many light stations Fresnel lenses have been replaced with modern plastic optics like this one at East Brother Lighthouse in California. Interestingly, the newer lenses rely on old-fashioned Fresnel technology.

haul of America's ill-equipped and, in many cases, sadly neglected lighthouses. As part of this effort, most lighthouses were fitted with sparkling new Fresnel lenses. Some of these lenses, installed during the years before the Civil War, remain in service to this day.

A Sophisticated Technology

Remarkably, Fresnel lenses are as effective and useful today as they were 150 years ago. This is a claim that can be made for very few devices. Few significant improvements have been made in the design of prismatic lenses since the days of Augustin Fresnel. Unlike so many other technologies—transportation, for instance—this one reached its peak of sophistication very early in the industrial revolution. Long before the development of space rockets, jet airliners, or automobiles, Fresnel lenses were already shining in lighthouse towers.

Although a Fresnel lens looks like a single piece of molded glass, it is not. The lens consists of individual prisms—sometimes more than a thousand of them—fitted into a metal frame. This makes them look like giant glass beehives.

Fresnels come in a variety of sizes, referred to as "orders." The huge first-order lenses, such as the one that formerly served at the Cape Canaveral Lighthouse (it is now on display at the Ponce Inlet Museum in Florida), are six feet or more in diameter and up to twelve feet tall. The smallest lenses, designated sixth-order, are only about one foot in diameter.

The larger and more powerful first-, second-, and third-order lenses were intended for use in coastal lighthouses. The smaller fourth-, fifth-, and sixth-order

Bodie Island Lighthouse at sunset

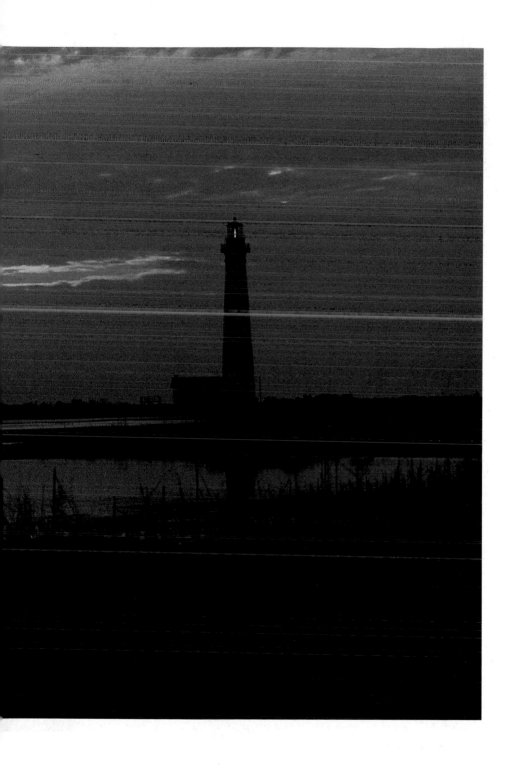

lenses saw use mostly in harbor and river lighthouses. Specially designed three-and-one-half-order lenses—a compromise between the larger and smaller sizes—were frequently used to guide vessels on the Great Lakes.

Although Fresnel lenses are as effective and powerful as any so-called modern optical device, they require considerable care and must be cleaned and polished frequently by hand. The larger Fresnels are quite heavy, sometimes weighing in at more than a ton. As a consequence, the mechanisms that turn flashing Fresnel lenses must be large and cumbersome. Despite their size, the old lenses are quite delicate, easily damaged, and almost impossible to repair. For all of these reasons, the efficiency-minded Coast Guard has replaced many Fresnels with plastic lenses or airport-type beacons that are lighter weight and easier to maintain. Many of the old lenses have ended up in museums, where the public can enjoy them.

Existing Fresnel lenses are practically irreplaceable. When destroyed by storms or vandalism, as, unfortunately, sometimes happens, the Coast Guard must put in their place a modern optic—or a Fresnel previously removed from another lighthouse. The cost of manufacturing new Fresnel lenses is prohibitively high and could run to millions of dollars.

During the nineteenth century, Fresnel lenses were hand ground and hand polished by the poorest classes of French laborers, including children. It is ironic that the handiwork of these unremembered workers can be counted among the most practical, durable, and handsome devices ever made. No one will ever know how many lives have been saved by these fine, old lenses or how many accidents were avoided because their guiding light could be seen on the horizon.

Since 1854 the Tibbetts Point Lighthouse in New York has marked the far eastern end of Lake Ontario and the entrance of the St. Lawrence River.

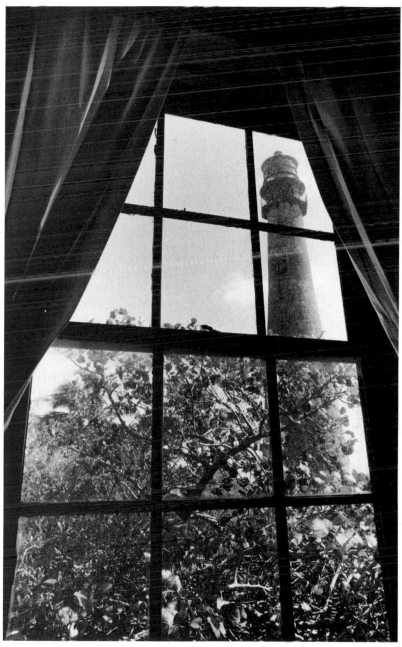

Cape Florida Lighthouse marks the far southeastern corner of the United States. It is the oldest surviving lighthouse in Florida, and has been restored to its original white appearance.

NORTHEAST

Portland Head Lighthouse

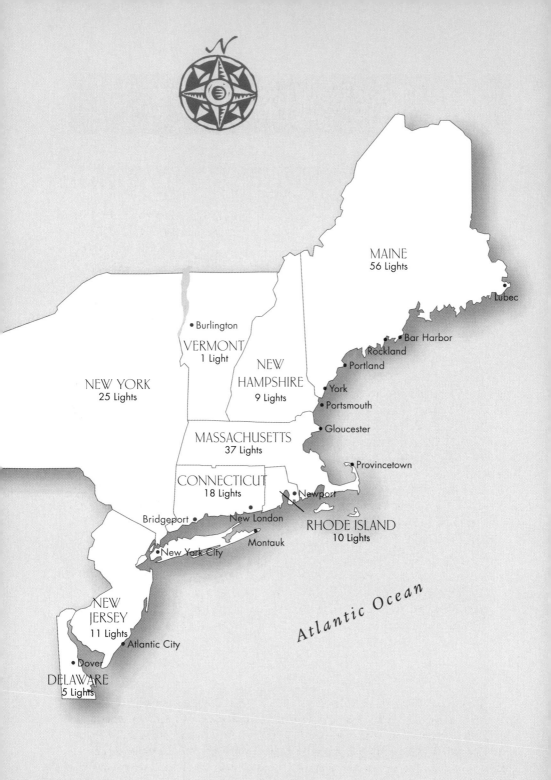

MAINE
56 Lights

• Lubec

• Burlington

VERMONT
1 Light

NEW
HAMPSHIRE
9 Lights

• Bar Harbor
Rockland •
• Portland

NEW YORK
25 Lights

• York
• Portsmouth

• Gloucester

MASSACHUSETTS
37 Lights

• Provincetown

CONNECTICUT
18 Lights

• Newport

Bridgeport •
• New London

RHODE ISLAND
10 Lights

• New York City
Montauk •

Atlantic Ocean

NEW
JERSEY
11 Lights

• Atlantic City

• Dover

DELAWARE
5 Lights

MAINE

■ WEST QUODDY HEAD LIGHT ■
Lubec (1808 and 1858)

Looking out across the Quoddy Narrows from its perch on a forty-foot cliff, West Quoddy Head Lighthouse anchors the easternmost point in the United States **(East Quoddy Head Light,** across the narrows, is on Canada's Campobello Island). Established in 1808, while Thomas Jefferson was still president, this is one of Maine's oldest light stations. The original rubblestone tower was torn down and rebuilt with brick in 1858. At that time the station received the third-order Fresnel lens that still guides ships and fishing vessels into Lubec Channel. The light

atop the forty-nine-foot, candy-striped tower flashes white four times each minute and can be seen from a distance of up to eighteen nautical miles.

Equipped with a strobe light and an electric eye that sense moisture in the air, the station's powerful foghorn occupies a separate brick building. Earlier fog signals here included a black-powder cannon, a 1,500-pound bell, and a steam whistle.

> *Travel information:* From U.S. Highway 1 turn toward Lubec on Route 189; then turn right at the sign for Quoddy Head State Park. The park charges a small entrance fee but offers world-class views of Grand Manan Channel, nature trails featuring real tundra, and a chance to walk the lighthouse grounds at leisure. Contact West Quoddy Head Light Keepers Association, P.O. Box 378, Lubec, ME 04652; (207) 733-4646.

■ LUBEC CHANNEL LIGHT ■
Lubec (1890)

Most vessels approaching the St. Croix River ports of Lubec, Eastport, and Calais use the narrow Lubec Channel, which separates Maine from Canada's Campobello Island to the north of Quoddy Head. To make this key passage safer, the U.S. government marked it with an open-water light station in 1890. Built on a massive caisson of concrete and iron, the station's brick-lined, cast-iron tower rises fifty-three feet above the water. When seen from a distance, lighthouses of this type resemble giant spark plugs.

In the past hardy keepers and their assistants lived year-round in cramped quarters on the lower level. The station was automated after a destructive oil fire in 1939.

For nearly eighty years the beacon was produced by a fifth-order, bull's-eye Fresnel lens rotated by a weight-driven clockwork mechanism. A plastic optic replaced the original lens in 1969. Now solar powered, the light remains active, flashing green ten times a minute.

Nick Salata, courtesy *Lighthouse Digest*

Travel information: Although closed to the public, the lighthouse can be seen from South Lubec Road, off Route 189 on the way to Quoddy Head State Park. The best views can be had from the roadside about one-half mile south of Lubec. Contact the St. Croix Historical Society, RFD 1, Box 93, Calais, ME 04619; (207) 454–2604.

■ WHITLOCKS MILL LIGHT ■
Near Calais (1909)

One of several small U.S. and Canadian beacons that formerly guided lumber freighters along the St. Croix River to the port of Calais, the Whitlocks Mill Lighthouse dates from 1909. Its twenty-five-foot masonry tower replaced an early stone lighthouse that had stood here since 1892. An automated optic replaced the fourth-order Fresnel lens in 1969. The light remains active, flashing green ten times a minute. The **St. Croix Lighthouse,** which at one time stood a few miles downriver from this one, was destroyed by fire in 1976.

Travel information: Travelers can see the tower from the St. Croix View Rest Area on U.S. Highway 1 a few miles east of Calais and about 5 miles northwest of the St. Croix Island International Historic Site.

■ LITTLE RIVER LIGHT ■
Near Cutler (1847 and 1876)

Established during the mid-nineteenth century, the Little River Light station served mariners for nearly 130 years before being shut down by the Coast Guard in 1975. Although one of the more attractive lighthouses on the coast of Maine, the thirty-five-foot iron tower and L-shaped Victorian dwelling stood empty and neglected for many years. The U.S. Coast Guard put the old light station up for sale during the 1990s, but at first there were no takers. Finally, the deteriorating lighthouse came under the wing of the American Lighthouse Foundation, which acquired the property in 2000. Although the badly weathered structures are still considered endangered, they are being restored.

Travel information: Located on an island near Cutler off Route 191 in far eastern Maine, the lighthouse cannot be seen from the mainland. However, local wildlife and sight-seeing cruises offer excellent views of the Little River Lighthouse as well as the **Machias Seal Islands Light Station** (1832) southeast of Cutler and the **Libby Island Light Station** near Machias; call (207) 259-4484. For more information on the American Lighthouse Foundation and its wide-ranging preservation efforts, contact P.O. Box 889, Wells, ME 04090; (207) 646-0515.

Courtesy Lighthouse Digest

■ PETIT MANAN LIGHT ■
Milbridge (1817 and 1855)

During the early nineteenth century, coasting schooners were often forced to heel hard aport to avoid the deadly rocks of Petit Manan Island. A lighthouse built there in 1817 did little to improve the situation. Shining from atop a rubble-stone tower only fifty-three-feet tall, its Winslow Lewis lamps were so limited in range that

Paula Roberts, courtesy Lighthouse Digest

sailors could barely see the beacon until they were almost upon the rocks. For more than a few mariners, the warning came too late.

In 1855 the Lighthouse Board sought to prevent further shipping losses by ordering construction of a soaring 119-foot brick-and-granite tower on Petit Manan. Fo-cused by a powerful second-order Fresnel lens, its flashing light pulsed a warning more than twenty-five miles out to sea. The Fresnel was replaced in 1972 by an automated optic of similar range. The light flashes six times each minute.

Travel information: From U.S. Highway 1 near Milbridge, turn south on Pigeon Hill Road and follow it to the Petit Manan Wildlife Refuge. A scenic 2-mile-long trail leads to the east side of Petit Manan Point, where visitors can enjoy an excellent view of the lighthouse.

■ PROSPECT HARBOR POINT LIGHT ■
Prospect Harbor (1850 and 1891)

Prospect Harbor Point Lighthouse looks much like a fisherman's cottage—except for the thirty-eight-foot conical tower rising from its seaward wall. Its design is appropriate since its beacon shines out mostly to lobster and sardine boats. Built in 1891, the two-story, wood-frame structure replaced an earlier granite lighthouse that first marked the point in 1850. Ironically, the stone light tower succumbed to the elements after little more than forty years, yet its wooden replacement perseveres, despite weathering over a century of storms. Nowadays, the dwelling serves as a guest house for visitors to the adjacent naval base. The light remains active, flashing red and white about ten times a minute.

Travel information: From U.S. Highway 1 follow either Route 186 or 195 to Prospect Harbor. Although open to the general public only on Memorial Day weekend, the lighthouse can be seen and photographed from several viewpoints in the village. The handsomely maintained dwelling occasionally serves as a vacation rental for military retirees. For information contact Navy Special Operations Command, Prospect Harbor, ME 04669; (207) 963-7700.

■ WINTER HARBOR LIGHT ■
Winter Harbor (1856)

Motorists on the perimeter road of Acadia National Park's Schoodic Point often notice a small white-brick light tower and attached Victorian keeper's dwelling. Located on Mark Island, just to the west of Schoodic Peninsula, this is the Winter Harbor Lighthouse, which served from 1856 until 1934, when it was decommissioned. At present the lighthouse is privately owned and maintained.

Travel information: From U.S. Highway 1 follow Route 186 through Winter Harbor to the Acadia National Park entrance—passes are required during the summer season. Parking areas about a mile south of the entrance afford excellent views of the lighthouse. Be sure to stop at Schoodic Point at the far end of the drive. On most days waves crash into the bare rocks of the point and spew high into the air. Don't feed the seagulls, or you'll have hundreds of them hounding you for handouts.

■ EGG ROCK LIGHT ■
Bar Harbor (1875)

The dramatic red flash of Egg Rock Lighthouse in Frenchman's Bay catches the attention of visitors to Acadia National Park. Once described as a "pillar of fire in the Atlantic," the beacon emanates from a barren ledge, which likely got its name from the countless seabird nests found there during mating season. The signal marks seaward approaches to Bar Harbor. Flashing red at five-second intervals, it can be seen from fourteen miles away.

The station's squat, forty-foot tower is far less awe-inspiring than its light. Built in 1875, the squared-off wooden dwelling and brick tower are more functional than scenic. An aeromarine beacon superseded the original fourth-order Fresnel lens when the light was automated in 1976.

Travel information: The light can be seen from several scenic overlooks along the Acadia National Park Loop Road on Mount Desert Island. Thundering surf, panoramic ocean views, and the East's loftiest headland—1,500-foot Cadillac Mountain—make this park one of America's must-see scenic wonders. The best time to avoid the summer throngs is before July 4 or after Labor Day. For information contact Acadia National Park, P.O. Box 177, Bar Harbor, ME 04609; (207) 288-3338. When you go, don't leave without sampling the boiled lobster in Bar Harbor or the popovers and tea at the Jordon Pond House.

■ BASS HARBOR HEAD LIGHT ■
Bass Harbor (1858)

Thought by many people to be the most picturesque lighthouse in America, this compact brick tower and attached wooden dwelling cling to a red-rock cliff near the entrance to Bass Harbor. Located on the western "quiet side" of Mount Desert

Island, well away from the tourist throngs of Bar Harbor and Acadia Park Island, Bass Harbor bobs with dozens of brightly painted lobster boats. The station's red light has guided the fisherman of this bucolic village since before the Civil War.

The original fourth-order Fresnel lens remains in place. Its light's focal plane lies about fifty-six feet above the water. The beam occults, or goes dark briefly, every four seconds. Panels outside the lens create the light's red color.

Travel information: Now used as a residence for Coast Guard personnel, the lighthouse is not open to the public, but visitors can enjoy it nonetheless. A small park surrounds the station property, and a paved walkway runs right up to the tower. On the far side of the station, a path connects the parking lot with a wooden stairway that leads down the side of the cliff to the reddish boulders below. The short but strenuous climb rewards the adventurous with extraordinary views of the channel and islands beyond and an unmatched opportunity to photograph one of the nation's prettiest lighthouses.

■ GREAT DUCK ISLAND LIGHT ■
Great Duck Island (1890)

Great Duck Island lies under siege by the Atlantic about five miles to the south of Bass Harbor. In part because of its remoteness, countless seabirds, including rare petrels and eider ducks, call the island home. For nearly a century the island was

also home to a tiny colony of lighthouse keepers and their families, who received weekly deliveries of mail and supplies from the mainland.

Established in 1890, the light is now automated. In 1986 a plastic lens replaced the fifth-order Fresnel lens that formerly crowned its forty-two-foot granite-and-brick tower. The light flashes red every five seconds.

Travel information: At present, the island and most of the station are owned by The Nature Conservancy, which maintains a bird sanctuary here. The island is off-limits to the public during the summer nesting season, but occasional bird-watching tours are conducted by the Maine chapters of The Nature Conservancy (207-729-5181) or Audubon Society (207-781-2330).

■ MOUNT DESERT ROCK LIGHT ■
Mount Desert Rock (1830, 1857, and 1893)

Relentlessly pounded by Atlantic waves, Mount Desert Rock surely ranks as one of the least hospitable places in America. Yet, for nearly 150 years, lighthouse keepers and their families lived on this open ocean ledge, which is only six hundred yards long and less than twenty feet above the water at its highest point. So barren was their home that friendly lobster fishermen brought them baskets of soil in the spring so that they could make a little garden in some rain-moistened crevasses among boulders.

Established in 1830 to warn ships away from this exceptionally dangerous obstacle more than twenty miles from the nearest land, the lighthouse at first consisted of only a two-story wooden cottage with a lantern on its roof. The light, provided by inefficient Winslow Lewis reflectors, often could not be seen in time to prevent wrecks.

In 1857 the Lighthouse Board had a stone tower built here, equipped with a third-order Fresnel lens. With a focal plane seventy-five feet above the water, the light was visible more than twenty miles away. Its range was sharply reduced in heavy weather, however. During a winter storm in 1902, the crew of the ocean tug *Astral* did not see the light at all, and their vessel slammed into rock. The keeper and his wife managed to save all but one of those onboard.

Courtesy U.S. Coast Guard

Keepers served at this isolated station until 1977, when the light was automated. At that time the old Fresnel lens was replaced by a plastic lens. The light flashes white four times each minute.

Travel information: Mount Desert Rock is, of course, very hard to reach, but whale-watching cruises operating out of Bar Harbor often take passengers within sight of the ledge and its lighthouse. For information contact the Bar Harbor Chamber of Commerce, P.O. Box 158, Bar Harbor, ME 04609; (207) 288-3393.

▪ BURNT COAT HARBOR LIGHT ▪
Swans Island (1872)

Burnt Coat Harbor may have gotten its name from a Revolutionary deserter.

Seeking refuge from the storm of war then breaking over the country, a soldier named Thomas Kench symbolically "burned his coat" and fled to the island in 1776. Vessels seeking refuge here from more natural storms have all too often ended up on the island's deadly rocks. To make the harbor—the primary anchorage for lobster men on Maine's sleepy Swans Island—easier and safer to reach, a lighthouse was built on Hockamock Head near its entrance in 1872.

At first a pair of range lights marked the safe channel, but these so confused local sailors that wrecks occurred even faster than before. To simplify matters, the Lighthouse Board ordered the smaller of the two towers pulled down in 1885. This left the square, thirty-two-foot, rear-range tower to guide vessels into the harbor. Still active, its white light occults, winking off briefly every four seconds.

Travel information: Swans Island can be reached via regularly scheduled ferries from Bass Harbor. For information contact the Maine State Ferry Service, P.O. Box 114, Bass Harbor, ME 04653; (207) 244-3254 or (800) 491-4883. The lighthouse is at the end of the main island road, a little less than 5 miles from the ferry slip. Services on the island are limited to a couple of small restaurants open only during summer, a general store open year-round, and a bed-and-breakfast handy for those who miss the last ferry to the mainland.

■ BEAR ISLAND LIGHT ■
Bear Island (1839, 1853, and 1889)

The Bear Island Light tower is only thirty-three feet tall, but it stands on the highest point of a rocky islet, elevating the focal plane of its signal to more than one hundred feet above the water. From its lofty perch, the little lighthouse guides fishing boats and pleasure craft into beautiful Northeast Harbor and ferries out to Acadia's timeless Cranberry Islands.

Two earlier lighthouses preceded the present tower and separate dwelling. The first was a rustic stone dwelling and tower built in 1839. The second, completed in 1853, had a separate brick tower that was apparently removed to make way for construction of the existing station in 1889. A plastic optic replaced the original fifth-order Fresnel lens during the 1980s.

Travel information: From the Northeast Harbor Marina, you can see the Bear Island Lighthouse in the distance. To reach Northeast Harbor, one of several extraordinarily scenic villages on Mount Desert Island, follow Route 3 and then Route 189 from Ellsworth. The deck of the Cranberry Island ferry offers a closer view of the lighthouse. For information on scheduled service from Northeast Harbor during summer, call (207) 276-3717 or (207) 276-5352.

■ BAKER ISLAND LIGHT ■
Baker Island (1828 and 1855)

Vessels plying the rock-strewn waters near Maine's legendary Mount Desert Island have long relied on the Baker Island Light. Since 1828 it has warned them away from the deadly shoals just off Little Cranberry Island and guided them safely into broad Frenchman Bay. The original wood-frame lighthouse was replaced in 1855 by the present forty-three-foot brick tower and separate dwelling.

When William Gilley, the station's first keeper, was dismissed after more than two decades of service, he took the government to court, claiming he owned the island and the lighthouse. Legal squabbling between the Lighthouse Service and the Gilley family went on for more than forty years before the government finally proved its clear title to the property. Baker Island now belongs to Acadia National Park.

The fourth-order Fresnel lens that at one time served here is now superseded by an automated plastic lens powered by batteries. These, in turn, are recharged by solar panels.

Travel information: Each summer, national park naturalists lead excursions to Baker Island that include a visit to the lighthouse. Contact Acadia National Park, P.O. Box 177, Bar Harbor, ME 04609; (207) 288–3338.

■ BLUE HILL BAY LIGHT ■
Green Island (1857)

Since before the Civil War, the Blue Hill Bay Lighthouse has survived wind, weather, and the encroaching sea on tiny Green Island near the entrance to Eggemoggin Reach. Completed in 1857, it served for almost eighty years before its work was taken over by a more easily maintained light mounted on a nearby steel-skeleton tower. In operation since 1935, the new steel light tower employs an automated fifth-order Fresnel lens. The still-standing old brick tower and attached cape-style dwelling are privately owned.

Courtesy Lighthouse Digest

Travel information: One of the hardest light stations in Maine to visit or photograph, the Blue Hill Bay Lighthouse is difficult to approach from the water and is probably best seen from the air. Aerial sight-seeing tours that include overflights of this and other lighthouses are available at the Hancock County/Bar Harbor Airport, off Route 3; call (207) 667–5534.

■ ISLE AU HAUT LIGHT ■
Isle au Haut (1907)

This lofty, rock-strewn island is often the first land spotted by mariners emerging from the open Atlantic. In 1604 French explorer Samuel de Champlain saw its densely forested hills rising blue above the ocean horizon and gave the place its name, Isle au Haut, or "high island." Despite its beauty and the abundance of food in the rich waters surrounding the island, Champlain found no one living there. The island is still sparsely populated. Only a few dozen hardy islanders live here year-round.

The Isle au Haut Lighthouse has served the island's scatter of resident watermen since 1907. The forty-eight-foot granite-and-brick tower rises from the rocks at the edge of the tide line on the island's Robinson Point. Still active, its light flashes red and white every four seconds. Nowa-

days the keeper's dwelling offers bed-and-breakfast rooms to island visitors in search of a truly unique experience.

> *Travel information:* Much of pristine Isle au Haut is part of Acadia National Park. Ferries from Stonington provide passenger access to the island; call (207) 367-6516. For rooms at the lighthouse, contact The Keeper's House, P.O. Box 26, Isle au Haut, ME 04645; (207) 367-2261.

■ EAGLE ISLAND LIGHT ■
Eagle Island (1838)

First lit in 1838 during the presidential administration of Martin Van Buren, the Eagle Island Light still guides vessels around Hardhead Shoals and into Penobscot Bay. One of a chain of lights near the mouth of the Penobscot River, including those at Dice Head and Fort Point, it marked a clear path through the rocky bay for a host of nineteenth-century freighters carrying lumber from mills in Bucksport and Bangor.

The short, whitewashed rubble-stone tower stands on a grassy cliff that helps elevate its light to more than a hundred feet above high tide. A fourth-order Fresnel lens that previously served here was removed in 1963 in favor of an automated plastic lens. The 1,200-pound brass fog bell was decommissioned at the same time, but not in a manner the Coast Guard might have hoped. It broke away, rolled over the cliff, and fell into the sea. A lobsterman later salvaged the huge bell and sold it to noted nature photographer Eliot Porter for use as a dinner bell.

> *Travel information:* Eagle Island Lighthouse is best seen from the water. Summer schooner cruises may pass the island (see Travel information for **Saddleback Ledge Light**). Keep in mind that Maine had several Eagle Islands. The one in Casco Bay, near Portland, was the home of Admiral Robert E. Peary, the first man to reach the North Pole.

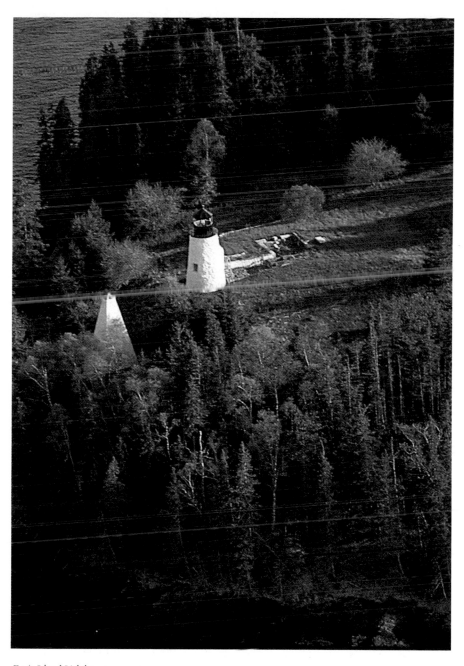

Eagle Island Lighthouse

■ SADDLEBACK LEDGE LIGHT ■
Isle au Haut (1839)

Saddleback Ledge, near Isle au Haut, is a bare scrap of rock exposed on all sides to the pounding sea. A forty-two-foot, cone-shaped stone tower has guarded the ledge since 1839, its flashing white light warning sailors in danger of collision with the rock against certain calamity. The lighthouse was automated in 1954, but until that time, keepers who had little or no contact with the outside world for weeks or even months at a stretch kept vigil here. Although the tower still clings precariously to the barren rock, all traces of dwellings and outbuildings have been swept away by wind, water, and time.

> *Travel information:* The Saddleback Ledge Lighthouse is a prominent feature of almost any cruise traversing the eastern approaches to Maine's impressive Penobscot Bay. Both two-day and weeklong schooner cruises are available in Camden, Rockport, and Rockland, Maine; (800) 533–9595. These cruises may or may not pass by Saddleback Ledge, but more than a few lighthouses will be on the itinerary.

Saddleback Ledge Light

■ DEER ISLAND THOROUGHFARE LIGHT ■
Stonington (1857)

All that remains of this pre–Civil War light station is the twenty-five-foot square brick tower on Mark Island. The light remains active, however, and guides fishing boats and pleasure craft into the thoroughfare that links Stonington to the Atlantic. A plastic lens now serves in place of the original fourth-order Fresnel.

Travel information: The lighthouse can be seen from the heights above Stonington, as authentic and hardworking a fishing village as you'll likely see anywhere along the Maine coast. While in town, stop in for some chowder at the Fisherman's Friend restaurant. Summer sight-seeing cruises from Stonington often pass by the tower; call (207) 367-6516.

■ DICE HEAD LIGHT ■
Castine (1829)

One of the oldest and most historic towns in America, Castine had its beginnings as a French fur trading station established in 1614. Seafaring nations long coveted the rocky heights above Dice Head, which domi-nates the entrance to the Penobscot River. Over the years the flags of four nations flut-tered above forts here, and several battles were fought for possession of the town.

In 1829 the Lighthouse Service built a rubble-stone-and-brick tower high up on the cliffs of Dice Head to guide lumber ships in and out of the Penobscot. The light also welcomed home the clipper ships of Castine captains on the last leg of adventurous trading cruises that took them as far away as China. A colonial cape dwelling, added to the station in 1858, was attached to the tower by a short, enclosed passageway. At the same time the origi-nal Winslow Lewis lamp-and-reflector system was replaced with a fourth-order Fresnel lens. Its powerful beacon could penetrate seventeen miles of storm-tossed Penobscot Bay waters. The Coast Guard discontinued the lighthouse in 1956, replacing it with a flashing beacon shining from a small skeleton tower located on the rocks beneath the cliffs. Unfortunately, the dwelling (as shown above) was badly damaged by fire in 1999.

Travel information: Anyone who appreciates history, old homes, and matchless ocean scenery will love Castine. To get there, turn off U.S. Highway 1 at Orland and follow Routes 175 and 166 to the town. The lighthouse is at the end of Battle Avenue.

■ FORT POINT LIGHT ■
Stockton Springs (1836)

During the nineteenth century as many as two hundred lumber ships might pass the square-towered Fort Point Lighthouse in a single day. Established in 1836 by order of President Andrew Jackson, the light pointed the way to the Penobscot River and beyond to Bangor, at that time the world's busiest lumber port.

Although not much taller than the attached keeper's dwelling, the thirty-one-foot tower stands on a high promontory, its light eighty-eight feet above the water. The lantern still contains the fourth-order Fresnel lens installed when the station was renovated in 1857. A fog-bell house stands nearby, one of the last of its kind.

Travel information: Turn off U.S. Highway 1 in Stockton Springs and follow East Cape Road to Fort Point State Park and the lighthouse. Park employees occupy the dwelling, but visitors may walk the grounds and enjoy a sweeping view of the Penobscot Bay. Nearby are the ruins of Fort Pownall, where British and American forces fought two battles during the Revolutionary War.

■ GRINDLE POINT LIGHT ■
Islesboro (1850 and 1874)

A narrow blade of rock more than ten miles long cleaves the upper reaches of Penobscot Bay. Known as Islesboro, it is summer home to many wealthy out-of-

staters (people from "away") as well as a community of Maine fishing folk. Most residents travel to and from the mainland via a car ferry that crosses over from Lincolnville several times each day. A small brick lighthouse marks the Islesboro ferry landing.

The square, thirty-nine-foot brick tower, built in 1874, replaced an earlier lighthouse in operation since 1850. The station was decommissioned in 1934. Under pressure from local traditionalists, however, the Coast Guard reactivated the old lighthouse in 1987. Residents and visitors can see its flashing green light from several points along U.S. Highway 1 near Lincolnville.

Travel information: The Islesboro ferry schedule varies, with only two daily round-trip crossings from January through May, up to seven each day during summer, and three or more daily from September through December. Contact the Maine State Ferry Service, P.O. Box 214, Lincolnville, ME 04849; (207) 734–6935. The lighthouse stands adjacent to the ferry slip. The Sailor's Memorial Museum, open daily in July and August, is located in the keeper's dwelling.

■ CURTIS ISLAND LIGHT ■
Camden (1835 and 1896)

During summer passenger schooners with masts taller and stouter than telephone poles crowd Camden's harbor and lend this charming coastal town a distinctly nineteenth-century feeling. On their way into the harbor, the schooners pass Curtis Island, with its tiny brick light tower and compact clapboard keeper's dwelling. The squat tower, only twenty-five feet tall, was built in 1896 to replace an earlier structure that had served for sixty years. The original fourth-order Fresnel lens remains in place. Its fixed green light is now solar powered.

Travel information: Located on the far side of the heavily forested island, the lighthouse is almost impossible to see from land. Harbor cruises often swing around the island so that their passengers can glimpse the little tower and dwelling. A range of granite mountains meets the sea at Camden, and visitors should definitely set aside time to enjoy the town and its picturesque setting. Several of Camden's schooners offer extended cruises, with ample opportunities to view and photograph Maine lighthouses. For more information on Camden or its schooners, call (800) 533–9595 or (207) 236–4404 (Camden Chamber of Commerce).

■ ROCKLAND BREAKWATER LIGHT ■
Rockland (1888 and 1902)

During the nineteenth century, prodigious quantities of lime and construction stone were shipped through the appropriately named port of Rockland, Maine. Freighters lying at anchor in Rockland's unprotected harbor were often at the mercy of high waves rolling in from the sea. To offset this danger the government built a breakwater in 1888, marking its outer end with a small trapezoidal light tower. In 1902 both breakwater and harbor signal were updated. Engineers extended the breakwater to its present length of more than a mile and constructed a more substantial lighthouse to warn mariners of its presence.

The station's square, twenty-five-foot tower rises from the corner of its two-story dwelling. The lighthouse stands on a platform of squared-off granite blocks. A modern optic now does the work of the fourth-order Fresnel lens that formerly produced its flashing white light.

> **Travel information:** From U.S. Highway 1 in Rockland, follow Waldo Road and Samoset Road to the Marie Reed Breakwater Park. Visitors can hike out the breakwater to the lighthouse. The lighthouse and its light, often stunningly beautiful at night, also can be seen from several points along the Rockland waterfront.
>
> Lighthouse lovers have another treat in store at Rockland. The Shore Village Museum on Limerock Street houses the most astounding collection of lighthouse lenses and equipment anywhere in America. Operated since the 1970s by Ken Black, a retired Coast Guard warrant officer, this delightful and highly informative museum focuses on lighthouse history and engineering. Contact the Shore Village Museum, 104 Limerock Street, Rockland, ME 04841; (207) 594–0311.

■ OWLS HEAD LIGHT ■
Rockland (1825)

Ferry passengers leaving Rockland often scan the headland at the mouth of the harbor, looking for its legendary owl. Anyone with a good imagination can see the old owl sculpted by nature into the rocks. A far more obvious feature of the promontory, however, is the short, white cylinder of its lighthouse. Built in 1825, this little lighthouse is beloved by mariners who, for the better part of two centuries, have followed its fixed white beacon to the safety of Rockland Harbor. The classic fourth-order Fresnel lens that has long served the station remains in place.

The station's especially powerful fog signal has also kept countless ships from crashing on the rocks. Spot, the family dog of a keeper who worked here during the 1930s, is credited with having saved more than a few fog-blinded mariners with his ceaseless barking. What is more, the keeper trained the clever mutt to pull on the fog-

bell rope whenever his sharp ears heard a vessel approaching.

Travel information: From Rockland take North Shore Road and follow signs to Owl's Head State Park. From the parking area a short drive along a highly scenic access road leads to the lighthouse. Keep in mind that this is an active Coast Guard facility. Also, be prepared to hold your ears, as the fog signal is so powerful it can damage hearing. The lighthouse can also be seen and enjoyed from the Vinalhaven ferry. For information, call (207) 596-2203.

■ BROWNS HEAD LIGHT ■
Vinalhaven (1832)

The Browns Head Lighthouse began marking the western approaches to Vinalhaven Island when Andrew Jackson was president. Completed in 1832 at a cost of only $4,000—including the adjacent dwelling—the twenty-foot stone tower became a permanent feature of the island landscape. To this day its fixed white light guides fishing boats and ferries. In 1902 the government strengthened the beacon by exchanging the existing fifth-order Fresnel lens for a more powerful fourth-order Fresnel, which remains in service.

Travel information: The Rockland/Vinalhaven ferries make three trips each way daily from April through October and twice daily during the rest of the year. The 15-mile crossing takes about seventy minutes. For ferry information contact the Maine State Ferry Service, P.O. Box 645, Rockland, ME 04841; (207) 596-2203. The light station is 6 miles north of Vinalhaven Village and about a mile off North Haven Road. The century-old dwelling is now a private residence.

While in Vinalhaven, don't miss the Historical Society Museum, which features the original Browns Head fog bell. Of particular interest to lighthouse lovers is Armbrust Hill, just south of the village. From here you can see the towers at Mantinicus Island to the southwest and Two Bush Island and Saddleback Ledge to the southeast.

■ HERON NECK LIGHT ■
Vinalhaven (1853)

Among the approximately one thousand hardy souls who live year-round on Vinalhaven Island, a considerable number are fishermen. Just as their forefathers

have for nearly one and a half centuries, these mariners depend on the lighthouse at Heron Neck to guide them into Carver's Harbor. Its fixed white and red beacon marks the entrance to Hurricane Sound as well as the approaches to Vinalhaven. A fifth-order Fresnel lens beamed out from atop the thirty-foot tower until replaced by a plastic lens in 1982. The Island Institute now owns the station and surrounding property, located on Green Island, just off the main island of Vinalhaven. A nonprofit organization, the institute is dedicated to preserving Maine's old maritime culture.

> *Travel information:* This lighthouse is very difficult to reach, but it can be seen from boats approaching Vinalhaven Island or entering Hurricane Sound. Summer cruises from Rockland or Stonington often feature views of the Heron Neck, **Goose Rocks,** or **Browns Head Lights.** For information and advice on these and other Maine attractions, call (800) 533–9595.

■ GOOSE ROCKS LIGHT ■
Vinalhaven (1890)

The Fox Island Thoroughfare separates Vinalhaven Island from the smaller North Haven Island and provides a shortcut for vessels passing between the east and west

Penobscot Bay channels. A killer ledge lurks just beneath the surface of this otherwise inviting passage. Since 1890, the ledge has been marked by an open-water light tower built atop an iron and concrete caisson. The fifty-foot cast-iron tower resembles the **Lubec Channel** "spark plug" **Lighthouse,** about a hundred miles to the east. It is difficult to imagine that keepers once lived and worked for months at a time in this confined space. Automated since 1963, the solar-powered beacon flashes red every six seconds.

> *Travel information:* The offshore tower can be seen from Calderwood Point on Vinalhaven Island, but is best seen by

boat. Summer cruises to this and other lighthouses in this area are available in Camden; call (207) 236-6250.

■ TWO BUSH ISLAND LIGHT ■
Rockland (1897)

Long ago, seamen heading north toward the west side of the Penobscot Bay scanned the horizon for a small island, barren except for a pair of scraggly pines. They knew that "Two Bush" Island marked a safe channel leading into the bay. In 1897 the government gave them a more substantial marker by building a forty-two-foot-tall, square brick light tower on the island.

For many years a fifth-order Fresnel lens served here, but in 1963 a modern optic was installed, and the station was automated. Later, a U.S. Army Special Forces team blew up the old keeper's dwelling as part of a training exercise. The tower still stands, however, and its light remains active, flashing white and red every five seconds. Its beacon can be seen from up to eighteen miles away.

Travel information: Often passengers can see Two Bush Island Lighthouse or its beacon from the Vinalhaven ferry or the decks of summer excursion boats headed for Matinicus Island or other coastal attractions. For ferry schedules and prices, call (207) 596-2203. For information on cruises call the Maine Visitors Bureau at (800) 533-9595.

■ MATINICUS ROCK LIGHT ■
Rockland/Matinicus Island (1827 and 1846)

Exposed to rain, wind, fog, and giant waves, Matinicus Rock seems an unlikely place to build a lighthouse of wood, but that is exactly what the Lighthouse Service did, throwing up two flimsy wooden towers in 1827. Surprisingly, the wooden towers survived almost twenty years; not until 1846 were they replaced by a pair of granite towers.

The new towers stood sixty yards apart, and, like their predecessors, they displayed two lights that appeared quite close together when seen from a distance. The builders hoped mariners could easily distinguish these key beacons from others along this especially dangerous portion of the Maine coast. Unfortunately, the Winslow Lewis lamps and reflectors used in these towers proved too weak for the station to serve its purpose effectively.

In 1857 the Lighthouse Board ordered the station's towers rebuilt and outfitted with third-order Fresnel lenses. Built with massive granite blocks, these towers have stood up to the worst the sea could throw at them for nearly one and a half centuries. Although the south tower still stands, it lost its job in 1924, when the Lighthouse Service decided to stop using twin lights and removed its lantern and lens. The north light still shines, warning mariners away from the rock with powerful white flashes, visible every ten seconds from up to twenty miles away. The north tower's old Fresnel was replaced by a plastic lens in 1983.

This is the light station where heroic teenager Abbie Burgess helped save her family and pet chickens during a tremendous storm in 1856 (see page 14).

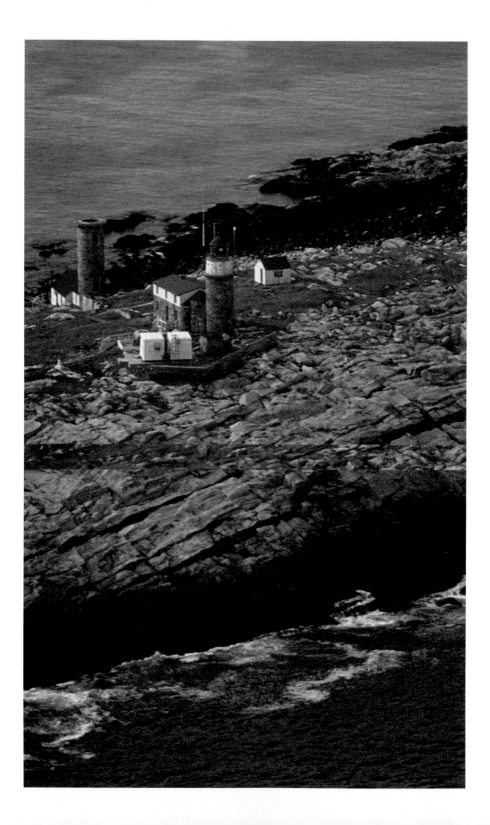

Travel information: The Fresnel lens from the old south tower can be seen at the excellent Shore Village Museum in Rockland; contact Shore Village Museum, 104 Limerock Street, Rockland ME 04841; (207) 594-0311. Excursions to Matinicus Rock are available during summer from Rockland. For information on available cruises, call the Maine Visitors Bureau at (800) 533-9595. The island is a favorite of bird-watchers since it is home to puffins, petrels, and other rare seabirds.

■ WHITEHEAD LIGHT ■
Thomaston/Sprucehead Island (1807 and 1852)

Established by order of President Thomas Jefferson in 1807, this is one of the oldest light stations in Maine. The forty-foot granite tower and adjacent wooden dwelling seen here today date from the 1850s when a third-order Fresnel lens replaced an outmoded lamp-and-reflector system. A two-thousand-pound fog bell once served here, and for many years it was rung by a mechanical contraption powered by the waves.

Ellis Dolph, one of Whitehead's early keepers, was fired for selling government lighting oil for personal profit. Dolph overstated the station's needs so that he could keep the oil and profits flowing.

Having guarded the southern entrance to Maine's Penobscot Bay for nearly two centuries, the Whitehead Light station on rugged Pine Island remains an active aid to navigation. While the Coast Guard maintains the station's light and fog signal, a private children's camp leases the keeper's house and other station property. Although the light was established in 1807, the existing, forty-one-foot conical granite tower dates to 1852. Replaced by a modern optic in 1982, the third-order Fresnel lens that served here for more than a century is now on display at the Shore Village Museum in Rockland.

Travel information: The tower can be viewed from the end of Sprucehead Point Road in Sprucehead, but is best seen from the water. Also visible from Sprucehead is the **Two Bush Island Lighthouse** (1897). However, the forty-two-foot Two Bush tower is located several miles offshore and is best seen from the water. The Shore Village Museum address is 104 Limerock Street, Rockland, ME 04841; (207) 594-0311.

(Opposite page) *Matinicus Rock Light*

■ TENANTS HARBOR LIGHT ■
Near Tenants Harbor (1857)

Built in 1857, the Tenants Harbor Lighthouse, southwest of Rockland, Maine, guided fishing boats and other vessels for more than seventy-five years. When the station was closed in 1933, its wooden cape dwelling and attached twenty-seven-foot brick tower were sold to private owners. For years, it was owned by the family of the famous artist Andrew Wyeth, who is said to have painted some of his best canvases while living here. Wyeth's son Jamie, also an artist, now lives and paints in the keeper's dwelling.

> *Travel information:* The lighthouse is on private property, but it can be seen from the water as well as from a landing off Route 131 in Tenants Harbor.

■ MARSHALL POINT LIGHT ■
Port Clyde (1832 and 1858)

The small stone lighthouse on Marshall Point serves Port Clyde, one of the loveliest and most bucolic fishing villages in America. Built in 1858, the signal replaced an earlier soapstone structure that had stood here since 1832. Rising from the water's edge, the thirty-foot tower looks much like the one at Isle au Haut with its upper section of brick and lower one of granite blocks. A wooden walkway at one time provided access to shore. A fifth-order Fresnel lens served here until 1980; now a modern optic sends out a fixed white light that can be seen from approximately twelve miles away.

> *Travel information:* This old tower is highly recommended for lighthouse lovers because of its peaceful setting and proximity to the Marshall Point Lighthouse Museum. Managed by the St. George Historical Society, this fine little museum displays artifacts and recounts the histories of the Marshall Point, **Whitehead, Tenants Harbor,** and **St. George Lighthouses.** The museum is free and open to the public May through October. Contact the Marshall Point Lighthouse Museum, P.O. Box 247, Port Clyde, ME 04855; (207) 372–6450.

> The tower and museum are located at the end of Marshall Point Road in Port Clyde. Reach them via Route 131 from U.S. Highway 1 in Thomaston. On the way to Port Clyde, stop in Tenants Harbor for a look at the Tenants Harbor Lighthouse. Decommissioned in 1934, it has served as both a home and art studio of Andrew and Jamie Wyeth.

■ MONHEGAN ISLAND LIGHT ■
Monhegan Island (1824 and 1851)

About a dozen miles from the Maine coast, the near-solid granite mass of Monhegan Island rises out of the Atlantic, its 150-foot cliffs towering over the waves. Since the 1620s, the one-and-a-half-mile-long island has been home to a hardy maritime community, and a scattering of lobstering and fishing families still live there. Theirs is a tradition-minded community, and even now most residences have no electric power.

The compact electric generator that supplies power to the modern optic of the Monhegan Island Light tower may seem out of place here. Located atop the cliffs, the forty-seven-foot tower emits a light with a focal plane nearly 180 feet above the waves. From this height it can be seen more than twenty miles away. The present tower, completed in 1851, replaced an earlier lighthouse that had served the island since 1824. Until 1959 a magnificent second-order Fresnel lens focused the light.

> *Travel information:* Excursions to Monhegan Island are available during summer from Boothbay Harbor (call 800–298–2284) or New Harbor (call 800–278–3346) and year round from Port Clyde (call 207–372–8848).

■ PEMAQUID POINT LIGHT ■
Damariscotta/Pemaquid Point (1827)

The unusual striated rock formations of Pemaquid Point look like ocean waves turned to stone—more than a few vessels lost in the fog have sailed up onto them with disastrous results. Established in 1827, the Pemaquid Point Light has prevented many such wrecks.

Built during the administration of John Quincy Adams, the stone tower had walls three feet thick. Despite their bulk the original walls did not stand up to the harsh local weather and had to be rebuilt in 1835 and again in 1857. The keeper's stone dwelling also suffered and was replaced in 1857 by the wood-frame cape that nowadays houses an excellent museum.

The thirty-eight-foot tower stands high on the rocks, placing the focal point of the light almost eighty feet above sea level. The station still employs its venerable fourth-order Fresnel lens; its flashing white light can be seen some fifteen miles away.

> *Travel information:* From U.S. Highway 1 at Damariscotta, follow Route 130 for 16 miles to the lighthouse. The keeper's dwelling now houses the Fisherman's Museum, which contains a fascinating array of nautical and lighthouse exhibits including a fourth-order Fresnel like the one in the lighthouse. The massive bronze fog bell from the old Manna Island

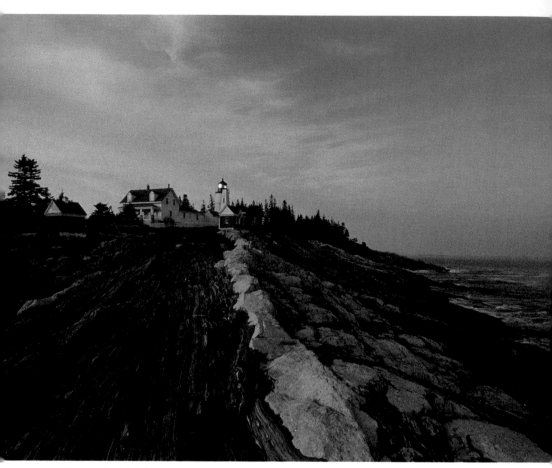

Pemaquid Point Light

station hangs outside. Contact the Fisherman's Museum, Pemaquid Point Road, New Harbor, ME 04554; (207) 677–2494. Cruises from nearby New Harbor pass by the active **Franklin Island Lighthouse** (1805) to the east of Pemaquid Point; call (800) 278–3346.

■ RAM ISLAND LIGHT ■
Near Boothbay Harbor (1883)

Located on rocky Ram Island, this light marks one of the key passages leading to Boothbay Harbor, now a popular summertime tourist destination. When the station was established in 1883, the seaside villages hereabouts were frequented mostly by fishermen. To help them avoid the ledges near the island, the government built a thirty-five-foot granite and brick tower and fitted it with a fourth-order Fresnel lens. Keepers lived in an L-shaped residence some distance inland. Although the station was automated many years ago, both the dwelling and tower remain standing. The Fresnel lens has been replaced by a modern optic, but the beacon is still in operation. It warns mariners with an alternating red light.

Travel information: The light can be seen from several parking areas along the shore road on Ocean Point at the end of Route 96 south of Boothbay Harbor. The Maine Maritime Museum in Bath operates summer cruises that pass Ram Island and other lighthouses along the mid-coast of Maine; call (207) 443-1316.

■ HENDRICKS HEAD LIGHT ■
Boothbay Harbor (1829 and 1875)

During an especially severe storm in the late 1860s, the Hendricks Head keeper pulled an ice-encrusted mattress from the waves. Inside, the astonished man found a crying baby and a note from a sinking schooner's desperate captain who had committed his tiny daughter "into God's hands." The keeper and his wife adopted the little girl, the lost ship's only survivor.

Established in 1829, the Hendricks Head Light no doubt helped prevent many other such losses. The present forty-foot, Federal-style brick tower and connected wooden dwelling were built in 1875 on the site of the original lighthouse, destroyed by fire earlier that year. The station's automated plastic lens displays a fixed white light with red sectors.

Courtesy Ben Russell

Travel information: From U.S. Highway 1 take Route 27 through Boothbay Harbor to Southport Island. The lighthouse can be seen from a public beach just off Beach Road. Visitors can see the **Burnt Island Lighthouse** (1857), with its flashing red light, from the waterfront in Boothbay Harbor and, in the distance, the **Cuckolds Lighthouse,** dating from the early 1800s. The **Ram Island Lighthouse** (1883), which resembles those at Isle au Haut and Marshall Point, can be seen from roadside overlooks along Route 96 in Ocean Point to the east of Boothbay Harbor. Cuckolds Lighthouse can also be seen from here.

■ SEGUIN ISLAND LIGHT ■
Georgetown (1795)

Among the oldest and most significant navigational stations in the eastern United States, Seguin Island Lighthouse stands on a rocky outcropping near the mouth of Maine's Kennebec River. Built by order of President George Washington, the lighthouse had John Polersky, an old Revolutionary War soldier, as its first keeper. The hard work and horrible weather ruined Polersky's health, and he soon died from the strain and exposure.

The lighthouse survived Polersky by many years but finally succumbed to a storm in 1820. The stone tower built in its place stood until 1857, when construction crews completed the present fifty-three-foot granite tower

on the island's highest point. The huge first-order Fresnel lens installed at that time still shines from its lofty perch 180 feet above the sea and can be seen from a distance of up to eighteen miles.

Travel information: The lighthouse cannot be seen easily from land, but the Maine Maritime Museum on Washington Street in Bath runs regular tour boats to Seguin Island during summer. The museum is a must-see attraction for anyone interested in maritime history, shipbuilding, or lighthouses. Contact the Maine Maritime Museum, 243 Washington Street, Bath, ME 04530; (207) 443–1316. Museum guides can direct you to several small, but interesting, lighthouses along the Kennebec River. These include the **Squirrel Point** (1898), **Perkins Island** (1898), **Pond Island** (1855), **Doubling Point** (1898), and **Doubling Point Range** (1898) **Lighthouses.** Most of them can be seen from Route 209 or side roads between Bath and Popham Beach.

Pond Island

Perkins Island

■ DOUBLING POINT RANGE LIGHTS ■
Arrowsic Island near Bath (1898)

These little range towers are only twenty-one and thirteen feet tall, respectively. Rather simply constructed of wood, they were placed on Arrowsic Island in 1898, the same year the nearby **Squirrel Point** and **Perkins Island** Light Stations were built. They are the only active range lights in the state of Maine. As with other range lights, the Doubling Point beacons help mariners stay within a narrow safe channel. Pilots try to keep the two lights stacked one atop the other. When the upper light slips out of the vertical either to the left or right, the approaching pilot steers in the opposite direction. Originally, both the small Doubling Point Range towers were equipped with fifth-order Fresnels, but these were replaced by plastic lenses when the lights were automated in 1979. The station's L-shaped wooden keeper's residence remains standing.

> *Travel information:* From U. S. Highway 1 follow Route 127 south and turn right onto Whitmore's Landing Road. At Doubling Point Road turn left and proceed to the station parking lot. While the towers are not open, visitors are welcome to walk along the station boardwalk to view and photograph these unusual structures.

■ HALFWAY ROCK LIGHT ■
Portland/Casco Bay (1871)

An open ocean tower somewhat like the one at Minot's Ledge in Massachusetts, the Halfway Rock Lighthouse marks a notorious sea hazard about ten miles from Portland, Maine's busiest seaport. Many ships caught by rocks here simply disappeared, the story of their loss never told—or even known. Congress appropriated $50,000 to mark the rocks in 1869, but the station took two years to build. The seventy-seven-foot tower's massive granite blocks dovetail in such a way that the walls grow even stronger when pounded by the waves. The station remains active, its automated lens flashing a red warning that can be seen for twenty miles.

Courtesy *Lighthouse Digest*

> *Travel information:* The lighthouse can be seen in the distance from high points in the city of Portland. Perhaps the best view is from the Portland Observatory on Congress Street. Otherwise it can only be viewed from the water.

The Portland area is rich in lighthouses, and harbor cruises, available mostly during summer, provide excellent views for photographing them. From cruise-boat decks you may see the **Portland Breakwater Lighthouse** (1875), **Spring Point Ledge Lighthouse** (1895), **Ram Island Ledge Lighthouse** (1905), and **Portland Head Lighthouse** (1791). For more information call Eagle Tours at (207) 774-6498, Bay View Cruises at (207) 761-0496, or the Portland Visitors Center at (207) 772-4994.

■ RAM ISLAND LEDGE ■
Cape Elizabeth (1873 and 1905)

Beginning in 1873, a beacon shining from atop a simple wooden tripod marked the dangerous Portland Ledge. It was replaced by the existing, much more substantial seventy-two-foot granite tower in 1905. Nearly 3,000 tons of granite were used in construction of the tower. A powerful third-order Fresnel lens served here for many years, but was replaced by a modern aeromarine beacon when the station was automated in 1959.

> *Travel information:* The Ram Island Ledge Lighthouse is located offshore about a quarter mile from the Portland Head Lighthouse. Follow Route 77 to Fort Williams Park, just south of South Portland.

■ PORTLAND BREAKWATER LIGHT ■
South Portland (1855 and 1875)

Classical Greek styling gives this little thirteen-foot tower the look of a giant chess rook. Despite its rather whimsical appearance, the tower and its beacon were a serious concern to mariners. The light alerted them to the presence of the Portland

Breakwater, at one time more than half a mile long. Built in response to a destructive storm in 1831, the breakwater was intended to protect the harbor, but since it was sometimes difficult to see, it posed a considerable threat to shipping. In 1855, a lighthouse was placed at the end of the breakwater to warn mariners. As the harbor was filled in over the years, the mainland marched steadily out toward the end of the breakwater with the result that the lighthouse now stands on dry land. The tower seen here today dates from 1875 when it replaced an earlier structure that was hauled away for use elsewhere as a watchtower. A small sixth-order Fresnel lens provided the beacon until the light was extinguished in 1942.

> *Travel information:* From Route 77 in South Portland, follow Broadway,

Breakwater Drive, and then Madison Street to the parking area for Bug Light Park and the lighthouse. This tower is one of several lighthouses highlighting Portland-area sight-seeing cruises; call (207) 761-0496.

■ PORTLAND HEAD LIGHT ■
South Portland (1791)

Among its first acts the U.S. Congress created a Lighthouse Establishment in 1789. Constructing the Portland Head Lighthouse became the first major project federal lighthouse officials undertook. Its eighty-foot fieldstone tower was completed in 1791, during George Washington's third year as president. Remarkably, it still stands and, despite numerous repairs and renovations over the years, looks much as it did in the late eighteenth century. A rambling, red-roofed keeper's residence stands beside the tower on a rocky, wave-swept headland. Together they form one of most beautiful and frequently photographed scenes in the East.

The Coast Guard removed the station's fourth-order Fresnel lens in 1989, the bicentennial year of the Lighthouse Service. A modern rotating beacon serves here now, its powerful flashing light seen for up to twenty-five miles. The dwelling now houses the Museum at Portland Head, where visitors can see an enormous second-order bivalve lens that once served here.

Travel information: The lighthouse is located in Fort Williams Park, off Route 77 near South Portland. Contact the Museum at Portland Head, P.O. Box 6260, Cape Elizabeth, ME 04107; (207) 799-2661. Fortunate passengers of airliners landing at Portland occasionally enjoy a stunning view of Portland Head and its two-century-old lighthouse.

■ CAPE ELIZABETH LIGHT ■
Cape Elizabeth (1828 and 1874)

The Cape Elizabeth Light station once guided mariners with two lights—one fixed, the other flashing. The twin lights, shining from towers spaced about 300 yards apart, allowed navigators approaching from any direction to quickly find their position on a chart. The first towers built here in 1828 cost the government only $4,250 and lasted for almost half a century. Finally, all but destroyed by wind, weather, and the sea, the deteriorated towers were replaced in 1874 by the handsome cast-iron towers that still stand. The Lighthouse Service stopped using twin beacons in 1924; afterward, only the east light was displayed. Although its second-order Fresnel lens was removed in 1994, the beacon remains in service, its flashing white light visible some fifteen miles away.

Travel information: Together with their gorgeous setting, the sixty-seven-foot Italianate Cape Elizabeth towers make this one of the loveliest and most distinctive lighthouses in America. It is located in Two Lights State Park, easily reached from Route 77 via Two Lights Road. Keep in mind that the residence and grounds are privately owned. A visit to Cape Elizabeth can be part of a compact lighthouse adventure including nearby **Portland Head** and several other lighthouses in the Portland area.

■ CAPE NEDDICK LIGHT ■
York (1879)

Just off Cape Neddick, near the old colonial town of York, Maine, lies a small, barren island long known to local fishermen as the "Nubble." Imaginative visitors say they can see the ghostly likenesses of people—perhaps sailors shipwrecked here long ago—in the fantastic shapes of the island's rock formations. Since 1879, the Cape Neddick Lighthouse, stationed on the island's highest point, has warned mariners of the deadly Nubble. From a forty-foot cast-iron tower, its flashing red light signals danger. A wood-frame residence connects to the tower by a covered walkway. Delightful miniature lighthouses decorate the balusters of the service gallery.

Travel information: From U.S. Highway 1 take Route 1A into York Beach. Turn right and follow Nubble Road to Nubble Point to enjoy a fine view of the lighthouse. Do not attempt to walk across to the island; the footing is dangerous, and tides may strand you. While in the area, don't miss the Lighthouse Depot in Wells, several miles north of York. This extraordinary shop is a treasure house of information and keepsakes related to Cape Neddick and lighthouses throughout the United States. Write to Lighthouse Depot, P.O. Box 427, Wells, ME 04090 or call (207) 646-3128. For mail orders call (800) 758-1444.

■ WHALEBACK LIGHTHOUSE ■
Kittery Point (1820, 1831, and 1872)

A scatter of ship-killing rocks and ledges obstruct the entrance to the Piscataqua River and the approaches to New Hampshire's Portsmouth Harbor. Prominent among these is Whaleback Ledge, located just off Kittery Point, Maine, across the river from Portsmouth. A lighthouse marked the ledge as early as 1820, but it was destroyed by a storm in 1830. A second Whaleback tower built the following year gave way in a gale during the late 1860s. The fifty-foot granite tower that marks Whaleback Ledge today was completed in 1872. Its fourth order Fresnel lens was replaced by a modern optic after the station was automated in 1963.

Travel information: From U.S. 1A in York Harbor, follow Route 103 south for about four miles. Turn left onto Gerrish Island Lane and follow it to Pochohantas Road and Fort Foster. The park at Fort Foster offers excellent views of the lighthouse. The Isle of Shoals Steamship Company runs cruises offering excellent views of Whaleback and other lighthouses in the area; call (800) 431-5500.

NEW HAMPSHIRE

■ PORTSMOUTH HARBOR LIGHT ■
Portsmouth (1771, 1884, 1804, and 1877)

Established in 1771, several years before the Revolution, the Portsmouth Harbor beacon has guided ships longer than all but a few lighthouses in North America.

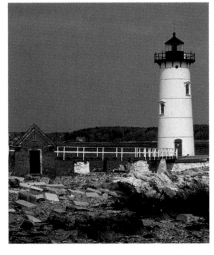

Although its light has burned almost continuously for more than two centuries, the lighthouse has evolved and changed substantially. At first it consisted of nothing more than a lantern hung from a pole on the grounds of a fort. By 1884 the light shone from atop an eighty-foot octagonal wooden tower, which eventually succumbed to rot and the concussions of the fort's mighty cannon. Rebuilt in 1804, it served until 1877, when the Lighthouse Service replaced it with a forty-eight-foot cylindrical structure made of bolted iron plates. This lighthouse still stands, its fourth-order Fresnel lens shooting out a fixed green beam visible from twelve miles away.

Over the years the Portsmouth Harbor Lighthouse has hosted many distinguished visitors, including General Lafay-ette, Daniel Webster, and Henry David Thoreau. But the most important—and likely the gruffest—personage to knock on the door here was President George Washington. He inspected the light station in 1789 and found its upkeep less than satisfactory. Not surprisingly, its keeper was summarily fired.

> *Travel information:* From U.S. Highway 1 in Portsmouth, follow signs to Fort Constitution or take Route 1B and Wentworth Road to the fort, which is now part of a Coast Guard base. Most of the base is off-limits, but the old colonial fort is open to the public. The lighthouse can be seen from its massive walls. However, the best view is from the water; contact Portsmouth Harbor Cruises at (800) 776-0915.

■ ISLES OF SHOALS LIGHT ■
Portsmouth (1821 and 1859)

The Isles of Shoals, consisting of a few barren scraps of rock a few miles seaward from Portsmouth, New Hampshire, have long attracted the adventurous and hardy of spirit. During the sixteenth century, European fishermen settled the isles to reap extraordinary harvests of cod. Later, Ralph Waldo Emerson, Nathaniel Hawthorne, and John Greenleaf Whittier came to enjoy the soul-expanding scenery and rustic hospitality of the old Appledore Hotel. A lighthouse marked the isles beginning in 1821. The existing fifty-eight-foot, brick-and-granite tower has stood since 1859. A second-order Fresnel lens once focused the

beacon, but it was replaced in 1987 with an automated optic. The station's batteries are recharged by solar panels.

> *Travel information:* Portsmouth-based tour boats offer excursions to the historic Isles of Shoals as well as special lighthouse cruises featuring **Portsmouth Harbor Lighthouse** (1877), **Whaleback Lighthouse** (1872), **Boon Island Lighthouse** (1852), and **Cape Neddick Lighthouse** (1879). Contact the Isles of Shoals Steamship Company, Box 311, Portsmouth, NH 03802-0311; (603) 431–5500 or (800) 441–4620.

■ LAKE SUNAPEE LIGHTS ■
New Hampshire Lake Country (1893)

For more than a century, Lake Sunapee in western New Hampshire has attracted vacationers who flock here to enjoy the lake's crystal-blue, spring-fed waters. During the nineteenth century, visitors arrived by train but traveled from place to place on the ten-mile-long lake by means of steamboats. A number of small lighthouses were built to make sure these vessels reached their destinations safely. Three of these extraordinary inland navigational aids remain, including the **Herrick Cove Lighthouse** (1890s) near the town of Sunapee. Octagonal

in shape, the small white tower still displays a modest light. The property and optic are maintained by the New Hampshire Department of Marine Control.

> *Travel information:* The lighthouse is located just offshore in Herrick Cove near Sunapee, New Hampshire. Cruises available in Sunapee offer an excellent view of the lighthouse as well as the **Burkehaven** (1893) and **Loon Island** (1960) towers; call (603) 763–4030.

VERMONT

■ COLCHESTER REEF LIGHT ■
Shelburne (1871)

Many might be surprised to hear of lighthouses in Vermont, but the state once had several important navigational beacons, most of them on Lake Champlain. While not considered one of the Great Lakes, Champlain is nonetheless big enough and sufficiently strategic to have been the site of decisive naval battles. A ragtag flotilla led by Benedict Arnold fought the British here during the early years of the Revolutionary War.

During the nineteenth century Burlington became a key industrial center and shipping point. Vessels moving southward toward the Burlington docks faced an array of three dangerous shoals about a mile off Colchester Point just north of the city. To mark them, workers built a combination light tower and dwelling atop a massive granite pier. A square structure with a mansard roof, it became a familiar site to commercial vessels and pleasure boaters navigating the middle reaches of the lake. Eleven successive keepers lived with their families in the four-bedroom dwelling.

Decommissioned in 1933, the lighthouse was allowed to deteriorate. During the 1950s, however, it was brought ashore, restored, and put on display at the Shelburne Museum. Today it stands near the steamer *Ticonderoga,* which plied the waters of the lake for many years.

> *Travel information:* Located off Highway 7 south of Burlington, the museum is open year-round, but winter hours are limited. Contact the Shelburne Museum, 5555 Shelburne Road, Shelburne, VT 05482; (802) 985-3346.

MASSACHUSETTS

■ NEWBURYPORT HARBOR LIGHT ■
Newburyport (1788 and 1898)

When this light station was established in 1788 (about the same time the U.S. Constitution was ratified), only ten other lighthouses stood in the entire country. Originally there were two towers here, their beacons serving in tandem as range lights to mark a safe channel in the Merrimac River. Only the thirty-five-foot, wood-frame rear-range tower still stands. In 1981 its fourth-order Fresnel lens was replaced by a plastic lens. The green light occults four times a minute.

Courtesy Lighthouse Digest

> *Travel information:* From U.S. Highway 1 in Newburyport, follow Route 1A and then Ocean Avenue onto Plum Island. The lighthouse is on the south end of the island in the Parker Ridge National Wildlife Refuge (978–465–5753). While in the area, don't miss the Custom House Maritime Museum

on Water Street in Newburyport. Among the featured exhibits is a fourth-order Fresnel lens similar to the one that once served Newburyport Harbor Light. Not far from the museum is the old **Newburyport Harbor Front Range Light** (1873) tower that at one time helped guide ships into the harbor.

■ CAPE ANN LIGHT ■
Rockport/Thatcher Island (1771 and 1861)

Among the oldest and most historic light stations in America, the twin Cape Ann Lights first beamed out their warnings in 1771, several years before the Revolution. Nearly a century and half later, the foghorn here may have saved the life of President Woodrow Wilson by preventing the wreck of his fog-blinded ship as it returned from Europe in 1919, following the Versailles Peace Conference that officially ended World War I. The two 124-foot granite towers that stand here now date from 1861. Only the south tower remains active, however, its flashing red beacon produced by a modern optic. The enormous first-order Fresnel lenses that formerly served here were removed in 1932.

Travel information: Thatcher Island is accessible only by boat, but you can see the towers from Route 127A near Rockport on Cape Ann. For information on occasional summer excursions to Thatcher Island contact the Thatcher Island Association, P.O. Box 73, Rockport, MA 01966; (978) 546-7697. Also near Rockport are the **Annisquam Harbor Lighthouse** (1897), off Route 127, and the **Straitsmouth Island Lighthouse** (1835), which can be seen from the Rockport waterfront. Both the above lights remain active.

■ EASTERN POINT LIGHT ■
Gloucester (1832, 1848, and 1890)

For more than 150 years, the Eastern Point beacon has guided Gloucester fishermen safely home from the sea. The tower and dwelling stand on the east side of the town's

harbor on a long, rocky point of land that forms a natural breakwater. Eastern Point's first 1832 lighthouse was completely renovated in 1848. The existing thirty-six-foot brick tower, built in 1890, projects a white light mariners can see from up to twenty miles at sea. The flashing signal helps mark dangerous Dog Bar Reef, near the harbor entrance.

Travel information: The light station is located at the end of Eastern Point Boulevard in East Gloucester. A stone breakwater extending from the end of the point offers the best viewing. The cast-iron **Ten Pound Island Light** tower (1881) and its flashing white light can be seen from the same breakwater. For cruises passing these historic lighthouses, contact the Friends of the Boston Harbor Islands at (781) 740-4290 or the Thatcher Island Association at (978) 546-7697.

■ TEN POUND ISLAND ■
Gloucester (1821 and 1881)

Having guided generations of mariners into Gloucester's harbor, the Ten Pound Island Light recently became a movie star as well as a navigational beacon. It was featured prominently in the hit action thriller *The Perfect Storm* released in 2000. A forty-foot stone tower, wood-frame dwelling, and several outbuildings were constructed on the island in 1821. The original tower was replaced by a thirty-foot-tall, brick-lined cast-iron cylinder in 1881. A fifth-order Fresnel lens served here for more than a century, but it has given way to a modern optic. The station remains operational, displaying a white light.

Travel information: Ferries and tourist cruises offer close-up views of the Ten Pound Island tower; call the Gloucester Chamber of Commerce at (978) 283–1601.

■ BAKER'S ISLAND LIGHT ■
Manchester-by-the-Sea (1798)

Established in 1798, during the administration of John Adams, America's second president, the Baker's Island Lighthouse originally displayed two beacons. Like the Matinicus Rock Lighthouse in Maine, the station consisted of two separate towers connected to a central keeper's dwelling. As an economy measure, one light was deactivated in 1870 and its tower torn down. The remaining fifty-foot-tall granite tower has survived, its lantern still displaying alternating red and white lights. A pair of Victorian-style keeper's dwellings, built in 1878, stand nearby.

Travel information: The lighthouse can be seen from Harbor Street or Boardman Avenue, off Route 127 in Manchester-by-the-Sea. For cruises passing this lighthouse, contact the Friends of the Boston Harbor Islands at (781) 740–4290 or the Boston Harbor Explorers at (617) 479–1871.

■ MARBLEHEAD LIGHT ■
Salem (1836 and 1895)

Built in 1836 for a mere $4,500, the original Marblehead Lighthouse was not much taller than an ordinary fisherman's cottage. It served effectively, however, until it was replaced in 1895 by the 105-foot steel-skeleton tower that dominates the

Marblehead beach today. The fixed green light, once focused by a fourth-order Fresnel lens, has been produced by a modern optic since 1960.

Travel information: From U.S. Highway 1 take Route 114 to Marblehead; then follow Ocean Avenue to its end near the lighthouse. A small park here provides an excellent view of the tower and of gorgeous summer sunsets.

■ DERBY WHARF LIGHT ■
Salem (1871)

Salem, best known now for its infamous witch trials, was once called "the Venice of the New World." This vigorous maritime community sent whole fleets of clipper

ships to China and India. When these vessels returned, spices, tea, and chinaware poured from their holds, bankrolling the fortunes of many an entrepreneur. Salem's cleverest trader was Elias Derby, likely America's first millionaire. Derby built the extensive wharf that still bears his name. Marking the far end of Derby Wharf is its small, square brick lighthouse, completed in 1871. The lamp in its small lantern room originally burned whale oil, but now a solar panel and batteries power its flashing red signal.

Travel information: Old Salem, with its fascinating cemeteries, museums, shops, wharf, and lighthouse, is located off Highway 1A, north of Boston. The lighthouse is in a small park at the end of the wharf off Derby Street. Nearby is the official Visitor Center for the Salem Maritime National Historic Site, a treasury of seventeenth- and eighteenth-century structures. Write to Salem Maritime National Historic Site, 193 Derby Street, Salem, MA 01970; (978) 740-1660.

The Winter Island Maritime Park, just north of Salem, features the tiny **Fort Pickering Lighthouse** (1872). The park also provides views of the **Hospital Point Range Lights** in Beverly (1872) as well as the Derby Wharf, **Marblehead,** and **Baker's Island Lighthouses.** Call (978) 745-9430.

■ HOSPITAL POINT RANGE LIGHTS ■
Beverly (1872 and 1927)

The Hospital Point Rear Range Light beams from the spire of Beverly's First Baptist Church, while the station's front-range light shines from atop a more conventional tower about a mile away. They form a vertically arrayed range light pair intended to help mariners keep safely within the narrow approach channel leading to Salem Harbor. The church-spire light, supplied by a small, automated optic, has shone since 1927. The steeple and spire place the light more than 180 feet above the water. The Hospital Point Front Range tower retains its original keeper's dwelling and third-order Fresnel lens.

Travel information: The Hospital Point Front Range Lighthouse is located in Beverly off Bayview Avenue. Although the station is not open to the public, it can be seen from Beverly's Lynch Park. The First Baptist Church and its spire light are located on Church Street in Beverly.

■ FORT PICKERING LIGHT ■
Salem (1872)

Since 1872, Salem's Fort Pickering Light-house has guided vessels headed for the city's bustling Derby Wharf. The old lighthouse remains in operation, display-ing a flashing white light with a focal plane twenty feet above the water. A con-ical brick tower, sheathed in iron to pro-tect it from the elements, it stands at the water's edge on Winter Island, site of important eighteenth-century fortifica-tions.

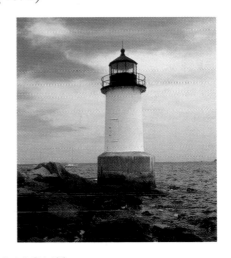

Travel information: From Salem, Winter Island Road will take you to Fort Pickering and its lighthouse.

■ BOSTON LIGHT ■
Boston (1716 and 1783)

The oldest navigational station in all of North America, Boston Lighthouse is a national treasure. Built in 1716 on Little Brewster Island at the entrance to the har-bor, it helped attract the fleets of trading ships that made Boston one of the world's most prosperous cities. Its light had been shining for almost sixty years by the time Paul Revere saw a different sort of beacon in the belfry of Boston's Old North Church and hurried off on his famous ride. The lighthouse was destroyed by the British during the Revolutionary War but was rebuilt in 1783. That post-Revolutionary tower still stands, its light continuing to guide ships more than 285 years after the station's inception.

The tower's extraordinary longevity is no accident. Aware the lighthouse could face other wars, not to mention fierce battles with Atlantic storms, the Boston masons who built the 1783 tower gave it fortresslike walls more than seven feet thick at the base. In 1853 its height was raised by fifteen feet and its stone walls lined with brick. Otherwise, except for reinforcing steel hoops added in 1983, the tower remains essentially unchanged.

Nearly as venerable as the tower itself is the second-order Fresnel lens installed here in 1859. It remains in service, producing a flashing white light visible from an impressive distance of more than twenty-seven miles at sea. Although the light was finally automated in 1998, the Coast Guard maintains an active station on the island.

Travel information: Little Brewster Island is part of Boston Harbor Islands State Park. Call the Friends of the Boston Harbor Islands at (781) 740-4290 or contact the Boston Harbor Islands Partnership at (617) 223-8666 for cruises offering close-up views of the Boston Lighthouse and nearby **Graves Ledge Lighthouse.** Airliners landing at Boston's Logan Airport offer thrilling views of these lighthouses and the **Long Island Head Lighthouse** (1919), near the inner harbor.

■ GRAVES LEDGE LIGHT ■
Boston (1905)

Gray and weather-streaked, the stone tower guarding Graves Ledge looks very old but dates only from 1905, making it a relatively young lighthouse. Some think the ledge received its rather ominous name because of tragedies such as the one that befell the schooner *Mary O'Hara* in 1941. During a blinding blizzard in January of that year, the

unlucky vessel rammed a barge and sank, leaving nineteen of her crew to drown or freeze. Actually the ledge is named for Thomas Graves, a prominent sea trader from colonial Massachusetts.

Built with massive granite blocks, the 113-foot tower easily withstands the ocean's pounding waves. The lighthouse was automated in 1976, and its huge, first-order Fresnel lens was exchanged for a modern lens. Seen from up to twenty-five miles at sea, the flashing white light is almost as powerful as that of the **Boston Light** on nearby Little Brewster Island.

Travel information: Refer to the preceding Boston Light travel information.

(Facing page) *Boston Harbor Light*

■ MINOTS LEDGE LIGHT ■
Cohasset (1850 and 1860)

Few navigational obstacles have snuffed out as many lives as Minots Ledge, a vicious shoal lurking just beneath the waves off Cohasset. Dozens of ships and countless smaller vessels wrecked on the ledge before anyone seriously considered marking the wave-swept shoal with a light. Finally, in 1850, Lighthouse Service crews completed an iron-skeleton tower, built on pilings hammered directly into the ledge. Thought able to withstand any Atlantic storm, the tower stood for less than a year before a mighty gale knocked it down, killing two assistant keepers.

The tower built in 1860 to take its place still stands, however. Its massive granite blocks dovetail, interlocking in such a way that the enormous pressures exerted on the walls by storm-driven waves actually strengthen them. Consisting of more than a thousand carefully shaped blocks, the tower weighs more than 2,300 tons.

Automated in 1947, the tower lost its second-order Fresnel lens, but not its unique one/one-two-three-four/one-two-three flashing sequence. Imaginative Cohasset folks read the flashes as I/L-O-V-E/Y-O-U and have given the Minot's beacon the nickname "Lover's Light."

Scituate Light

Travel information: The tower and "Lover's Light" can be seen from beaches off Atlantic Avenue in Cohasset. A few miles south of Cohasset is the **Scituate Lighthouse** (1811). Although discontinued in 1960, it is well maintained. From Route 123 follow signs to Scituate Harbor. For cruises see the Boston Harbor Light travel information.

■ PLYMOUTH LIGHT ■
Plymouth (1769, 1803, and 1843)

One of America's earliest lighthouses, the original Plymouth Light station showed two beacons, one each from a pair of small wooden towers only a few feet apart. The lights were not very effective at guiding mariners, but they did attract some unwanted attention from a British frigate that fired on the station during a Revolutionary War battle in 1778.

Courtesy Lighthouse Digest

When the lighthouse accidentally burned to the ground in 1801, its replacement, built two years later, also sported double towers. These were replaced in 1843 by yet another set of twin towers—the double light helped mariners distinguish the lighthouse signal from other nearby beacons. Each tower was thirty-nine feet tall and fitted with its own fourth-order Fresnel lens. One of the towers was dismantled in 1924, but the other still stands. Its light remains active, flashing white and red twice a minute.

Travel information: The lighthouse is located near the end of the Gurnet, a sandy peninsula reaching several miles into Plymouth Bay. Cruises taking visitors within easy viewing distance of the lighthouse depart from piers along Water Street in Plymouth. Also near Plymouth is the still active **Duxbury Lighthouse** (1871), a caisson-type structure located north of the Plymouth inner harbor.

■ CAPE COD (HIGHLAND) LIGHT ■
Cape Cod/Truro (1798 and 1857)

A whorl of sparkling sand deposited by glaciers of the last ice age, legendary Cape Cod is one of the world's most famous geological features. Extending far out into the stormy Atlantic from the southeastern corner of Massachusetts, the peninsula poses a formidable threat to seafaring vessels. Hence, Cape Cod became home to a remarkable array of lighthouses. The oldest and best known of these is the Cape Cod—also known as Highland—Lighthouse, established in 1798. Although its tower was only thirty feet high, the focal plane of its light, shining from atop a high, sandy bluff, was more than 150 feet above sea level. From this height whaling ships and schooners could see it more than twenty miles out at sea.

Wind and water, the same forces that built the bluffs, also eat away at them, and by the 1850s threatened to undercut the lighthouse and dump it into the sea. In 1857 a new sixty-six-foot tower was built more than five hundred feet from the nearest cliff. The erosion did not stop, however, and by the 1990s the cliffs were within 110 feet of the tower's foundation. To save the lighthouse a committee of local preservationists raised $1.5 million to move the lighthouse back from the cliffs and out of danger. An extraordinary engineering feat, the move was completed in 1997.

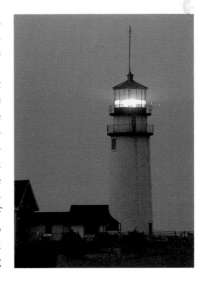

These days an aeromarine beacon produces the powerful flashes of the Cape Cod Light, but until 1945, a huge, first-order Fresnel lens served here. The light has a range of about twenty-three miles.

> *Travel information:* Anyone interested in lighthouses, history, or beautiful scenery should pay the Cape and this facility a visit. The Cape Cod Lighthouse offers ample parking, a museum, and a scenic overlook. From U.S. Highway 6 in Truro, follow the CAPE COD LIGHT signs. Contact the Highland Museum and Lighthouse, P.O. Box 486, Truro, MA 02666; (508) 487–1121.

■ RACE POINT LIGHT ■
Cape Cod/Provincetown (1816 and 1876)

Hundreds of ships have ended their days on Race Point, which forms Cape Cod's westward knuckle. Vessels must round the point to reach Provincetown Harbor a few miles to the southeast, and over the years more than a few have tried and failed. No doubt, countless others have been saved by the Race Point Light, established in 1816.

The existing forty-five-foot-tall cast-iron cylinder replaced the original rubble-stone tower in 1876. Built on a foundation at beach level, the tower elevates its fourth-order flashing white light only forty-one feet above sea level, limiting its range to just over fifteen miles.

> *Travel information:* From U.S. Highway 6 in Provincetown take Race Point Road to Race Point Beach. Two miles

Courtesy Lighthouse Digest

of soft sand separate the parking area from the lighthouse, a hike recommended only for veteran walkers (wear old shoes). The **Long Point Lighthouse** (1875) and **Wood End Lighthouse** (1873) can be seen from the Provincetown waterfront. Now managed and maintained by the American Lighthouse Foundation, the Race Point Station is open to the public and available for overnight stays; call (781) 740-4290.

■ NAUSET BEACH LIGHT ■
Eastham (1838, 1877, and 1923)

The steadily crumbling cliffs above Nauset were once marked by the **Three Sisters of Nauset** (1838 and 1892), an unusual array of three separate light towers and beacons. Eventually, the Sisters were threatened by erosion and had to be removed. In

1923, the existing, forty-eight-foot, cast-iron tower was brought to Nauset from Chatham, where it had been part of a twin-tower, two-light system since 1877. In time, the replacement tower itself stood in danger of falling over the cliffs, and in 1996 the ninety-ton structure was moved to a safer location. Now owned by the National Park Service, the lighthouse is once more displaying its flashing red and white light.

> *Travel information:* From Route 6 in Eastham, follow Brackett Road, Nauset Road, Cable Road, and then Ocean View Drive to the Nauset Lighthouse parking area. The partially restored Three Sisters towers are in a small nearby park. Contact the Cape Cod National Seashore at (508) 255-3421.

■ CHATHAM LIGHT ■
Cape Cod/Chatham (1808, 1836, and 1877)

The large number of navigational beacons beaming seaward from Cape Cod tended to confuse mariners. Maritime officials struggled to give the lights distinctive characteristics. After 1808, a pair of matched towers at Chatham marked the town's busy harbor with a rare double light. Then, in 1836, an even more unusual triple beacon—the Three Sisters—went into service at nearby Nauset Beach.

Built on a high, sandy bluff, the original wooden Chatham towers eventually fell victim to erosion. Relocated or rebuilt more than once, they were finally replaced in 1877 by two forty-eight-foot cast-iron cylindrical towers on more stable ground across the harbor. In 1923 lighthouse officials moved one of these iron towers to Nauset Beach, where it took the place of the famed Three Sisters Light.

Chatham's exceptionally powerful flashing beacon can be seen from up to thirty miles at sea. Its distant twin tower at Nauset Beach displays an alternating white and red light with a range of about twenty miles.

Travel information: Chatham's Main Street leads directly to the lighthouse. For the **Nauset Beach Lighthouse,** turn off U.S. Highway 6 onto Brackett Road and follow signs to the beach. The tower and dwelling are closed to the public but can be viewed from the adjacent Cape Cod National Seashore parking lot. A short, paved walkway leads to the retired **Three Sisters** towers. For more information on the lights, Cape Cod, or the National Seashore, call (508) 255-3421 or (508) 349-3785.

■ NOBSKA POINT LIGHT ■
Woods Hole (1829 and 1876)

At Woods Hole near Cape Cod's far southwestern tip, the Nobska Point Light warns ships away from a pair of vicious shoals called the Hedge Fence and L'Hommedieu. The first lighthouse built here was a simple stone cottage with a lantern on top, but in 1876 the Lighthouse Board approved a new tower for the

Nobska station. Its iron shell was built in a shipyard and brought to Woods Hole in four sections. Once in place, the forty-foot tower was lined with brick and fitted with the fourth-order Fresnel lens that still focuses its light. Sailors near the shoals see a red beacon, whereas those in safe water see a white one.

Travel information: The Nobska Point Lighthouse is located off Nobska Road in Woods Hole, south of Falmouth.

■ BRANT POINT LIGHT ■
Nantucket (1746, 1757, and 1901)

America's second-oldest lighthouse (after Boston) owes its existence to a town meeting held on Nantucket Island in 1746. Tired of seeing their whaling ships miss the Nantucket Harbor and pile up on nearby beaches, the island folk approved spending two hundred English pounds to construct a small wooden light tower. The little lighthouse burned to the ground several times during its more than 250 years of service, but it was always rebuilt. Shining from a height of only twenty-six feet above the water, its occulting red light has a range of about ten miles.

Much more impressive, although not necessarily as historic, are the lighthouses at Great Neck, on Nantucket's northernmost point, and Sankaty Head, near the village of Siasconset. The aeromarine beacon atop the 1850 **Sankaty Head Light** tower is visible up to twenty-four miles at sea. The **Great Point Light** station dates from 1748, but the existing rubble-stone tower was built in 1818. Its third-order Fresnel lens is still in use, flashing white and red twelve times a minute.

Courtesy U.S. Coast Guard

Travel information: A popular summer tourist destination, Nantucket Island can be reached by ferry from Hyannis. For fares and schedule contact the Steamship Authority at (508) 771-4000 or Hy-line Cruises, Ocean Street Dock, Hyannis, MA 02601; (508) 778-2600. While on the island, don't miss the Nantucket Whaling Museum; (508) 228-1894. Although Nantucket mariners no longer hunt whales on the high seas, local shops and restaurants may turn you into one with their fattening and delicious lobster, ice cream, and pastries.

■ SANKATY HEAD LIGHT ■
Nantucket Island (1850)

Perched atop a line of soaring cliffs, the seventy-foot brick tower of Sankaty Head Lighthouse dominates Nantucket's southeastern shore. Built in 1850, the tower was fitted with a Fresnel lens, the first in Massachusetts. For years this large second-order lens was rotated by a clockwork mechanism driven by weights. In 1950, the historic lens was replaced by a smaller modern optic. The light remains in operation, shining out to sea from an overall height of 158 feet. The flashing white beacon can be seen from up to twenty-four miles away.

Courtesy Bob and Sandra Shanklin

Travel information: Nantucket can be reach via ferry from Hyannis on Cape Cod; call (508) 771-4000. The light station is located off Baxter Road on the east side of the island.

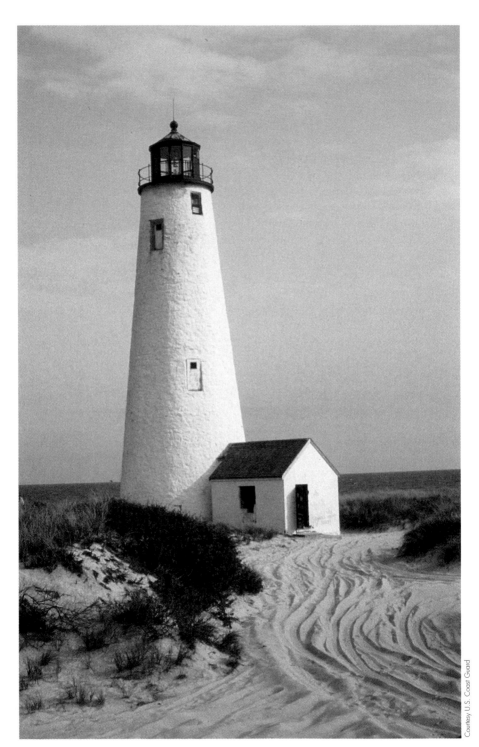

Great Point Light

■ GAY HEAD LIGHT ■
Martha's Vineyard (1799 and 1856)

Of the several lighthouses on Martha's Vineyard, the oldest and most impressive is the one standing atop the color-streaked cliffs at Gay Head. Built during the final

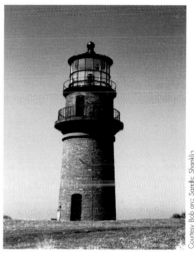

year of the eighteenth century, the first light-house here was an eight-sided wooden structure. The existing brick tower was built in 1856. Because its approximately fifty-foot tower rises from the considerable height of a cliff, the lighthouse sends out a beam with a focal plane more than 170 feet above sea level. Mariners can see its alternating red and white beacon from up to twenty-five miles away.

> *Travel information:* Ferries to Martha's Vineyard are available from Falmouth or Hyannis. For schedules and fares call the Woods Hole Steamship Authority at (508) 548-3788 or the Martha's Vineyard Chamber of Commerce at (508) 693-0085.

Courtesy Bob and Sandra Shanklin

■ EDGARTOWN HARBOR LIGHT ■
Edgartown on Martha's Vineyard (1828 and 1875)

The cast-iron tower that now marks Edgartown Harbor on Martha's Vineyard originally stood at Ipswich, well to the north of Boston. Constructed in 1875, it was pulled

down and shipped to Edgartown in 1939. The relocated tower replaced the station's historic 1828 Cape Cod–style lighthouse, which had been destroyed by a hurricane. For many years a fourth-order Fresnel lens served this station and the mariners who depended on its beacon to guide them to Edgartown. The classic lens was removed in 1988 and replaced by a modern optic.

> *Travel information:* Martha's Vineyard can be reached by ferry from Falmouth or Hyannis; call (508) 548-3788. The lighthouse is located on the north side of the island near Edgartown. Also on Martha's Vineyard are the **Cape Poge Lighthouse** (1893), **East Chop Lighthouse** (1877),

Courtesy Bob and Sandra Shanklin

and **West Chop Lighthouse** (1818). The Martha's Vineyard Historical Society Museum in Edgartown maintains excellent lighthouse displays, including a Fresnel lens; call (508) 627-4441.

■ BUTLER FLATS LIGHT ■
New Bedford (1898)

Built in open water atop a concrete-filled cast-iron caisson, the Butler Flats Lighthouse marks the main channel used by vessels approaching New Bedford. Completed in 1898, the station has a brick, rather than cast-iron, tower. The original Fresnel lens still guides vessels with its flashing white beacon—visible from about four miles away.

Travel information: The lighthouse can be seen from the New Bedford waterfront or from the Martha's Vineyard ferry.

■ CLARK'S POINT LIGHT ■
New Bedford (1804 and 1869)

Intended to guide vessels to New Bedford, the original Clark's Point Lighthouse served for more than sixty years before relinquishing its view of the water to a great stone fort. Begun during the Civil War, the fort eventually blocked the tower's beacon with its massive walls. Consequently, maritime authorities ordered the lantern room removed from the forty-two-foot stone tower and placed on the walls of the fort. This makeshift arrangement worked well enough, and the Clark's Point Light remained in operation until 1869, when the nearby Butler Flats Lighthouse was completed. The City of New Bedford is restoring the fortress lighthouse as a historical monument.

Travel information: The fort and lighthouse remain closed to the public while restoration work continues. However, both can be seen from East Rodney French Boulevard in New Bedford.

■ BORDEN FLATS LIGHT ■
Fall River (1881)

Set atop a massive open-water caisson, the Borden Flats Lighthouse points the way to Fall River, Massachusetts, known to many as the home of Lizzie Borden, the famous New England spinster who was accused of murdering her parents with an ax. Although Lizzie was acquitted of the crime, her story continues to fascinate murder mystery fans. Far less famous is the cast-iron, sparkplug-style Borden (named for Lizzie's family) Flats Lighthouse, which dates from 1881. The old station remains in operation, guiding mariners with a flashing white light visible from eleven miles away. Originally focused by a fourth-order Fresnel lens, the light is now produced by a modern optic.

Travel information: The light can be seen from the Fall River waterfront.

RHODE ISLAND

■ NEWPORT HARBOR LIGHT
Newport (1824, 1842, and 1865)

At least three different lighthouses have stood on Newport's Goat Island. The most recent, completed during the Civil War, is a thirty-five-foot, octagonal granite structure. Its fifth-order Fresnel lens remains in use and produces a flashing green light. Many lighthouses have survived gales and high water. This one, however, also survived being rammed by a World War I–vintage U.S. submarine in 1922. This accident destroyed the old keeper's dwelling.

Also in Newport are the **Castle Hill Lighthouse** (1890) and **Lime Rock Lighthouse** (1854). The famous lighthouse keeper Ida Lewis lived and served at the latter station for more than half a century. Having rescued at least half a dozen drowning sailors, children, and even a hapless sheep from the icy waters off Lime Rock, Lewis found herself on the cover of *Harper's Weekly* in 1869. Later that same year she played host to President Ulysses S. Grant.

> *Travel information:* The lighthouse is on Goat Island beside the Hyatt Hotel, near historic downtown Newport. Parking is free, and visitors are allowed to walk the grounds. The still active Castle Hill Lighthouse is reached via a short trail from the Castle Hill Cove Marina. The old Lime Rock Lighthouse, now home of the Ida Lewis Yacht Club, is located off Wellington Avenue. Several Newport harbor cruises offer excellent views of the city's lighthouses.

■ ROSE ISLAND LIGHT ■
Newport (1870)

The lofty suspension towers and bright lights of the Newport Bridge, completed in 1969, made the century-old Rose Island Light redundant. The Coast Guard discontinued it in 1971, and the fine, old combination tower and dwelling might have been torn down except for the tireless efforts of Newport preservationists. Located on a small island just south of the bridge, the station has been handsomely refurbished and relit as a private aid to navigation.

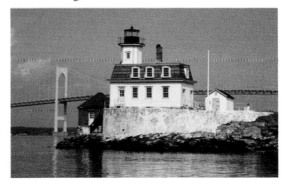

Travel information: Newport harbor cruises nearly always feature a close look at the Rose Island Lighthouse. For tours or to stay overnight in the lighthouse—a unique opportunity to sample the life of a lighthouse keeper—contact the Rose Island Lighthouse Foundation, Box 1419, Newport, RI 02840; (401) 847-4242.

■ POMHAM ROCKS LIGHT ■
Providence (1871)

No longer active, the combination residence and tower clings to an exposed rock beside the main Providence shipping channel. Its fourth-order Fresnel lens was removed when the station was discontinued in 1974. Nowadays the station is owned by an oil company.

Travel information: Unfortunately, this interesting structure is closed to the public but it can be seen from the East Bay Bicycle Path in East Providence. To the southwest of Providence is the **Warwick Lighthouse** (1827), in Warwick, off Route 117. Its occulting green light remains active.

■ BEAVERTAIL LIGHT ■
Jamestown (1749 and 1856)

America's third-oldest light station marks the entrance to Newport Harbor and Narragansett. During the 1600s notorious pirate Captain William Kidd used this area as a hideout. Captured by the British in Boston, he was eventually hanged. A century later, the British would treat the Beavertail Lighthouse as roughly as they had Captain Kidd, burning it when they abandoned Newport Harbor during the Revolutionary War.

The existing fifty-two-foot, square granite tower dates from 1856. A modern optic replaced its classic fourth-order Fresnel lens in 1991 and emits a flashing white signal.

Travel information: This particularly historic and scenic lighthouse is located in Beavertail State Park. Take the Jamestown exit off Route 138 (just across the Newport Bridge from Newport) and follow Beavertail

Road to the park and lighthouse. The keeper's dwelling now serves as a museum. Contact the Beavertail Lighthouse Museum, P.O. Box 83, Jamestown, RI 02835; (401) 423-3270.

■ POINT JUDITH LIGHT ■
Point Judith (1810, 1816, and 1857)

A crude wooden tower, Point Judith's first light tower was blown over by a gale in 1815. Its replacement, completed the following year, was built with stone. The existing fifty-one-foot, octagonal granite-block tower was completed in 1857. One of the earliest of America's flashing beacons, its lamps and reflectors were at one time rotated by a clockwork mechanism powered by 288-pound weights. This lighthouse guards what was once one of America's most heavily trafficked stretches of water. More than 22,000 vessels passed Point Judith in 1907 alone. A fourth-order Fresnel lens installed here before the Civil War remains in service.

Travel information: The station can be reached off U.S. Highway 1 via Route 108 and Ocean Road. Visitors are welcome to walk the grounds.

■ WATCH HILL LIGHT ■
Watch Hill (1807 and 1855)

The first tower at Watch Hill was used as a lookout for possible invasion from the sea during King George's War (1744-48). The first lighthouse came into existence in

1807, when a local carpenter erected a round wooden tower and fitted it out with whale-oil lamps. In 1857 the Lighthouse Board had a square, fifty-one-foot granite tower and attached dwelling built; they equipped the tower with a fourth-order Fresnel lens. An automated modern lens serves the station now.

Travel information: From U.S. Highway 1 take Route 1A to Avondale and then Watch Hill Road. The station is located at the end of Lighthouse Road, actually a narrow, paved drive leading off Larkin Road just beyond the village. There is a small museum on-site, containing the station's original Fresnel lens. Museum open limited hours in July and August. Contact Watch Hill Lighthouse Museum, Watch Hill, RI 02891.

■ BLOCK ISLAND SOUTHEAST LIGHT ■
Block Island (1875)

This redbrick octagonal tower and attached Victorian/Gothic residence built in 1875 looks like the setting for a nineteenth-century romance novel or, perhaps, a vampire yarn. After lording over Block Island's Monhegan Bluffs for more than a

century, however, the historic lighthouse became the focus of a different sort of drama. By 1990 galloping erosion had eaten the high, crumbling bluffs away to within a few feet of the structure's foundation. To keep it from tumbling into the sea, preservationists raised almost $2 million to have the venerable building moved to safety. Lifted by jacks onto rollers, the two-thousand-ton lighthouse was pushed back several hundred feet and out of harm's way.

Block Island Southeast Light

Although the tower is only fifty-two feet tall, the height of the cliffs places the light a whopping 260 feet above sea level. This helps give its first-order Fresnel lens a range of more than twenty miles. The lens in use here today at one time served in North Carolina's **Cape Lookout Lighthouse.**

Block Island North Light

On the opposite side of the six-mile-long island is the **Block Island North Lighthouse** (1867), a fifty-foot-tall granite building on Sandy Point. Three earlier lighthouses stood on the point, one of them a rare double-towered structure. Although moved to a nearby skeleton tower in 1973, the station's light has been restored to the original structure—now a lighthouse museum.

Travel information: Block Island is a page out of America's past. To visit its quaint inns, shops, and lighthouses, you must take a ferry from New London, Connecticut, or Point Judith, Rhode Island. Call (401) 783–4613. For lighthouse hours call (401) 466–5009.

CONNECTICUT

■ STONINGTON HARBOR LIGHT ■
Stonington (1824 and 1840)

The thirty-five-foot stone tower and dwelling marking Stonington Harbor, completed in 1840, replaced an earlier structure undercut by erosion. The existing station served until 1900, when it was decommissioned. Old buildings are venerated in New England, as is this one, which serves today as a historical museum.

Not far to the west of Stonington along U.S. Highway 1 is the well-known Mystic Seaport, a living maritime-history museum with its own operating lighthouse—a replica of the Brant Point tower on Nantucket.

Travel information: Stonington and its Old Lighthouse Museum are located off U.S. Highway 1, near the eastern extremity of coastal Connecticut. Mystic Seaport is just off I-95 and U.S. Highway 1 in the town of Mystic. Its old whaling ships, shops, maritime exhibits, and the **Mystic Seaport Lighthouse** (replica) are well worth the admission fee; call (860) 572 0711. The museum offers a river and harbor cruise, which provides a glimpse of the distinctive **Morgan Point Lighthouse** (1869), now a private residence.

■ NEW LONDON HARBOR LIGHT ■
New London (1760 and 1801)

When the whale-oil lamps of the first New London Lighthouse were lit in 1760, only three other light towers marked the coasts of colonial America. When the existing structure replaced the original sixty-foot stone tower, nearly two generations later, America still had only a few lighthouses. Now approaching its third century of service, the gracefully tapered eighty-nine-foot stone tower still employs

New London Harbor Light

New London Ledge Lighthouse

its 1857 fourth-order Fresnel. Interestingly, the original station was financed by a public lottery.

Marking a dangerous shoal near the harbor entrance is the remarkable **New London Ledge Lighthouse** (1909). Its French Empire architecture is more suggestive of an old-money aristocratic town home than a hardworking lighthouse. This still-active station displays a white and red beacon, as does the much older harbor lighthouse. It reputedly has a resident ghost, that of a former keeper who, forsaken by his wife, jumped to his death from the tower.

> *Travel information:* You can see the New London Harbor Lighthouse from Pequot Avenue near Ocean Beach. The dwelling and grounds are privately owned and closed to the public. The New London Ledge Lighthouse is difficult to see from the shore. The best view is from the deck of New London's Block Island or Avery Point Ferry; call (401) 783-4613. The U.S. Coast Guard Academy, reached via Briggs Street and Monhegan Avenue in New London, is well worth a visit, especially as it contains a fine, first-order Fresnel lens. Also worth seeing is the **Avery Point Light** (1943), located on the campus of the University of Connecticut in Groton. The modest Avery Point tower was built by the Coast Guard to honor America's lighthouse keepers.

■ LYNDE POINT LIGHT ■
Old Saybrook/Fenwick (1803 and 1838)

Thomas Jefferson was president when the whale-oil lamps of the Lynde Point Light station were first lit in 1803. The original octagonal wooden structure stood until 1838, then was replaced by the existing sixty-five-foot dressed-stone tower. Although automated today, the station's classic fifth-order Fresnel lens remains in operation, sending out a fixed white light with a range of fourteen miles.

(Opposite page) *Mystic Seaport Lighthouse*

At the end of a nearby stone jetty extending into the Connecticut River is the **Saybrook Breakwater Lighthouse** (1838). The fifty-foot cast-iron tower resembles a giant chess rook. A plastic lens focuses its flashing green light, warning vessels away from a sandbar at the mouth of the river.

Courtesy U.S. Coast Guard

Travel information: From U.S. Highway 1 in Old Saybrook, follow Route 154 to the gracious, old-time residential community of Fenwick. Both lighthouses are closed to the public but can be seen from Route 154. Various Connecticut River cruises provide fine views of these and other lighthouses; contact the Old Saybrook Chamber of Commerce at (860) 388–3266.

■ FAULKNER'S ISLAND LIGHT ■
Near Guilford (1802)

Local preservationists are struggling to save what remains of this venerable light station, but they face a significant challenge. Ravaged by fire in 1976, Connecticut's second-oldest lighthouse is now threatened by erosion—interestingly enough, made worse by burrowing rabbits. The octagonal fieldstone structure was built in 1802 to guide coasting vessels and warn them away from ship-killing rocks lying just off the mainland.

Travel information: The island is now a bird sanctuary, and there is no regular access to the public. Those interested in Faulkner's Island preservation efforts should contact Faulkner's Light Brigade, P.O. Box 199, Guilford, CT 06437.

■ SOUTHWEST LEDGE LIGHT ■
New Haven (1877)

Built in a Baltimore shipyard, the Southwest Ledge tower was exhibited at the 1876 Centennial Exposition before being shipped to Connecticut. The forty-five-foot steel cylinder stands on a concrete-and-steel caisson at the end of New Haven's east breakwater. Its flashing red light, produced by a plastic lens, remains active.

Courtesy U.S. Coast Guard

The centerpiece of New Haven's Lighthouse Park is the **Five Mile Point Lighthouse**, built in 1840 and decommissioned in 1877. An earlier lighthouse had served New Haven since 1805. Although out of service for more than a century, the tower has survived the ravages of time and urban growth.

> *Travel information:* From I-95 follow Townsend Avenue and then Lighthouse Road to Lighthouse Park, which is open year-round during daylight hours. The Southwest Ledge Lighthouse is more than a mile from shore but can be seen from the park.

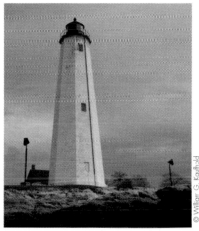

Five Mile Point Lighthouse

■ STRATFORD SHOAL LIGHT ■
Bridgeport (1877)

A rocky shoal lurks just beneath the surface of Long Island Sound, about halfway between Bridgeport, Connecticut, and the shores of Long Island. Over the centuries it has claimed the vessels of many unwary seamen who expected to find relative safety in the sound. In 1837, the Lighthouse Service marked the shoal with a lightship, and then, in the mid-1870s, with a permanent lighthouse.

Completed in 1877, the Stratford Shoal Lighthouse stands on a concrete-filled caisson built atop a foundation of granite blocks held together with iron staples. The caisson serves as a platform for the Victorian-style dwelling with attached tower. The station's aeromarine beacon displays a flashing white light easily seen from both shores.

To the north is the **Stratford Point Lighthouse** (also known to locals as Lorship Light), flashing from a thirty-five-foot brick tower built in 1881. A few miles away, marking the Bridgeport Harbor with a flashing green light, stands the diminutive twenty-one-foot tower of the **Tongue Point Lighthouse** (1891). To the west, near Fairfield, is the **Penfield Reef Lighthouse,** an Empire-style combination tower and dwelling built in 1871. Its flashing red light warns vessels away from a collection of jagged rocks known locally as "the Cows."

> *Travel information:* The Stratford Shoal Lighthouse cannot be seen easily from land but can be viewed from the decks of ferries that link Bridgeport to Long Island. Stratford Point Lighthouse is located on Prospect Drive, off Route 113 near the Bridgeport Airport. You can view Tongue Point Lighthouse from Bridgeport's Sound View Drive. The Penfield Reef Lighthouse can be seen from Calf Pasture Park in Fairfield. Seaside Park in Bridgeport also provides a view of the Penfield Reef station as well as access to the historic, but no longer active, **Black Rock Harbor Lighthouse** (1823).

■ SHEFFIELD ISLAND LIGHT ■
Norwalk (1828 and 1868)

Established in 1828 and rebuilt in 1868, this handsome, two-story stone dwelling and steeplelike tower served as a lighthouse until 1900. Restored and cared for by the Norwalk Seaport Association, the old lighthouse is now open to the public.

Travel information: Summer excursions to Sheffield Island, now a wildlife refuge, are available. Contact the Norwalk Seaport Association, 132 Water Street, South Norwalk, CT 06854; (203) 838–9444. From Sheffield Island or Norwalk's Crescent Beach, you can see the alternating red and white flash of **Green's Ledge Lighthouse** (1881). To the west is the privately owned **Stamford Harbor Lighthouse** (1882).

© William Kaufhold

NEW YORK

■ RACE ROCK LIGHT ■
Near Fishers Island (1879)

Built at great expense and through almost superhuman effort during the late 1870s, this lighthouse marks an extraordinarily dangerous shoal known as Race

Rock Reef. Strong currents rushing back and forth between Long Island Sound and the Atlantic make this area a nightmare for seamen. Building a lighthouse over the wave-swept shoal was thought impossible, but the government finally took on the project. Construction crews labored for years to build up an artificial island of concrete and stone. On this they erected a granite dwelling and attached square tower. On February 21, 1879, eight years and $278,716 after work began, the Race Rock Light split the night for the first time, sixty-seven feet above the water. The flashing red signal still warns mariners away from the shoals; its pulse is visible from a distance of up to twenty miles.

> *Travel information:* Whereas Race Rock Lighthouse can be reached only by water, you can see it from Watch Hill, Rhode Island, and several points along the Connecticut coast. Ferries operating between New London, Connecticut, and Block Island or Orient Point on Long Island often pass within sight of the station. For schedule and fares call (401) 783-4613.

■ MONTAUK POINT LIGHT ■
Montauk (1797)

President George Washington personally ordered construction of the Montauk Point Lighthouse at the strategic far-eastern tip of Long Island. Washington's successor, John Adams, was in office when the project was completed in 1797. The sandstone tower and adjacent two-story dwelling cost $22,300, a sizable fortune at the time. The young United States government got its money's worth, however—the still operational seventy-eight-foot tower has now passed its two-hundredth birthday.

The station's flashing white light, produced nowadays by an aeromarine beacon, shines out toward the open Atlantic from a height of 168 feet above the water. Its guidance is heartily welcomed by seamen, none of whom want to come near the

Cedar Island Lighthouse

Courtesy Bob and Sandra Shanklin

killing sands and surf of Montauk, where ships have been known to "melt away like butter."

Travel information: The lighthouse is in Montauk State Park at the end of Route 27. Since 1987, when the last resident keepers left the station, the dwelling has served as a maritime museum, where visitors may view fascinating historical exhibits and a marvelous array of Fresnel lenses and other lighting devices. Contact Montauk Point Lighthouse Museum, Box 112, Montauk, NY 11954; (631) 668-2544. To the west in Cedar Point County Park, off Route 114, is the granite block **Cedar Island Lighthouse** (1868), abandoned since 1934.

■ ORIENT POINT LIGHT ■
Orient Point (1899)

A caisson-type structure, sometimes described as a "coffeepot" light, Orient Point Lighthouse marks Oyster Pound Reef, one of Long Island's most feared navigational obstacles. Completed in 1899, the tower took two years to build and cost $30,000, six times the original estimate. Keepers in the past lived and worked in the cramped cast-iron tower, only twenty-one feet in diameter at the base. Automated since 1954, the station warns vessels away from the reef with a flashing white light, visible from up to seventeen miles.

Travel information: You can see the Orient Point "coffeepot" Lighthouse from the ferry landing at the end of Route 25. The church-and-steeple-style **Plum Island Lighthouse** (1869), which is no longer active, is visible to the east of the land-

ing. The ferry that provides passage to New London, Connecticut, offers an excellent view of both lighthouses. On the way across the sound, passengers also get a look at the impressive eighty-foot, granite-block **Little Gull Island Lighthouse** (1867). For schedules and fares call (860) 443-5281.

■ HORTON POINT LIGHT ■
Southold (1790 and 1857)

George Washington identified Horton Point as the likely site of a lighthouse while still a young military officer serving in the French and Indian War. Years later, as president, Washington helped fulfill his own prophecy by commissioning a lighthouse for the point. The fifty-eight-foot granite tower that stands here today, however, was built in 1857. It remains in service, its flashing green light reaching out across Long Island Sound from a total height of just over one hundred feet above the water.

© William Kaufhold

Travel information: From Route 48 in Southold, turn north onto Sound View Avenue and follow the signs to Horton Point Lighthouse Museum. The keeper's dwelling houses this excellent museum filled with nautical artifacts; call (631) 765-5500. A few miles east, at the entrance to Orient Harbor, is the **Long Beach Bar Lighthouse** (1993), a replica of the original 1870 screw-pile lighthouse that burned to the ground in 1963. It can be seen from several points in the town of Orient as well as from nearby Shelter Island.

■ OLD FIELD POINT LIGHT ■
Stony Brook (1823 and 1868)

This lighthouse marks one of several fingers of land that stretch northward to menace shipping in Long Island Sound. The granite combination tower and dwelling seen here at present was completed in 1868. It replaced an earlier, though similar, structure that had served since 1823. The station was deactivated in 1933, but was placed back in service in 1991. The building now serves as the Old Field Village Hall.

Courtesy Bob and Sandra Shanklin

Travel information: The lighthouse, owned by the Village of Old Field, is closed to the public. It can be seen from Old Field Road north of Setauket. A better view is from aboard the Bridgeport (CT) to Port Jefferson ferry; call (631) 473–0286 or (203) 335–2040.

■ FIRE ISLAND LIGHT ■
Fire Island (1826 and 1858)

In 1850 the freighter *Elizabeth* struck a shoal and sank almost in the shadow of the Fire Island Lighthouse, which had guided shipping along the south shore of Long Island for almost twenty-five years. Sea captains had long complained that the seventy-four-foot light tower was too short to give adequate warning of the shoals. The tragic loss of the *Elizabeth* along with most of her crew brought a general public outcry to which Congress quickly responded. The entire Lighthouse Service was soon under close scrutiny, and a Lighthouse Board was formed to revamp the nation's sadly deteriorated system of navigational lights.

The Lighthouse Board approved the construction of a new brick tower more than twice as high as the original. When completed in 1858, it stood 180 feet above the island sands. Focused by a first-order Fresnel lens, the light could now warn mariners as far as twenty-five miles from the coast.

Long ago, the station's flashing white beacon earned it the nickname "Winking Woman." The lighthouse stopped winking in 1974, when the station was decommissioned. Rapidly deteriorating, the abandoned lighthouse was on the point of being demolished when a local preservation society came to the rescue. Happily, it has been restored and relighted, and it is now a prime seashore attraction. The residence now serves as a visitors center and maritime museum.

Travel information: From Route 27A take the Robert Moses Parkway onto Fire Island and follow signs to parking for the lighthouse. Contact the Fire Island Lighthouse Preservation Society, Box 4640, Captree Island, NY 11702; (516) 321–7028.

(Facing page) *Fire Island Lighthouse* Courtesy William Kaufhold

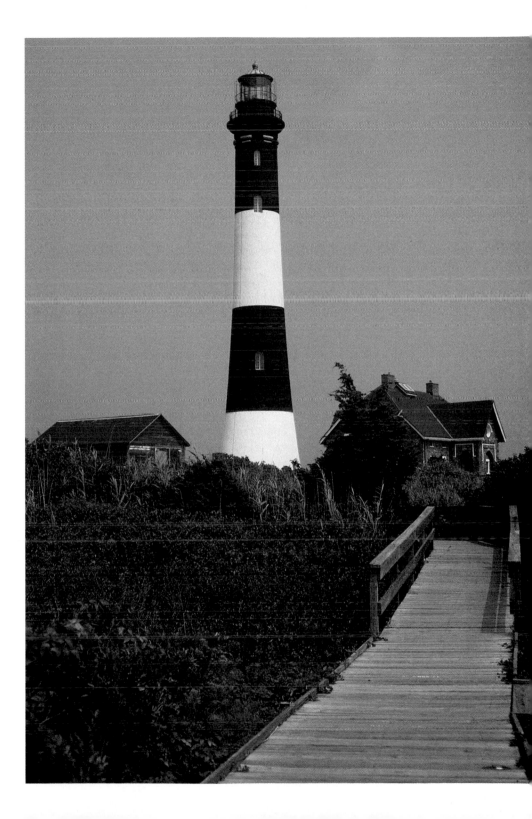

■ EATON'S NECK LIGHT ■
Asharoken (1799)

One of only a handful of surviving eighteenth-century light towers, Long Island's Eaton's Neck Lighthouse near Asharoken remains in operation after nearly two hundred years of service. Established to guide ships through the western reaches of Long Island Sound, it dates from the administration of John Adams, the nation's second president. Constructed of fieldstone, it was lined with protective walls of brick during the years following the Civil War. The station's Winslow Lewis Argand lamp-and-reflector system gave way in 1858 to a third-order Fresnel lens. That same fine old lens still shines from a height of 144 feet above the waters of the sound. Its fixed white light can be seen from about eighteen miles away.

Courtesy Bob and Sandra Shanklin

Travel information: Despite its historic nature and presence on the National Register of Historic Places, the Eaton's Neck Light station is not readily open to visitors. You can get special permission to visit, however, by contacting the U.S. Coast Guard Station, Eaton's Neck, Northport, NY 11768; (631) 261-6959. The **Huntington Harbor Lighthouse** (1912) in nearby Lloyd Harbor, New York, can be seen from Lloyd Harbor Road. To the west, near the terminus of Long Island Sound, are the **Execution Rocks Light** (1850), located off Sands Point on Long Island, and **Stepping Stones Light** (1877), located off Kings Point.

■ CONEY ISLAND LIGHT ■
Brooklyn (1890)

This distinctly blue-collar lighthouse was assigned the task of guiding New York City garbage barges to the watery dumps in the Atlantic. Established in 1890, the light also guided hulking iron freighters to their Coney Island loading docks.

The sixty-eight-foot tower consists of a central cylinder crowned by a gallery and lantern room and braced by four steel legs. Originally, this workmanlike structure operated as the rear member of a pair of range lights. The front-range light was taken out of service shortly before the turn of the twentieth century, but the rear-range light remains in operation to this day, displaying a flashing red light visible more than fifteen miles away.

Travel information: From I-278 follow the Prospect Parkway and Ocean Parkway to Coney Island. The lighthouse is on Surf Avenue between Forty-sixth and Forty-seventh Streets in the community of Seagate. The fourth-order Fresnel lens, which focused the Coney Island Light until the station was automated in 1989, is on display in the South Street Seaport Museum in lower Manhattan. Another attraction of this famous maritime museum is the **Lightship Ambrose** (Number 87), launched in 1907. Call (212) 748-8600.

Coney Island Light

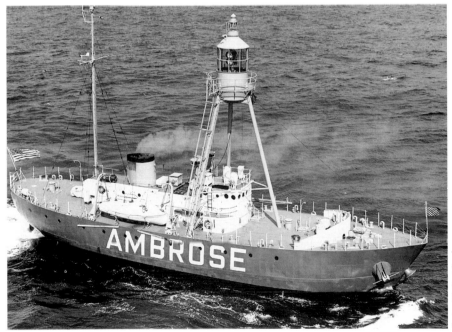

■ ROBBINS REEF LIGHT ■
New York City (Staten Island) (1839 and 1883)

A coffeepot-style, cast-iron tower, the existing Robbins Reef Lighthouse replaced an
earlier stone structure in 1883. Located on a
massive stone pier in the middle of the main
channel through the Upper New York Bay,
the light remains active, guiding vessels in
and out of the great city's busy harbor. The
original fourth-order Fresnel lens was
replaced by a modern optic when the station
was automated in 1966. This offshore lighthouse is famous for keeper Kate Walker,
who took over the job from her husband
when he died in 1885 and faithfully watched
the light for the next thirty-four years.
Walker handled even the most physically
taxing keeper's chores unassisted, and she is
credited with saving as many as seventy-five
lives.

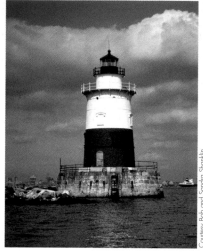

Courtesy Bob and Sandra Shanklin

> *Travel information:* The best way to see this lighthouse is from the decks
> of the Staten Island ferry; call (212) 806–6940.

■ STATUE OF LIBERTY ■
New York (1886)

Dedicated in 1886 and commissioned as a harbor light that same year, the Statue
of Liberty is probably the world's most famous lighthouse. The light in the bronze
lady's torch guided ships in and out of the harbor for many years and is still hailed
as a guiding light by many landlubbers. The lady herself is 151 feet tall; she lifts her
lamp a spectacular 305 feet above the ground, making this one of America's loftiest navigational lights. Particularly hardy visitors may choose to climb the 354 steps
leading to the statue's crown. Those who pay homage to Lady Liberty owe much of
their deep attachment to her to Emma Lazarus's famous inscription on the
pedestal: ". . . GIVE ME YOUR TIRED, YOUR POOR, YOUR HUDDLED MASSES YEARNING TO
BREATHE FREE . . . SEND THESE, THE HOMELESS, THE TEMPEST-TOSSED TO ME, I LIFT MY LAMP
BESIDE THE GOLDEN DOOR!"

> *Travel information:* The ferry to Liberty Island and its statue leaves from
> Battery Park at the lower tip of Manhattan. Passengers can also view the
> cast-iron coffeepot-style **Robbins Reef Lighthouse** (1839). Its flashing
> green light remains in operation. For information on the Statue of Liberty
> National Monument, call (212) 363–3200; for ferry schedules, call (212)
> 269–5755.

(Facing page) *Statue of Liberty* Courtesy *Lighthouse Digest*

▪ JEFFREY'S HOOK LIGHT ▪
New York City (1920)

There may be no greater architectural contrast than that presented by New York's "little red lighthouse" beside the Hudson and the mighty George Washington Bridge soaring overhead. Built in 1920, the diminutive cast-iron tower took the place of a pair of stake lights, which had stood here since 1889. Only eleven years later, completion of the bridge's massive, 3,500-foot central span made the lighthouse obsolete.

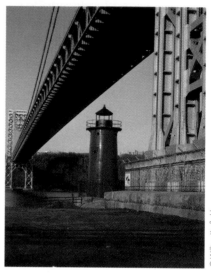

© William Kaufhold

The Coast Guard intended to auction off the tower as scrap metal and would have done so if not for the public outcry, raised in part by publication of Hildegarde Hoyt Swift's classic children's book *The Little Red Lighthouse and the Great Gray Bridge*. The Jeffrey's Hook structure still stands as a sort of monument to the little and forgotten things of this world.

Travel information: The long-abandoned tower, kept painted bright red by New York City park workers, stands directly under the George Washington Bridge on the Manhattan side of the Hudson. Take the Fort Washington exit off Riverside Drive. For tours call (212) 304-2365.

▪ ROUNDOUT CREEK LIGHT ▪
Kingston (1880 and 1915)

The Hudson River used to have as many lighthouses as some entire coastal states. One of the best known marked the harbor entrance of the inland port city of Kingston. The first light station was established here in 1880, but the current fifty-two-foot square brick tower and attached dwelling date only from 1915. Known

locally as Roundout Two, the lighthouse stands on a concrete pier surrounded by the river's swirling waters. The Hudson River Maritime Center leases the building for use as a museum depicting the lives of river lighthouse keepers and their families.

Courtesy Bob and Sandra Shanklin

Travel information: Reach Kingston via I-87 (New York Thruway) or Route 9.

For museum hours contact the Hudson River Maritime Center at (845) 338-0071. Downriver a few miles from Kingston is the **Esopus Meadows Lighthouse** (1879), now undergoing restoration by local preservationists. Located in mid channel, it cannot be reached from land but can be seen from points along Route 9 on the east side of the river.

Esopus Meadows Lighthouse

■ SAUGERTIES LIGHT ■
Saugerties (1836 and 1869)

Floodwaters and ice were always problems for lighthouses on the Hudson. The Saugerties Lighthouse, established in 1836, held up to the annual beatings for nearly thirty years before finally succumbing during the 1860s. Engineers built the two-story brick dwelling and attached tower that replaced it in 1869 on a massive stone caisson to shield it from the river's destructive floes. This strategy succeeded, and the lighthouse remained safe and relatively dry until the station was decommissioned eighty-five years later.

Travel information: Handsomely restored by the Saugerties Lighthouse Conservancy, the lighthouse is now a museum open to the public on weekends. The conservancy now works to preserve other lighthouses. You may contact the organization at (914) 247-0656. Well to the north of Saugerties, and more than a hundred miles from the sea, is the **Hudson City Lighthouse** (1874). Located in midchannel, it cannot be reached from land but can be seen from either Hudson City on Route 9 or Athens on Route 385.

Hudson City Lighthouse

■ STATEN ISLAND LIGHT ■
New York City/Staten Island (1912)

The ninety-foot octagonal brick tower rises from high ground that lifts its light more than 230 feet above sea level. Built in 1912, the structure is Edwardian in character. Interestingly, its huge, second-order bivalve lens was imported from England rather than France. Still in use today, the bull's-eye lens produces a fixed white beacon used as a rear-range light. The front-range beacon shines from the **West Bank Lighthouse** (1901), a cast-iron tower built on a concrete caisson more than five miles away.

Travel information: Although closed to the public, you can approach the Staten Island tower by way of Lighthouse Avenue, off Richmond Road. The West Bank Lighthouse is located in the open waters of the Lower Hudson Bay. The historic **New Dorp Lighthouse** (1856), a wooden combination tower and dwelling, is now a private residence. It can be seen from Altmont Street, off Richmond Road. From the Gateway National Recreation Area and Great Kills Park off Hylan Boulevard, you can spot the coffeepot-style **Old Orchard Shoal Lighthouse** (1893), rising on a caisson about three miles to the southeast. Its flashing white and red light remains active.

NEW JERSEY

■ SANDY HOOK LIGHT ■
Highlands/Sandy Hook (1764)

On the evening of June 11, 1764, a keeper trudged up the steps of the recently completed Sandy Hook Lighthouse and lit its lamps for the first time. Today—more than two-and-one-third centuries later—the light at the top of the eighty-five-foot stone tower still burns each night, making this the oldest continuously operating lighthouse in America. The **Boston Lighthouse,** completed in 1716, was blown up by the British during the Revolutionary War and had to be rebuilt. The Sandy Hook tower almost suffered the same fate as its older Boston counterpart when Continental soldiers tried but failed to blow it up to keep it out of British hands.

A large, open-panned lamp with forty-eight separate wicks provided the station's light during the eighteenth century. Later, a Winslow Lewis Argand lamp and reflector served here and then, after 1857, a third-order Fresnel lens. The old Fresnel remains in service, displaying a fixed white light with a range of about twenty miles.

Travel information: Follow Route 36 to Highlands Beach and follow signs to this lovely and historic light station. Contact the Gateway National Recreation Area, P.O. Box 530, Highlands, NJ 07732; (732) 872-0115.

Courtesy William Kaufhold

■ HIGHLANDS (NAVESINK) LIGHT ■
Highlands (1828 and 1862)

Henry Hudson first noted the distinctive hills of New Jersey's upper elbow and used them as daymarks during his 1609 voyage of exploration. Mariners have used these highlands for navigation ever since. In 1828 the U.S. government made the navigator's work easier by placing lights in a pair of fortresslike stone towers atop the hills. In 1838 these towers became the home of America's first Fresnel lenses. An enormous first-order lens sent out its light from the north tower, while a revolving bull's-eye-type second-order lens flashed from its neighbor.

Rebuilt during the early Civil War years, the twin light towers were relit in 1862. Interestingly, the new south tower was given a square shape, whereas the north tower was octagonal.

In 1898 the north tower was taken out of service and the south tower fitted with an experimental first-order Fresnel lens. One of the largest lenses ever used in an American lighthouse, it weighed more than seven tons and was wide enough (almost ten feet in diameter) to fit a comfortable room inside it. Shining from an elevation more than 240 feet above sea level, this extraordinarily powerful light could be seen up to twenty-five miles at sea. The light and station were deactivated in 1953.

In 1899 Guglielmo Marconi used a transmitter and mast located not far from the Highlands Lighthouse to conduct the first practical demonstration of his wireless. Using the air rather than a wire to carry the dots and dashes of Morse code, he relayed to New York City the results of the America's Cup races being run off Sandy Hook.

Travel information: From exit 117 off the Garden State Parkway, follow Highway 36 and the signs to Twin Lights State Historic Site and Museum. The museum recounts the extraordinary history of this light station. Contact Twin Lights Museum, Lighthouse Road, Highlands, NJ 07732; (732) 872–1814.

■ SEA GIRT LIGHT ■
Sea Girt (1896)

With its weathered brick walls, pitched roof, and spacious balustered porch, the Sea Girt Lighthouse looks much like other homes in this seaside community. Unlike neighboring houses, however, this one wraps around two sides of a square, forty-foot tower with a gallery and a small lantern perched on top.

Now operated as a private aid to navigation, this homey-looking lighthouse was built in 1896 to guide fishing boats and other vessels into the shallow Sea Girt Inlet. The light also filled in a dark stretch of coast between the **Barnegat** and **Highlands Lights.** The lantern shone out from its fourth-order Fresnel lens until 1945, when the Coast Guard discontinued the light. During the 1980s, the Sea Girt Lighthouse Committee raised enough money to restore the structure. It has been relit as a private aid to navigation.

Travel information: From the Garden State Parkway just south of I–95, take the Highway 34 exit and drive south for approximately six miles. Take Route 71 north to Sea Girt and follow Beacon Bouelvard to the lighthouse.

■ BARNEGAT LIGHT ■
Long Beach Island (1835 and 1857)

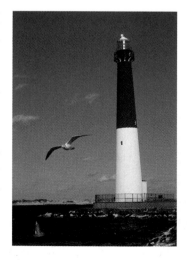

The original Barnegat tower, completed in 1835, was the work of famed lighthouse contractor Winslow Lewis. Only about twenty years after the station's lamps first burned, however, a government inspector declared the workmanship shoddy and the light woefully inadequate—even though Lewis had designed the lamps and reflectors himself. The inspector was none other than George Meade, a U.S. Army engineer, who some years later would lead the Union Army to victory at Gettysburg. Meade's call for a new and better lighthouse at Barnegat went unheeded, but only a year later a storm knocked down the old Lewis tower. Meade probably smiled at the news.

The soaring, 172-foot-tall brick tower seen at Barnegat nowadays was completed in 1857 under

(Facing page) *Sea Girt Light* © William Kaufhold

the watchful auspices of the Lighthouse Board. With the fate of the original light-house fresh in their minds, designers of the new tower gave it two walls, the outer one more than four feet thick. The project cost $45,000, with another $15,000 for a first-order Fresnel lens. The height of the tower and power of its lens gave the light such a boost that it was occasionally seen from as far as thirty miles at sea. The light stayed in service until 1944.

> *Travel information:* From the Garden State Parkway, take Route 72 to Long Beach Island, turn left, and drive to Barnegat Lighthouse State Park at the far northern end of the island. Visitors may climb the tower of "Old Barney," as local residents call it, for a small fee. Call (609) 494–2016. The station's old first-order lens is the primary attraction of the nearby Barnegat Light Museum.

■ ABSECON LIGHT ■
Atlantic City (1857)

The bright lights of Atlantic City's gaming palaces are dim by comparison to the powerful flash of the Absecon Lighthouse in its heyday. Focused by a first-order Fresnel lens with a focal plane almost 170 feet above the ocean, the beacon could be seen from more than twenty miles away.

Congress ignored demands for a light to mark this stretch of the New Jersey coast for decades before finally providing $35,000 for the project in 1854. Flooded foundations and dried-up funding delayed the work for almost three years. It took a $12,000 supplemental federal appropriation and the engineering skills of George Meade to complete the lighthouse. Keeper Daniel Skull first lit the lamps inside the station's big lens in early 1857. The station's name, Absecon, honors an Indian tribe that at one time lived on the New Jersey coast.

On several occasions erosion threatened to undermine the tower's foundation. It survived the Atlantic's worst storms and tides, however, only to succumb to what is often described as progress. By 1933 the beacon could no longer be distinguished from the lights of the burgeoning city that then surrounded it. In 1933 the Coast Guard abandoned the station, deeding it to the city.

> *Travel information:* Located at the intersection of Rhode Island and Pacific Avenues in Atlantic City, the Absecon Lighthouse fell into a sad state of disrepair over the years. Fund-raising efforts underway since the early 1990s, however, are aimed at returning the lighthouse to its former glory and opening it to the public as a tourist attraction.

■ HEREFORD INLET LIGHT ■
North Wildwood (1874)

With its long porch, delicate balusters, and four-story square tower pushing up through its pitched roof, this fanciful, stick-style lighthouse strongly suggests the Victorian era that produced it. Completed in 1874 at the relatively modest cost of $25,000, the unusual structure proved a solid piece of work. An 1889 hurricane swept away entire nearby communities but spared the little lighthouse, along with eighteen storm refugees who huddled within its surprisingly sturdy walls.

Despite numerous storms and a couple of nearly disastrous fires, the Hereford Inlet Light remained in service for ninety years. In 1964 the Coast Guard discontinued the station, replacing it with a far less attractive skeleton tower. With the property restored and maintained by city and state funds, the station's fourth-order Fresnel lens is now active once more as a private aid to navigation.

> *Travel information:* The lighthouse is located in North Wildwood, just off Central Avenue between Chestnut and First Streets. It is open to the public during summer. Hours vary.
>
> Oddly enough, this seemingly unique structure has two near-twins. One is the **Point Fermin Lighthouse** in Southern California. The other, located in Nags Head, North Carolina, is a replica and serves as the home of Lighthouse Gallery and Gifts, founded by Bruce Roberts, one of the authors of this book.

■ CAPE MAY LIGHT ■
Cape May Point (1824, 1847, and 1859)

The 157-foot tower of the Cape May Lighthouse soars above the flat, sandy New Jersey coast and the blue Atlantic beyond. Built in 1859, the distinctive white tower still guides ships along the coast and into Delaware Bay. The enormous tower replaced two earlier structures, dating from 1824 and 1847 respectively.

Exactly 199 steps lead from the ground floor to the lantern room, where an extraordinarily powerful aeromarine beacon flashes its white signal every fifteen seconds. Vessels more than twenty-five miles away can see its light.

Like several other light towers along the New Jersey coast, this one is of double-wall construction. Built on a foundation of stone blocks, the giant tower is twenty-seven feet wide at the base and precisely half that wide at the top. These dimensions give the tower its graceful, tapered appearance.

Perhaps the tower's beauty and the romantic nature of its ocean setting account for its apparent influence on young lovers. Over the years numerous marriage proposals have been offered—and accepted—in the lantern room.

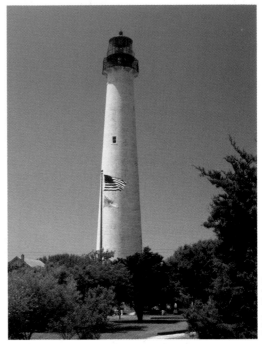

© William Kaulhold

Travel information: Follow the Garden State Parkway south until it ends in Cape May. The lighthouse is in Cape May Point State Park on Lighthouse Avenue, just off Sunset Boulevard. A visitors center is open daily much of the year but only on weekends during cold-weather months. Contact Cape May Lighthouse, Lighthouse Avenue, Cape May Point, NJ 08204; (609) 884–5404. The park is a protected natural area of considerable diversity and beauty. Step gently here, but enjoy.

■ EAST POINT (MAURICE RIVER) LIGHT ■
South of Millville (1849)

Although severely damaged by fire in 1971, the East Point Lighthouse still marks New Jersey's Maurice Cove and the mouth of the Maurice River. Completed in 1849, the station consists of a two-story brick dwelling with an octagonal tower on its roof. A sixth-order Fresnel lens once served here, but the light is now produced by a modern optic.

Travel information: The station is located on East Point Road in Maurice River Township, about an hour south of Millville, New Jersey. The Maurice River Historical Society leases the property and is restoring the building; call (856) 691–5934. Farther up the Delaware Bay are the historic **Maih Maull Shoal** (1913) and **Finns Point Rear Range** (1877) Lighthouses.

Courtesy H. Kent Edwards

■ TUCKER'S ISLAND LIGHT ■
Tuckerton (1868 and 1999)

Built in 1868, the Tucker's Island Lighthouse was swept out to sea along with much of the surrounding community during the 1920s. A replica of the original two-story dwelling and tower now serves as a key attraction of Tuckerton Seaport, a fascinating museum complex consisting of sixteen re-created historic structures. The lighthouse serves as an interpretive center.

Travel information: From the Garden State Parkway, take exit 58 and follow Route 539 to Tuckerton; then follow Route 9 to the Tuckerton Seaport; call (609) 296-8868.

DELAWARE

■ LISTON REAR RANGE LIGHT ■
Fort Penn (1877)

Range lighthouses operate in pairs to mark channels for shipping. Arrayed one behind the other, with the rear light on a higher plane, the beacons appear in perfect vertical alignment to pilots who steer their ships in the middle of a safe channel. If the upper light appears to tilt either to the left or the right of vertical, the vessel is straying out of the channel in the direction indicated, and the pilot must correct the course.

Liston Light

Fourteen Foot Bank Lighthouse

Over the years, several range lights have served ships moving through the Delaware Bay. Among the most remarkable of these is the Liston Rear Range Light, built in 1877 and still active. A 120-foot black giant with steel-skeleton frame, it held a second-order Fresnel lens until 1976, when it was automated and fitted with an aeromarine beacon. The companion front-range light shines from a forty-foot tower near the river's edge.

Travel information: From U.S. Highway 13 turn eastward toward Fort Penn on Route 2. The Liston light station is located less than a mile from the turn. From Bowers Beach southeast of Dover, the **Fourteen Foot Bank Lighthouse** (1888) can be seen standing on a huge concrete caisson surrounded by the waters of the bay.

■ HARBOR OF REFUGE LIGHT ■
Lewes (1896 and 1926)

Ships sailing along the northeast coast of the United States are often caught in the grip of powerful storms. As early as the 1820s, government maritime officials planned a harbor of refuge where ships could ride out major gales. They created a harbor at Lewes, near the southern entrance to Delaware Bay, by building an extensive series of breakwaters.

A pair of cylindrical iron light towers built in 1926 mark the harbor breakwaters. The seventy-six-foot Harbor of Refuge Lighthouse replaced an earlier tower built in 1896. It remains active, flashing white and red twelve times a minute. The nearby forty-nine-foot **Delaware Breakwater Lighthouse** was preceded by several different towers and navigational aids, the earliest dating from 1834. No longer an active light, it serves as a daymark.

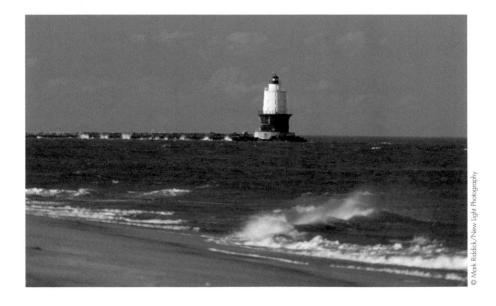

© Mark Riddick/New Light Photography

For many years the **Cape Henlopen Lighthouse,** an old stone colonial tower established in 1767, had guided ships into Delaware Bay and pointed the way to its safe harbors. Eventually, erosion undermined the historic structure, and it finally collapsed during a storm in 1926. No trace of it remains.

Travel information: To view or photograph the harbor lights, follow U.S. Highway 9 to its end at Cape Henlopen State Park, just east of Lewes. The park features delightful ocean scenery and is open year-round during day-light hours. Harbor cruises are available in nearby Lewes, where one can also visit the lightship *Overfalls* (1838). The Lewes Historical Society restored the *Overfalls,* which spent most of its operational life in New England. Contact the Overfalls Maritime Museum, Lewes, DE 19958; (302) 644-4646.

■ FENWICK ISLAND LIGHT ■
Fenwick Island (1858)

The famed Mason-Dixon Line not only runs right through the light station prop-erty, it starts here. The lighthouse, built half in the North and half in the South in 1858, helps guide ships into Delaware Bay with its occulting white signal.

Like the **Barnegat** and **Cape May Lighthouses** to the north, this one has a double-walled tower. The brick structure rises eighty-seven feet above the island sands, placing the focal plane of its light nearly ninety feet above the water. The third-order Fresnel lens is the station's original optic. Eclipser panels roll around the lens on a dolly, causing it to occult, or wink, about four times a minute.

Travel information: Located on Route 528 at the Delaware bor-der north of Ocean City, Maryland, the lighthouse and its small museum are open to the public, but hours are very limited. For more about the Fenwick Island Lighthouse, contact P.O. Box 6, Selbyville, DE 19975; (410) 250-1098. For a museum schedule call (302) 436-8410.

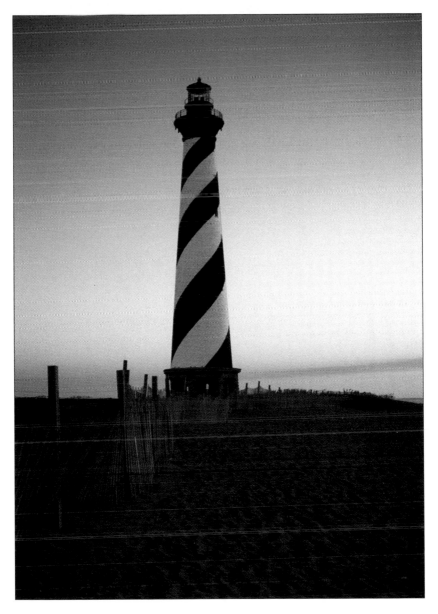

Cape Hatteras Lighthouse before it was moved

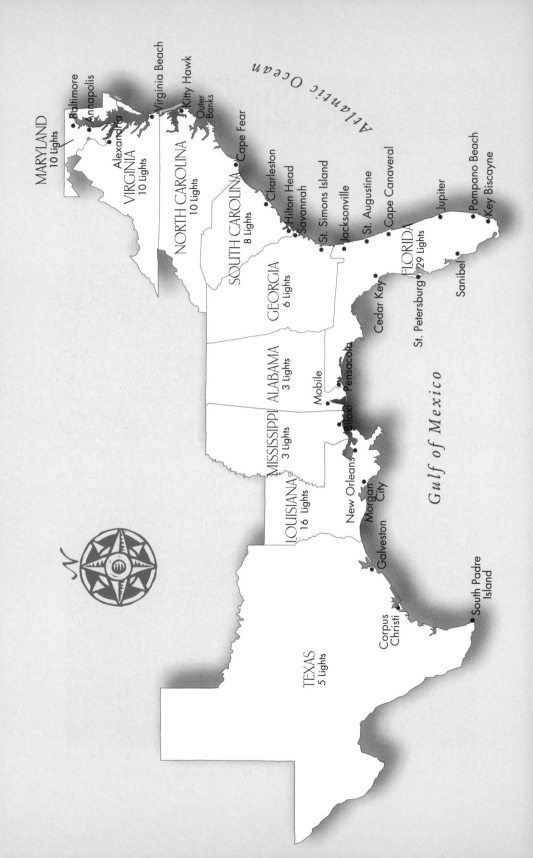

Atlantic Ocean

MARYLAND
10 Lights

Baltimore
Annapolis

Alexandria

VIRGINIA
10 Lights

Virginia Beach
Kitty Hawk
Outer Banks

NORTH CAROLINA
10 Lights

Cape Fear

Charleston

SOUTH CAROLINA
8 Lights

Hilton Head
Savannah

GEORGIA
6 Lights

St. Simons Island
Jacksonville
St. Augustine
Cape Canaveral

FLORIDA
29 Lights

Jupiter

Pompano Beach
Key Biscayne

Sanibel

Cedar Key

St. Petersburg

ALABAMA
3 Lights

Mobile
Pensacola

MISSISSIPPI
3 Lights

Biloxi

Gulf of Mexico

LOUISIANA
16 Lights

New Orleans
Morgan City
Galveston

TEXAS
5 Lights

Corpus Christi

South Padre Island

MARYLAND

■ CONCORD POINT LIGHT ■
Havre de Grace (1827)

Two years after he built the original **Thomas Point Lighthouse**—and botched the job—contractor John Donohoo was hired to erect a light tower on Concord Point at Havre de Grace. Donohoo completed the thirty-two-foot stone tower in less than a

year for $3,500. Apparently he learned from his earlier mistakes. This tower still stands, no less solid than when its lamps were first lit in 1827.

Originally, the lantern held a set of lamps and sixteen-inch reflectors. Later, these were exchanged for a fifth-order Fresnel lens. At present the tower displays a fixed white light as a private aid to navigation.

All the keepers of this lighthouse were members of the same family, that of war hero John O'Neil. During the War of 1812, O'Neil made a quixotic one-man stand against an entire British fleet. Miraculously, he survived and, as a reward, was named keeper of the Concord Point Light. The job passed down from one generation of O'Neils to the next until the light was automated in the 1920s.

> *Travel information:* The lighthouse sits in a small park beside the Susquehanna River in the town of Havre de Grace. The tower is open for tours on weekend afternoons from April through October; other times only by appointment. Contact the city of Havre de Grace at (410) 939-1498.

■ TURKEY POINT LIGHT ■
Elk Neck (1833)

Turkey Point juts southward into the Chesapeake Bay near its far northern end. A modest masonry light tower has marked the point since 1833, its beacon guiding ships headed for the Susquehanna River. John Donohoo built the conical stone tower and a nearby keeper's dwelling for $4,355. Although only thirty-eight feet tall, the tower stands on a one-hundred-foot bluff, making its light far more effective.

Several female lighthouse keepers served here, including Mrs. Harry Salter, appointed to the post by President Calvin Coolidge in 1925 after the death of her husband, the previous keeper. She was the last female keeper in the old Lighthouse Service.

Travel information: The lighthouse is located in pristine Elk Neck State Park, a major game preserve. Take the Route 272 exit off I-95, several miles north of the Susquehanna Bridge. The tower is accessible by way of a twenty-minute walk on a park hiking path.

■ SEVEN FOOT KNOLL LIGHT ■
Baltimore (1855)

The oldest of the Chesapeake Bay's surviving screw-pile light towers, the Seven Foot Knoll Lighthouse was completed in 1855. Most of the bay's other screw-pile lighthouses had octagonal, cottagelike dwellings, but this one looks more like a huge, red cheese hoop-shaped box.

Built to mark a dangerous shoal near the entrance to the Baltimore harbor, the lighthouse stood on eight iron piles hammered and screwed into the muddy bottom of the bay. Designed for a third-order Fresnel lens, it received a less powerful fourth-order lens instead. Keepers lived and worked in a round-walled, one-story dwelling. A short cylindrical tower rose from the flat roof of the building.

First automated and then abandoned by the Coast Guard, Seven Foot Knoll served mariners as an active light and daymark for more than 130 years. Eventually, it was donated to the city of Baltimore for use as a museum. In 1988 the 220-ton

Lightship Chesapeake

Seven Foot Knoll Light

structure was cut from its pilings and barged to its current location at Pier Five in the city's popular Inner Harbor district.

Travel information: From I-95 take the Pratt Street exit and follow signs to the Baltimore Inner Harbor. The lighthouse is at the end of Pier Five, not far from the permanent berth of the **Lightship *Chesapeake*** (1930), now a floating navigational museum. Call the Baltimore Maritime Museum at (410) 396-3453 or call (410) 837-4636 for Baltimore tourism information.

■ THOMAS POINT LIGHT ■

Annapolis/Thomas Point (1825, 1838, and 1875)

Vessels moving through the middle reaches of the Chesapeake Bay must swing wide to avoid a treacherous bank of shoals just off Thomas Point near Annapolis. Since 1825, lighthouses have marked this obstacle. Two of these were built onshore by legendary lighthouse contractor Winslow Lewis. The first Lewis tower proved nearly useless, so he built another some thirteen years later. But the light, provided by a lens-and-reflector system of Lewis's own design, remained too weak to adequately warn ships approaching the shoals.

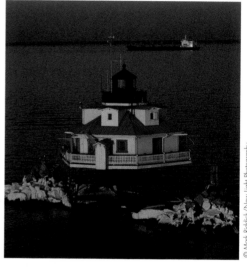

In 1875 the Lighthouse Board decided to move the light offshore and place it where it would be most effective—out in the bay, directly over the shoals. The new lighthouse was a small hexagonal building held above the water by iron legs anchored to screw piles. Abandoned, the Lewis tower on the point eventually collapsed, but for more than a century the lighthouse on the shoals has weathered storms, floods, and ice floes. Its flashing beacon still guides ships.

Travel information: The best way to see this open-water lighthouse is from a boat. Sight-seeing cruises out of Annapolis, Maryland, often pass the station. Contact the Tourism Council of Annapolis and Anne Arundel County, One Annapolis Street, Annapolis, MD 21401; (410) 280-0445.

■ SANDY POINT SHOAL LIGHT ■

Skidmore (1883)

With its mansard roof and pitched dormer windows, the Sandy Point Shoal Lighthouse looks more like an old Victorian townhouse than a navigational marker. Its location is distinctly maritime, however. It rests on a caisson, completely surrounded by the choppy waters of the Chesapeake Bay. The seemingly out-of-place structure and its flashing light mark a troublesome shoal off Sandy Point, near where the Chesapeake Bay Bridge now connects Maryland's eastern shore region with the rest of the state.

The Lighthouse Board established a light station onshore at Sandy Point in 1858, but it was of limited use to pilots trying to avoid the shoal, especially in fog or stormy weather. In 1883 the light was moved directly over the shoal to maximize its effectiveness. A combination tower and dwelling, the structure rises more than fifty feet above the waters of the bay. It remains in operation, displaying a white flash ten times every minute.

© Mark Ridd cv/New Light Photography

Travel information: The lighthouse is off-limits to the public but can be seen from Sandy Point State Park, accessible from an exit off U.S. Highway 50, just west of the Chesapeake Bay Bridge tollbooths. The park is also an excellent place to have a picnic and enjoy the bay scenery.

■ HOOPER STRAIT LIGHT ■
St. Michaels (1867 and 1879)

For more than forty years, beginning in 1927, a lightship marked a crooked channel of Hooper Strait. But in 1867 the Lighthouse Board built a modest screw-pile tower to guide shipping. Ten years later a massive ice floe swept the little lighthouse off its piles and carried it five miles down the bay. A tender found the wreckage and managed to salvage the lens and some of the equipment.

A larger, hexagonal lighthouse replaced the crushed tower by the autumn of 1879, and it remained in service for three quarters of a century. Deactivated in 1954, it was eventually acquired by the Chesapeake Bay Maritime Museum in St. Michaels on the Maryland eastern shore. To move the forty-four-foot-wide structure down the Chesapeake to St. Michaels, museum officials had it cut in half, like a giant apple, and loaded onto a barge. Reassembled and restored to like-new condition, the lighthouse now stands on Navy Point beside the museum.

Travel information: To reach the museum and lighthouse, take U.S.

Highway 50 and then Route 33 to St. Michaels. Signs point the way to Navy Point and the museum. Contact the Chesapeake Bay Maritime Museum, P.O. Box 636, St. Michaels, MD 21663; (410) 745-2916.

■ COVE POINT LIGHT ■

Solomons (1828)

Among the oldest light towers on the Chesapeake Bay, the Cove Point Lighthouse marks the entrance to the Patuxent River. The conical, fifty-one-foot brick tower is the work of John Donohoo, who built several of the Chesapeake's historic light-houses. The Cove Point tower is among his best—it has stood intact since 1828.

Erosion threatened the structure almost from the start. During the 1840s retaining walls were built to hold back the eroding tides, which they have managed to do for more than 150 years. The tireless Chesapeake, however, has now cut to within a few feet of the foundation and may yet claim its victim.

Travel information: Although the light is now automated, Cove Point remains an active Coast Guard facility and is off-limits to the public. You *can* view the lighthouse through the station fence. Follow Maryland Route 4 to Solomons and then Cove Point Road to the lighthouse. Helpful information may be obtained from the Calvert Lighthouse Museum in Solomons; (410) 326-2042.

■ DRUM POINT LIGHT ■

Solomons (1883)

American taxpayers have known few such bargains as the hexagonal, cottage-type Drum Point Lighthouse, which cost only $5,000 to build. Completed in 1883, the

little lighthouse served faithfully for nearly eighty years. Its fourth-order Fresnel lens, which likely cost more than the light-house itself, warned mariners until 1962, when the station was taken out of service.

During its active years the light marked a sandy spit that threatened vessels passing Drum Point. Now it is part of the Calvert Maritime Museum.

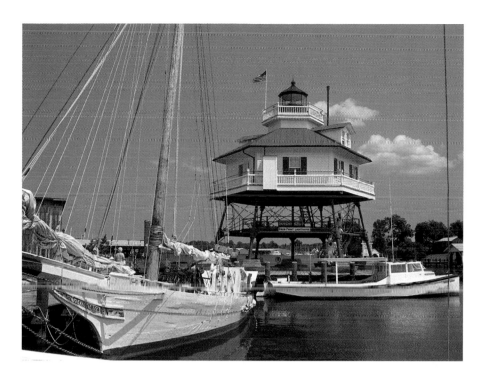

Travel information: Follow Route 4 to Solomons. The museum and lighthouse are near the bridge across the Patuxent River. The lighthouse has been wonderfully restored and furnished in early 1900s style. Contact the Calvert Maritime Museum, Box 97, Solomons, MD 20688; (410) 326-2042.

From Solomons the **Point Lookout Lighthouse** (1830) can be reached via a half-hour drive across the Patuxent Bridge on Route 4 and then southeastward along Route 235 and Route 5 to Point Lookout State Park. Deactivated in 1966, the old lighthouse is under restoration by the state. From the park drive back

Point Lookout Lighthouse

toward Washington, D.C., on Route 5 to the small town of Callaway; turn south on Route 249 and drive to Piney Point, where an authentic John Donohoo light tower still stands. Deactivated in 1964, the **Piney Point Lighthouse** (1836) presently serves as a museum. Call (301) 769-2222.

VIRGINIA

■ ASSATEAGUE ISLAND LIGHT ■
Assateague Island (1833 and 1867)

In 1831 Congress appropriated funds for a lighthouse a few miles south of the Maryland border on Assateague Island. Its chief duty was to warn ships away from a series of shoals that extend seaward like knife blades from the island. But when completed two years later, the forty-five-foot stone tower and its Winslow Lewis lamp-and-reflector system proved far too weak to perform this task effectively.

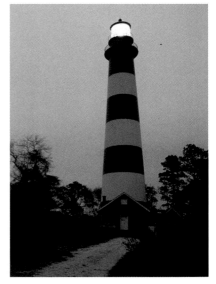

During the 1850s the Lighthouse Board launched a determined campaign to upgrade lighthouses along America's coasts. As part of this comprehensive effort, the board decided to rebuild the Assateague tower, but the Civil War interrupted the project. Hence, the new 142-foot tower was not ready for service until October 1867. When its first-order Fresnel lens finally began to shine, however, mariners saw an immediate improvement in the station's beacon, which they were now able to spot from more than twenty miles at sea. An automated aeromarine beacon replaced the old Fresnel in 1961.

Travel information: Take U.S. Highway 13 and Route 175 to Chincoteague; then follow the signs to the Chincoteague National Wildlife Refuge on Assateague Island. A quarter-mile trail leads from the lighthouse parking lot to the base of the tower. Contact the Chincoteague National Wildlife Refuge, P.O. Box 62, Chincoteague, VA 23336; (757) 336–6122.

■ CAPE CHARLES LIGHT ■
Smith Island (1828, 1864, and 1894)

A pair of light stations mark the Virginia Capes. Dating from 1792, the two-century-old **Cape Henry Light** on the southern lip of the capes is the elder of the two. The younger, Cape Charles Light, marks the northern side of the capes on Smith Island. Established in 1828, it has shone for more than 170 years.

The giant, 190-foot steel-skeleton tower that stands on Smith Island now is Cape Charles station's third tower. The first, a fifty-five-foot stone structure, was always woefully inadequate. Its light, supplied by outmoded lamps and reflectors, was rarely visible more than a dozen miles away. A 150-foot brick replacement tower was built during the Civil War, despite a destructive assault on the station in 1862 by a Confederate raiding party. Completed in May 1864, it served for thirty years before coastal erosion forced the government to relocate the station.

The huge skeleton tower that took its place is more than a mile inland. Its pyramidal steel superstructure is intended to protect the tower from high winds. A winding staircase inside a nine-foot-wide steel cylinder provides access to the lantern room. The flashing white light has an effective range of about twenty-five miles.

Travel information: Even the Coast Guard has trouble getting to this light station on remote Smith Island. Not surprisingly, the station is closed to the public. Motorists, however, can see the lighthouse as they cross the 17-mile-long Chesapeake Bay (toll) Bridge on U.S. Highway 13. The first-order Fresnel lens that served here until the station was automated in 1963 is now on display at the Newport News Mariners Museum; (800) 581-7245.

■ JONES POINT LIGHT ■
Alexandria (1855)

On the south shore of the Potomac, just downriver from Washington, D.C., stands a small rectangular building with white-washed wooden walls, pitched roof, and raised porch. Except for the tiny lantern perched on its roof, the little building might be taken for a nineteenth-century country schoolhouse. Instead, it is the Jones Point Lighthouse, built in 1855 to guide trading ships, tugs, and barges into the then-thriving port of Alexandria. Deactivated in 1926, after more than seventy years of service, the lighthouse stood unused for much of the twentieth century. Recently, however, it was handsomely restored and relit as a private aid to navigation.

Travel information: From U.S. Highway 1 just south of I–95/495 and the Wilson Bridge, look for signs to Jones Point. In addition to the lighthouse, the small grassy park at Jones Point offers sweeping Potomac River views and a stone that marks a corner of the original, ten-mile-square federal district (Alexandria and the southwest side of the district voted to rejoin Virginia in 1846). The U.S. Park Service can provide information on visiting the lighthouse; call (703) 289–2500.

■ NEW POINT COMFORT LIGHT ■
Mathews (1804)

Completed in 1804, the New Point Comfort Light did not, as its name implies, replace the Old Point Comfort Light. Instead, the two lighthouses, both built at about the same time, take their names from the separate headlands where they have stood guard now for nearly two hundred years. Built on a small island near the entrance to Mobjack Bay, the New Point Comfort Lighthouse pointed the way up the Chesapeake toward Baltimore. Deactivated during the 1950s, it now serves only as a daymark.

Travel information: Virginia's Mathews County restored the lighthouse as a memorial to local mariners who lost their lives at sea. It can be reached only by boat. However, it can be seen from a boardwalk in New Point Comfort Preserve at the end of Route 600 in Bavon. Several miles to the north is the **Wolf Trap Lighthouse.**

New Point Comfort Light

■ WOLF TRAP LIGHT ■
Chesapeake Bay (1870 and 1893)

In 1691 a Chesapeake shoal ensnared the HMS *Wolfe* and has been known ever since as the Wolf Trap. A bright red, octagonal lighthouse, built on an enormous concrete-and-iron caisson, now guards the shoal. The light flashing from its fifty-two-foot tower warns vessels against being trapped like the *Wolfe*. A cottage-style, screw-pile lighthouse placed here in 1870 had a misadventure of its own when a mighty ice floe swept it down the Chesapeake during the winter of 1893. A lighthouse tender found it bobbing in the waves out toward the Virginia Capes. Protected by its massive caisson, the current structure is far less vulnerable.

Travel information: The Wolf Trap Lighthouse can be reached only by boat. It can be seen from the water, but it is off-limits to the public.

■ OLD POINT COMFORT LIGHT ■
Fort Monroe (1802)

Among the earliest lighthouses constructed on the Chesapeake Bay was the fifty-four-foot tower erected in 1802 at Fort Monroe. The light marked the mouth of the James River and the entrance to Hampton Roads.

Because of its strategic location, the lighthouse has seen plenty of conflicts. During the War of 1812, British troops seized the fort and used the lighthouse as a watchtower. Half a century later, the ironclad *Virginia* steamed past the Point Comfort Light on its way to do battle with the *Monitor*. Following the Civil War, Confederate President Jefferson Davis was imprisoned in a cell not far from the tower.

Fort Monroe remains an active military post to this day. Its lighthouse is still on duty, displaying a flashing red light with a range of about fifteen miles.

Travel information: Fort Monroe can be reached from Norfolk via I-64, Route 169, and Route 143. The sentry at the gate can point the way to the lighthouse. Although the tower is not open to the public, visitors are more than welcome at the nearby Casement Museum, which celebrates the fort's rich and often somber history. Contact the Casement Museum, P.O. Box 341, Fort Monroe, VA 23651; (757) 727-3391.

■ NEWPORT NEWS MIDDLE GROUND LIGHT ■
Newport News (1891)

Built on an open-water caisson, this lighthouse warns ships away from the dangerous "Middle Ground," an L-shaped shoal in the heart of Hampton Roads, one of the nation's busiest harbors. Shaped something like a coffeepot without a handle, the thirty-five-foot tower displays a flashing white light.

Travel information: The lighthouse can be seen from Route I-664 as it crosses the James River, and it is a featured attraction of Hampton/ Newport News harbor cruises. On Museum Drive, just off U.S. Highway 60 in Newport News, is the excellent Mariner's Museum, which tells the story of humanity's long—and occasionally stormy—relationship to the sea. On display here is the huge first-order Fresnel lens from the **Cape Charles Lighthouse.**

■ *PORTSMOUTH* LIGHTSHIP ■
Portsmouth (1916)

Known to the Coast Guard as Lightship *LV 101*, this sturdy vessel served for forty-eight years at stations off the Delaware, Maryland, Massachusetts, and Virginia coasts. As with other lightships, it marked dangerous obstacles and key navigational

points where it was impossible or too expensive to build a lighthouse. Among its unusual features is a hollow lightmast, allowing internal access to its optic. Retired in 1960, the *LV 101* became the *Portsmouth* Lightship, a floating maritime museum. Present-day visitors will find the crew's quarters, galley, and engine room all shipshape, as if the *Portsmouth* were ready to go to sea at a moment's notice.

Travel information: The *Portsmouth* Lightship and Museum are part of the Art Center complex on the Portsmouth waterfront. Contact the Portsmouth Lightship Museum, London Slip, Portsmouth, VA 23704; (757) 393-8741. From Ocean View Avenue in nearby Norfolk, one can see the **Thimble Shoal Lighthouse** (1912). The three-level tower rests on a caisson and displays a flashing white light.

■ CAPE HENRY LIGHT ■

Virginia Beach (1792 and 1881)

In 1774 the colonies of Maryland and Virginia decided to mark the entrance to the Chesapeake Bay with a lighthouse, a project under consideration for almost a century. Tons of stone were piled up at Cape Henry, the selected site. But before construction could begin, the Revolutionary War brought a stop to all such public works. The effort did not get under way again until 1791, when the now-independent nation's first federal Congress appropriated $24,077 to see it completed.

Hired by Secretary of Treasury Alexander Hamilton, contractor John McComb hoped to use the original stockpile of stone for the tower but soon discovered that the large blocks had sunk deep into the sand. Nonetheless, using freshly quarried

New Cape Henry Light

sandstone, he completed the ninety-foot tower in less than a year. It was a solid piece of work. The McComb tower has stood for more than two centuries, through several wars and countless gales. The Confederates put the light out at the beginning of the Civil War, but the Union had its whale-oil lamps burning again by 1862.

During the 1870s cracks appeared in the tower's octagonal walls. Fearing it would collapse, the Lighthouse Board had a second, much taller tower built just south of the original. This cylindrical cast-iron structure, more than 150 feet tall, was ready for service in 1881. Its first-order Fresnel lens, a magnificent optic becoming a lighthouse of such importance, still flashes its white signal every twenty seconds.

Old Cape Henry Light

Travel information: The Cape Henry towers are located in historic Fort Story, reached off U.S. Highway 60 in Virginia Beach via Atlantic Avenue. Visitors can climb the two hundred steps to the top of the old 1792 tower—concerns over the stability of the original lighthouse proved unwarranted. Contact Old Cape Henry Lighthouse, 4401 Wisheart Road, Virginia Beach, VA 23455; (757) 422-9421.

Also of interest in Virginia Beach is the Virginia Lifesaving Museum on Atlantic Avenue. Celebrating the old U.S. Lifesaving Service, it is filled with lifesaving equipment. Photographs and displays recount stories of shipwreck and bravery. Call (757) 422-1587.

NORTH CAROLINA

■ CURRITUCK BEACH LIGHT ■
Corolla (1874)

Near the border between the North Carolina and Virginia coasts, the mighty Gulf Stream sweeps in close to the mainland. To avoid fighting its powerful northeasterly current, captains of southbound ships must steer perilously close to land. Sometimes they come too close—with disastrous results. To warn mariners to keep their ships at a safe distance, the Lighthouse Board erected a series of three tall coastal sentinels along this dangerous stretch of coast: the 193-foot Cape Hatteras tower (1870), 163-foot Bodie Island tower (1872), and 158-foot Currituck Beach tower, completed in 1875.

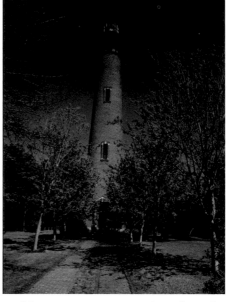

Strategically placed about halfway between the Cape Henry, Virginia, and Bodie Island lights, the Currituck Beach Lighthouse illuminated one of the last remaining dark stretches of southern coastline. Stout walls, almost six feet thick at the base, help the tower withstand Atlantic storms. To distinguish it from neighboring lighthouses, its red bricks were left unpainted, and they remain so. The twelve-foot-tall lantern at the top still holds the station's original first-order, bull's-eye Fresnel lens. The automated light flashes white every twenty seconds and can be spotted from up to nineteen miles away.

Travel information: From Kitty Hawk turn north off U.S. Highway 158 (the Outer Banks Highway) onto NC 12 and drive approximately 20 miles to the village of Corolla. The lighthouse, on the left, can be seen from the road. Visitors may climb the tower's 214 steps for a small fee—the extraordinary view from the gallery is well worth the price. The station is open to the public every day except Sunday during warm-weather months. For information write to Currituck Beach Lighthouse, P.O. Box 58, Corolla, NC 27927 or call (252) 453-4939. To schedule tours call (252) 453-8152. Lucky visitors may catch a glimpse of wild-horse herds on nearby beaches.

■ BODIE ISLAND LIGHT ■

Bodie Island (1848, 1859, and 1872)

It is hard to imagine a contractor being instructed to do a poor job, but that was the case with Francis Gibbons, builder of the first Bodie Island Lighthouse. Despite a thick layer of mud under the construction site, a penny-pinching U.S. Treasury official ordered Gibbons to drive no piles, so Gibbons built on a shallow foundation of brick. Not surprisingly, his tower began to lean out of plumb almost as soon

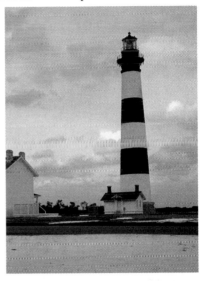

as he finished it in 1848. The leaning tower of Bodie Island was rebuilt in 1859, but its replacement lasted only two years. Confederate troops blew it up during the opening months of the Civil War.

The soaring 163-foot tower seen at Bodie Island today rests on a granite foundation set atop iron pilings and a grillage of pine timbers. This technique (also employed at Cape Hatteras) enables the tower to stand straight, as it has since 1872. Automated in 1931, when its beacon was electrified, the Bodie Island Lighthouse remains vital to navigation. The lantern retains its original giant lens. Its twice-a-minute white flashes shine out to a distance of eighteen miles.

Chicamacomico Lifesaving Station

Travel information: Located off Route 12 about 17 miles north of Rodanthe, the scenic Bodie Island Lighthouse is open daily to the public. The National Park Service operates a small museum in the keeper's dwelling (1893). Contact the Cape Hatteras National Seashore, Route 1, P.O. Box 675, Manteo, NC 27954; (252) 473-2111.

Visitors to the Bodie Island Lighthouse will want to stop at Rodanthe for a look at the **Chicamacomico Lifesaving Station** (1911), now a fascinating museum dedicated to the old U.S. Lifesaving Service. The station and museum are open May through September on Tuesday, Thursday, and Saturday; call (252) 978-1552.

■ CAPE HATTERAS LIGHT ■

Hatteras Island (1803 and 1870)

Two mighty ocean rivers, the cold Labrador Current and steamy Gulf Stream, oppose each other just off Cape Hatteras. The violent seas and killer shoals thrown up by their interaction have claimed at least 2,300 ships, causing sailors to dub these waters "the Graveyard of the Atlantic."

Congress authorized a lighthouse for the cape in 1794, but political squabbling over selection of a contractor delayed the project for years. Fighting storms, mosquitoes, and outbreaks of yellow fever, construction crews finally had the ninety-five-foot stone tower standing by late 1803. Not tall enough to be seen from the vicious Diamond Shoals that extend several miles seaward from the cape, this first Hatteras lighthouse was never considered adequate. Reporting to the Lighthouse Board in 1851, a Navy inspector called it "the worst light in the world." Following the Civil War, the board replaced it with a new, 193-foot brick tower painted with distinctive spiral stripes.

Built on a granite foundation set atop iron pilings and a grillage of pine timbers, the big brick tower withstood many hurricanes; however, the lighthouse faced a much more serious threat from the sea. Once almost a third of a mile from the Atlantic, the Cape Hatteras Lighthouse teetered at the very edge of the tides by the late 1990s. That's when the U.S. Park Service launched a $12 million effort to save the old tower by moving it beyond the reach of the ocean's threatening waves. The move, completed during the spring and summer of 1999, became one of the most celebrated events of the year.

Fortunately for those who love this lighthouse and for mariners who, almost two hundred years after its construction, still depend on its guidance, the Cape Hatteras Lighthouse still stands. Its light shines each night, flashing white every seven and a half seconds from an elevation of 191 feet above high water. In clear weather sailors can spot it from a distance of almost twenty-four miles.

Travel information: The lighthouse is located just off Route 12, near the village of Buxton on Cape Hatteras. A keeper's dwelling houses a visitors center and museum dedicated to the history of the station and Outer Banks. From the beach sharp-eyed visitors may be able to see the **Diamond Shoals Lightship** (1967), which rests on steel pilings directly over the shoal and looks something like an offshore oil rig. Contact the Cape Hatteras National Seashore, Route 1, Box 675, Manteo, NC 27954; (252) 473-2111.

Courtesy U.S. Coast Guard

Diamond Shoals *Lightship*

■ OCRACOKE LIGHT ■
Ocracoke (1803 and 1823)

The first Ocracoke Lighthouse went up in 1803, the same year the original Cape Hatteras tower was completed. It stood on Shell Castle Island, where British colonial forces cornered and killed the notorious pirate Blackbeard early in the eighteenth century. Lightning destroyed the lighthouse in 1818. The existing sixty-five-foot conical brick tower near Ocracoke Village was completed in 1823. Automated in 1955, the Ocracoke Lighthouse displays a fixed white light with a focal plane about seventy-five feet above high water that can be seen from fourteen miles away.

© Mark Riddick/New Light Photography

Travel information: Ocracoke Island is accessible only by ferry from Cedar Island, Swans Quarter, or Hatteras Island. Schedules vary. Contact the North Carolina Department of Transportation, Ferry Division, 113 Arendell Street, Morehead City, NC 28557; (800) 293-3779. The lighthouse is located off NC 12 on Lighthouse Road, about a mile north of the main ferry. A small parking area allows visitors access to the station grounds and tower. For additional information contact the Cape Hatteras National Seashore at Route 1, P.O. Box 675, Manteo, NC 27954; (252) 473-2111. For the Ocracoke Island Visitors Center call (252) 928-4531.

■ CAPE LOOKOUT LIGHT ■
Cape Lookout (1812 and 1859)

Completed in 1812, the first Cape Lookout Lighthouse was of unusual design, with interior walls of brick enveloped in an outer cocoon of wood. Although it cost $20,678 to build—a small fortune at the time—and stood more than a hundred feet tall, its light was surprisingly weak. It offered little assistance to mariners trying to avoid the cape, long ago nicknamed "Horrible Headland" because of the many shoals just offshore.

To improve the light the Lighthouse Board had the present 156-foot tower built in 1859, fitting it with a first-order Fresnel lens. During the Civil War troops retreating from nearby Fort Macon shot out the lens, but it was soon replaced. In 1967, some years after the station was automated, the big Fresnel lost its job to an airport-style beacon. The light flashes white every fifteen seconds and can be seen from up to twenty-five miles away.

> *Travel information:* The lighthouse is located on Core Banks Island, now part of Cape Lookout National Seashore. The island can be reached only by passenger ferry; contact Barrier Island Transportation Service, P.O. Box 400, Harker Island, NC 28531. For other information contact Cape Lookout National Seashore, 131 Charles Street, Harker Island, NC 28531; (252) 728-2250. An interesting maritime museum in nearby Beaufort houses a fourth-order Fresnel lens. Contact the North Carolina Maritime Museum, 315 Front Street, Beaufort, NC 28516; (252) 728-7317.

■ BALD HEAD (CAPE FEAR) ISLAND LIGHT ■
Bald Head Island (1794 and 1818)

Although its lantern has been dark since 1935, the 110-foot-tall Bald Head Island Lighthouse remains a majestic structure, its octagonal brick tower rising ninety feet above the mostly flat island. Established in 1796 on Bald Head Island at the mouth of the Cape Fear River, this light station was North Carolina's first.

Bald Head Light

After a tornado toppled the original lighthouse in 1812, it was replaced by a fortresslike stone tower with brick walls five feet thick and a seven-foot-deep brick-and-sandstone foundation. Unlike many light towers, the interior of the shaft was not open but, instead, consisted of a series of five storage and work rooms stacked one atop the other. The lantern room at the top originally housed whale-oil lamps and reflectors said to produce a fixed white light seen from eighteen miles at sea.

Known to seamen as "Old Baldy," the lighthouse was deactivated in 1935. In 1985 the Old Baldy Foundation refurbished the structure and fitted it with a copper dome.

Travel information: The lighthouse is located on Bald Head Island, which can be reached by passenger ferry; call (800) 234-1666. Ferry service is also available from Southport for visits to historic Fort Fisher on Federal Point. The ruins of the **Price's Creek Range Light** can be seen, but the area is not open to

Price's Creek Range Light

Courtesy U.S. Coast Guard

Shipwreck near the site of the Federal Point Lighthouse

the public. Contact the Old Baldy Foundation, Bald Head Island, Southport, NC 28461; (910) 457-7481.

■ OAK ISLAND LIGHT ■

Caswell Beach (1958)

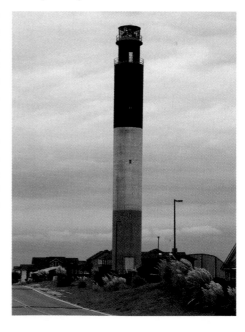

Built during the late 1950s, this 155-foot, reinforced-concrete tower houses a modern optic that produces an extraordinary fourteen million candlepower. Under normal conditions its flashing white light can be seen from up to twenty-four miles away.

Travel information: From U.S. Highway 17 near Wilmington, follow Route 133 to Caswell Beach. Located on an active Coast Guard station, the lighthouse is closed to the public.

SOUTH CAROLINA

■ GEORGETOWN LIGHT ■
Georgetown (1801 and 1812)

Built for $7,000 on land donated by Revolutionary War patriot Paul Trapier, the

original Georgetown Lighthouse consisted of a seventy-two-foot cypress tower, a small, two-story keeper's dwelling, and a tank for storing the whale oil that fueled the lamps. Completed in 1801, the tall wooden tower collapsed in a gale just five years later.

The eighty-seven-foot brick tower here today dates from 1812. Constructed at a cost of more than $17,000—a hefty figure at the time it was built to last, and it has weathered nearly two centuries of Atlantic storms. Refurbished in 1857 when it received a fourth-order Fresnel lens and again in 1867 to repair Civil War damage, the lighthouse still displays its flashing white light. The station's resident ghost reputedly climbs up and down the tower's steps on occasion. Now automated and fitted with a solar-powered modern optic, the station remains an active aid to navigation.

> *Travel information:* The best way to see the lighthouse is via a tour boat from Georgetown. For information or reservations, write to Captain Sandy's Tours, P.O. Box 2533, Pawley's Island, SC 29585; (843) 527-4106.

■ CAPE ROMAIN LIGHT ■
McClellanville (1827 and 1858)

In 1827 the government established a light station on Cape Romain to warn mariners of threatening shoals some nine miles to the southeast. Noted contractor Winslow Lewis built the first Cape Romain Lighthouse for approximately $7,500, equipping the sixty-five-foot, conical brick tower with lamps and reflectors he had designed himself. The Lewis optic proved insufficient, however, and when a new, more powerful reflector system also failed to do the job, officials decided to rebuild the lighthouse.

Completed in 1858, only a few years before the

Civil War, the second Cape Romain Lighthouse owns the dubious distinction of being built by slave labor. Its magnificent 150-foot, octagonal brick tower still stands despite a tilted foundation, which causes it to lean queasily out of plumb, like the famed tower of Pisa.

A first-order Fresnel lens cast light at least nineteen miles into the night, more than enough to warn ships away from the shoals. Damaged by Confederate forces in 1861, the lighthouse remained dark throughout the Civil War but was fully repaired and back in operation by 1866. Automated in 1937, the light was discontinued ten years later. Buoys now mark the notorious shoals.

> *Travel information:* The lighthouse is located north of Charleston on Lighthouse Island, part of a protected coastal wild area, and can be reached by boat from McClellanville. Contact the Cape Romain National Wildlife Refuge, 5801 Highway 17 North, Awendaw, SC 29429; (843) 928-3368.

■ MORRIS ISLAND LIGHT ■
Charleston (1767, 1837, and 1876)

Among the oldest, most gracious cities in America, Charleston, South Carolina, was the site of one of America's earliest lighthouses, established in 1767. The black-and-white banded tower now on Morris Island was built in 1876, but a copper plate on

its cornerstone reads, THE FIRST STONE OF THIS BEACON WAS LAID ON THE 30TH OF MAY 1767 IN THE SEVENTH YEAR OF HIS MAJESTY'S REIGN, GEORGE III. The existing 161-foot brick tower—inactive since 1962—rests on a concrete foundation eight feet thick and set atop piles driven fifty feet into the mud. This solid underfooting helped save the lighthouse when an earthquake leveled much of Charleston in 1885. Replaced in 1962 by the Charleston Light on Sullivans Island, the abandoned tower is now threatened by erosion. Among the most-endangered lighthouses in the United States, the old banded tower may eventually succumb to the tide. Preservationists still hope to save it, however, and funds are being raised for a rescue effort.

> *Travel information:* Follow U.S. Highway 17 south from Charleston, then East Ashley Street to its end. The lighthouse stands about one hundred yards off the nearby beach. The **Charleston Lighthouse** on Sullivans Island can be seen across the harbor. If you would like to help preserve the historic Morris Island tower, write to Save the Lighthouse, P.O. Box 12490, Charleston, SC 29422 or call (843) 795-8911.

■ CHARLESTON LIGHT ■

Sullivans Island (1962)

Unlike the old Morris Island station, which predates the Revolution, the Charleston Light, on Sullivans Island near Fort Moultrie, is a product of the rock 'n' roll era. Built in 1962, the 140-foot triangular tower is fashioned of reinforced concrete clad in aluminum siding. Coast Guard service personnel travel via the nation's only lighthouse elevator to the station's modern optic, which can generate a sizzling twenty-eight million candlepower. The flashing white beacon marking the entrance to Charleston Harbor is visible up to twenty-six miles at sea.

Travel information: Follow Route 703 through Mount Pleasant to Sullivans Island and follow the signs toward Fort Moultrie. As you approach the fort, you'll see the tower on the left about two blocks off Middle Street. The tower is closed to the public, but visitors are welcome to walk the station grounds.

While in the area, be sure to visit Fort Moultrie National Monument; call (803) 883-3123. The fort took part in Revolutionary War and Civil War battles. Edgar Allan Poe was once stationed here as was, interestingly enough, William Tecumseh Sherman.

■ HUNTING ISLAND LIGHT ■

Hunting Island State Park (1859 and 1875)

The Hunting Island Light had beamed for only two years when the Civil War plunged it into darkness. By the end of the war, the station had mysteriously disappeared. Lighthouse officials assumed it was blown up by Confederates or, more likely, felled by erosion.

With the island's rapidly eroding shoreline in mind, the Lighthouse Board commissioned the station's cast-iron replacement tower—completed in 1875—to be built in sections that could be taken apart and reassembled elsewhere if necessary. When erosion threatened in 1885, the tower was safely moved about a mile inland. A second-order Fresnel lens served here until the station was decommissioned in 1933.

Travel information: Take U.S. Highway 21 east from Beaufort to Huntington Island State Park; (803) 838-2011. Visitors are allowed to climb the 180 steps to the service gallery.

■ HARBOUR TOWN LIGHT ■
Hilton Head (1970)

The ninety-foot, red-and-white-striped tower of the Harbour Town Lighthouse is the visual centerpiece of the popular Sea Pines resort on Hilton Head Island. Its white light flashes every two and a half seconds to mark the Inland Waterway and Calibogue Sound. Completed in 1970, Harbour Town Light was the first privately financed light tower built since the early 1800s. Visitors who climb the tower steps will find at the top a gift shop and an excellent spot to view Hilton Head.

Travel information: Follow U.S. Highway 278 until it ends at Sea Pines Plantation. Contact Sea Pines Resorts, P.O. Box 7000, Hilton Head Island, SC 29938; (843) 785-3333.

■ HILTON HEAD REAR RANGE (HAIG POINT) LIGHT ■
Hilton Head Island (1881)

First marked during the Civil War by a Union Navy lightship, Hilton Head received a pair of land-based range lights in 1881. The lantern room of a tall skeleton tower housed one light and a second, lesser tower was perched atop a house. Braced iron legs help the ninety-five-foot rear-range tower withstand gales. Keepers climbed the 112-step spiral staircase, winding upward through a central steel cylinder, to reach the hexagonal wooden lantern room, which once held a Fresnel lens. Both lights were retired from service in 1932. A pair of keeper's dwellings built near the rear-range tower during the late 1800s are said to be haunted. According to popular legend the ghost is that of Caroline Fripp, the daughter of an early keeper.

Travel information: The rear-range tower is located in exclusive Palmetto Dunes, a gated and guarded residential community closed to the public except by permission; call (800) 845-8001. The supposedly haunted dwellings have been moved to nearby Harbour Town, where they house businesses, including a popular delicatessen.

■ HAIG POINT REAR RANGE LIGHT ■

Freeport (1872)

So many battles were fought on Daufuskie Island that locals began calling it the "Place of Blood." During the early 1800s a pair of range lights on Bloody Point guided vessels to the island, where cotton and sugar plantations then prospered. At one time lighted by candles and later by kerosene lanterns, the Bloody Point Range Lights served mariners for more than a century before being extinguished in 1922.

Beginning in 1872, a second pair of range lights were established on the opposite side of the island on Haig Point. One light was fastened on a pole far out in the water, while the rear-range light shone from a twenty-five-foot-tall tower atop the keeper's dwelling. The government deactivated the Haig Point Range Lights in 1934. Now a private club, the restored lighthouse is owned by the International Paper Company and operates as a private aid to navigation.

Travel information: You can reach Daufuskie Island via scheduled cruises from Hilton Head. Contact Adventure Cruises, Shelter Cove Harbour, Hilton Head Island, SC 29928; call (843) 785-4558. The Haig Point Lighthouse can be seen from Calibogue Sound but is closed to visitors. The building that formerly served as the **Bloody Point Rear Range Lighthouse** (1883) still stands, but it has been moved away from the water.

GEORGIA

■ TYBEE ISLAND LIGHT ■
Tybee Island (1791, 1857, and 1867)

Shortly after General James Oglethorpe founded the colony of Georgia in 1733, he ordered construction of a tall wooden tower on Tybee Island to guide ships into the Savannah River. Destroyed by storms and rebuilt several times, the tower was finally lighted with a lamp in 1791. That same year the wooden structure caught fire and burned to the ground. "It was so hot I was not able to Tarry for a moment," said the keeper, who escaped without injury.

Rebuilt, this time with brick instead of wood, the Tybee Island Lighthouse served faithfully until retreating Confederate troops burned it in 1861. Following the Civil War, masons restored the tower, encircling the 154-foot octagonal structure with massive brick walls nearly twelve feet thick at the base. In 1867 the lantern was fitted with the same first-order Fresnel lens that still serves the station, giving the light a range of about twenty miles. Handsomely restored during the 1990s, the Tybee Island tower has been painted in a distinctive black-white-black color scheme.

> *Travel information:* Follow U.S. Highway 80 from Savannah to Tybee Island. The lighthouse, which can be seen from miles away, is located at the north end of the island in old Fort Screven. Contact the Tybee Island Lighthouse and Museum, P.O. Box 366, Tybee Island, GA 31328; (912) 786-5801.

■ COCKSPUR ISLAND LIGHT ■
Savannah (1849)

During the late 1840s the Lighthouse Service established a pair of light towers marking the key north and south channels of the Savannah River. The North Channel Light, built on Oyster Bed Island, was destroyed during the Civil War. Despite being caught in a tremendous artillery duel between Union batteries on Tybee Island and the big Confederate guns at nearby Fort Pulaski, the South Channel Lighthouse survived. The thirty-five-foot-tall lighthouse served continuously until 1949, when it was retired at the ripe old age of one hundred. Although restoration work was done in 2000, the tower continues to be threatened by high water.

Travel information: Located on Cockspur Island, a scrap of semidry land, the lighthouse can be seen from the U.S. Highway 80 bridge east of Savannah. Nearby Fort Pulaski, completed in 1848, is well worth a visit. The brick-and-stone fort took eighteen years to build but only a few days to fall to Union forces during an 1862 artillery duel. For information contact Pulaski National Monument, P.O. Box 30757, Savannah, GA 31410; (912) 786-5787.

■ SAPELO ISLAND LIGHT ■
Sapelo Island (1820)

Few places along the U.S. East Coast are as wild as Georgia's Sapelo Island, a natural treasure trove of tall marsh grass, pristine beaches, and gnarled coastal forests. An eighty-foot brick-and-stone tower, the first Sapelo Island Light tower was the work of Winslow Lewis, who built so many of America's early lighthouses. Lewis billed the government $17,000, a price that included one of his patented lamp-and-reflector optics. During the early 1850s the government raised the tower by ten feet and installed a fourth-order Fresnel lens.

In 1905 a giant steel-skeleton tower took over the work of the original lighthouse. Deactivated in 1933, the later structure was dismantled and shipped to Lake Superior for use in the Apostle Islands. The earlier light tower still stands; it was restored and relighted in 1998.

Travel information: The Georgia Department of Natural Resources maintains Sapelo Island as a wildlife and nature preserve and offers a variety of nature tours; call (912) 437-3224. Privately operated lighthouse tours are available from Meridian, Georgia, reached via Route 99, off I-95; call (912) 638-6732. In addition to the original Lewis tower, Sapelo Island is also home to the tiny, iron-legged **Sapelo Front Range Lighthouse** (1877).

■ ST. SIMONS ISLAND LIGHT ■
St. Simons Island (1810 and 1872)

Built in 1810, the first St. Simons Lighthouse was a white, seventy-five-foot-tall structure, covered with tabby, a stucco-like cement made of crushed oyster shells. Topped by an iron lantern containing an oil lamp suspended by chains—a fire prevention measure—it marked the St. Simons Sound. Confederate troops destroyed the tower and all the station outbuildings as they retreated from the island in 1862.

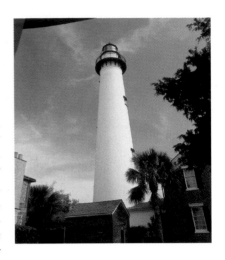

Outbreaks of a mysterious illness, probably malaria, that repeatedly decimated work crews delayed construction of a new lighthouse for years. The 104-foot brick tower and adjacent dwelling were finally completed in 1872. The St. Simons Island Lighthouse remains in service to this day, its third-order, L. Sautter Company Fresnel lens still in place. The beacon flashes white once a minute and has a range of twenty miles.

According to legend the ghost of a former keeper haunts the station. Killed more than a century ago in a duel with his assistant, the keeper is said to walk the tower steps at night.

> *Travel information:* Charming St. Simons Island is reached by causeway from Brunswick. On the island follow Kings Way and Beachview; then turn right onto Twelfth Street. The fascinating Museum of Coastal History, located in the old brick keeper's residence, displays a fourth-order Fresnel lens. Contact the Coastal Georgia Historical Society, P.O. Box 1136, St. Simons, GA 31522; (912) 638-4666.

■ LITTLE CUMBERLAND ISLAND LIGHT ■
Little Cumberland Island (1820 and 1838)

Winslow Lewis, America's most prolific lighthouse builder, received a contract in 1819 to erect a light tower and dwelling on Georgia's Little Cumberland Island. For $17,000 Lewis delivered a fifty-foot brick tower, a small brick keeper's dwelling, and a Lewis-style optic for the lantern, all ready for service by July 1820.

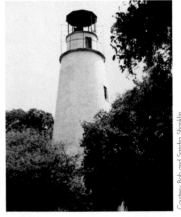

In 1838 the Lighthouse Service decided to build a new tower on the island's northernmost point—the original station stood on the south end of the island. While the new lighthouse was under construction, the old one taken apart brick by brick, shipped to Florida, and reassembled on Amelia Island, where it still stands.

The new, sixty-foot tower had brick walls supported by heavy cross-timbers, but eventually they were replaced with iron braces. In 1903 a sparkling, third-order Fresnel lens supplanted the old Lewis-style lamps-and-reflector optic. During the Civil War Confederate troops damaged the lens and the tower, putting the station out of service until repairs were completed in 1867. The station was discontinued and abandoned in 1915.

Travel information: Little Cumberland Island is a private residential community, and neither the island nor the lighthouse is open to the public. Tour cruises, however, from nearby Jekyll Island pass within sight of the tower. Contact Coastal Expeditions at (912) 265-0392.

FLORIDA

■ AMELIA ISLAND LIGHT ■
Old Fernadina Beach (1839)

In 1838 the Lighthouse Service dismantled the tower that had marked Georgia's Little Cumberland Island since 1820 and reassembled it on Amelia Island, near the mouth of the St. Marys River. Renovated in classic Victorian style in 1885, Florida's northernmost lighthouse is a graceful structure. A gleaming black lantern crowns the white, sixty-four-foot brick tower. A third-order Fresnel lens placed here in 1903 still shines each night, displaying a flashing light. Navigators approaching the dangerous shoals in nearby Nassau Sound see a white flash, whereas others see a red flash.

Travel information: Used as a private residence for Coast Guard personnel, the lighthouse is closed to the public. Although you can see this historic structure from Route A1A in Old Fernadina Beach, perhaps the best way to enjoy the sight is on an evening walk along one of Amelia Island's lovely beaches, with its warm beacon flashing in the distance.

■ ST. JOHNS RIVER LIGHT ■
Mayport (1830, 1835, and 1859)

A simple oil lamp hung on a pole was likely the first navigational light used to guide ships into the untamed St. Johns River, now a bustling thoroughfare for commercial freighters, fishing boats, and pleasure craft. The river's first official lighthouse, completed in 1830, was among the first light towers in what was then the Territory of Florida. The structure cost the government $24,000 but lasted little more than five years. Surging tidal currents quickly undermined its foundation, and it was torn down in 1835. That same year a second lighthouse was built, but by the early 1850s, nearby sand dunes had piled up so high that the beacon could no longer be seen from the sea.

Completed in 1859, the river's third lighthouse was a sixty-six-foot brick tower fitted with a third-order Fresnel lens. Its lamps burned regularly until 1864, when Confederate gunners shot out the light in hopes of blinding federal gunboats. The light was quickly restored following the Civil War. In 1887 brick masons added fifteen feet to the tower, raising it to a height of eighty-one feet. The light served until 1929, when a lightship moored seven miles from the mouth of the St. Johns replaced it. The old tower remains in excellent shape, although almost twenty feet of it is now underground—buried during construction of a runway for the adjacent Mayport Naval Air Station.

Travel information: Located on the Mayport Naval Air Station, the lighthouse is closed to the public. As of this writing the base itself is closed due to security considerations. For current status and other information, contact the Public Affairs Office, Mayport Naval Air Station, P.O. Box 280032, Mayport, FL 32228-0032 or call (904) 270–5226.

■ ST. AUGUSTINE LIGHT ■
St. Augustine (1824 and 1874)

Shortly after the United States acquired Florida from the Spanish in 1819, a federal customs collector placed a lantern in an old stone tower to guide American ships to St. Augustine. A more conventional seventy-three-foot brick tower soon replaced this rather primitive lighthouse, but its weak reflecting optic projected light only a short distance beyond the harbor entrance.

Although darkened during the Civil War, the St. Augustine Lighthouse survived the conflict— only to be flattened by tidal erosion. Before the tower collapsed, the government established a new light station on nearby Anastasia Island. The keeper lit the lamps inside its first-order Fresnel lens on October 15, 1874. From atop this new, 165-foot brick tower, a combination fixed and flashing light shot its beam through some twenty-five miles of darkness. The same lens remains in operation today. Painted in distinctive black-and-white barber-pole stripes, the tower helps guide mariners during the day.

Travel information: Follow Route A1A and Old Beach Road to Lighthouse Avenue. The beautifully restored brick keeper's residence houses an excellent museum that celebrates the history of the lighthouse and coastal Florida. For a gull's-eye view of the Atlantic and the old Spanish town of St. Augustine, visitors may climb the 219 steps to the service gallery. Contact the St. Augustine Lighthouse and Museum, 81 Lighthouse Avenue, St. Augustine, FL 32084; (904) 829-0745.

■ PONCE DE LEON INLET LIGHT ■
Ponce Inlet (1887)

The first lighthouse at Ponce Inlet, then called Mosquito Inlet, collapsed in an 1835 storm before its lamps were ever lit. Half a century passed before the government once more attempted to establish a major coastal light here, this time on an Olympian scale. Using red brick shipped south from Baltimore, construction crews erected an impressive 168-foot tower, completing it in 1887. In the lantern room a first-order Fresnel lens focused the light provided by a five-wick kerosene lamp designed by none other than George Meade, the famed lighthouse engineer and Civil War general.

The Coast Guard discontinued the light in 1970 as an economy measure, replacing the grand old brick tower with a simple steel tower at the Smyrna Dunes Coast Guard station. Nearby high-rise construction, however, soon rendered the new light ineffective, and in 1983, the Ponce de Leon Inlet Lighthouse was recommissioned. An aeromarine beacon now produces the flashing white light, which has a range of seventeen miles.

Travel information: Its tower, dwellings, and other outbuildings beautifully restored, the light-station complex comprises one of the finest lighthouse museums in America. A special exhibit building houses an enormous first-order, clamshell-type Fresnel lens that once served at Cape Canaveral. Also on display is the third-order lens used at Ponce de Leon Inlet after 1933. Contact the Ponce de Leon Inlet Lighthouse Museum, 4931 South Peninsula Drive, Ponce Inlet, FL 32127; (386) 761-1821.

■ CAPE CANAVERAL LIGHT ■
Cape Canaveral (1848 and 1868)

Thrusting eastward into the Atlantic, Cape Canaveral poses a formidable threat to ships moving along the Florida peninsula. Yet when the Lighthouse Service marked the cape with a sixty-five-foot brick tower in 1848, it perhaps did more harm than good. The light proved so weak that captains often ran their vessels aground on nearby shoals while searching for the signal. The Civil War cut short efforts to correct this unhappy situation.

After the war the Lighthouse Board gave the Cape Canaveral station high priority. They constructed a cast-iron cylinder tower fitted with a first-order Fresnel lens. Shining from atop the 145-foot brick-lined tower, the light could be seen from eighteen miles away, a distance sufficient to keep ships away from the shoals. In 1893 beach erosion forced relocation of the lighthouse to a new site about a mile inland.

A modern, automated beacon replaced the massive glass Fresnel lens in 1993. Sailors still use the light to navigate safely around the Canaveral shoals, but nowadays they often see other bright lights on the cape—rockets rushing skyward from the Kennedy Space Center.

Courtesy NASA

Travel information: Located on an active Air Force base, the lighthouse is off-limits to casual visitors. However, it can be seen from the nearby Kennedy Space Center. Contact Spaceport U.S.A./Visitors Center, Kennedy Space Center, FL 32899; (321) 452-2121.

▪ JUPITER INLET LIGHT ▪
Jupiter (1860)

Robert E. Lee surveyed the site for the Jupiter Inlet Light station. George Meade designed and supervised construction of the 125-foot Jupiter tower. The two Army engineers would eventually square off against each other as commanding generals of opposing armies at Gettysburg, Pennsylvania, with General Meade emerging as victor.

The Jupiter Inlet Light also played a role in the Civil War. Established just prior to the fratricidal conflict that plunged much of America into darkness, the Jupiter Inlet Light was snuffed out by Confederate raiders after burning for little more than a year. Following the war, keeper James Armour found the station's first-order Fresnel lens hidden in a nearby creek. He soon restored the lens to its proper place and had the light back in operation by the end of 1866. The big lens still remains in use, its flashing white light visible from twenty-five miles away.

Nature as well as war have battered the structure. A 1928 hurricane knocked out both the primary and emergency electric power, forcing keeper Charles Seabrook to reinstall the station's old mineral lamps. When the keeper fell ill from exhaustion, his sixteen-year-old son climbed the swaying tower's steps to rotate the lens by hand and keep the light burning.

Travel information: Now open to the public as a key attraction of the nearby history museum, the bright red tower is located in Jupiter Lighthouse Park, reached via Route 707 off U.S. Highway 1. The museum is in Burt Reynolds Park, off U.S. Highway 1 in Jupiter. Contact the Florida History Center and Museum, 805 North U.S. Highway One, Jupiter, FL 33477; (561) 747 8380.

■ HILLSBORO INLET LIGHT ■
Pompano Beach (1907)

Looming dramatically above Hillsboro Inlet near Pompano Beach, this cast-iron skeleton tower fits right into the local scenery but is not a Florida native. A Chicago foundry fabricated the 137-foot tower and barged it down the Mississippi to St. Louis, where it delighted crowds at the 1904 Exposition. After the fair the government bought the lighthouse, took it apart, and reassembled it on faraway Hillsboro Inlet. The first-order Fresnel lens, purchased by the government in 1907 for $90,000, still functions, displaying a flashing white light with an impressive range of twenty-eight miles.

Travel information: This lighthouse is not open to the public but can be viewed from the A1A bridge over Hillsboro Inlet or from the beach on the south shore.

■ CAPE FLORIDA LIGHT ■
Key Biscayne (1825)

A Seminole war party attacked the Cape Florida Lighthouse in 1836, killing the keeper's assistant and torching the tower. Keeper John Thompson survived by retreating to the lantern room sixty feet above the ground as the tower steps below him went up in flames. The fortuitous arrival of a U.S. Navy warship saved the badly burned Thompson from certain death by starvation or exposure.

The threat of Indian attack made repair of the lighthouse impossible for nearly ten years. Despite the fire and a decade of neglect, the original hollow-walled brick tower remained standing. After raising the height of the tower to ninety-five feet, the Lighthouse Service restoration crew had the station back in operation by the end of 1846.

Courtesy Mark Riddick/New Light Photography

Its light extinguished in 1878 when the **Fowey Rocks Lighthouse** was completed, the Cape Florida tower languished dark and empty for more than twice as long as it had served as an active aid to navigation. At present, however, the tower is handsomely refurbished, thanks to $1.5 million in privately donated and state-matching funds raised by the Dade County Heritage Trust. Given a fresh coat of stucco and white paint, the gleaming tower was relit during the Miami Centennial celebration in July 1996.

Travel information: The lighthouse is located on Key Biscayne, southeast of downtown Miami. From I-95 follow the Rickenbacker (toll) Causeway and Crandon Boulevard. Contact the Bill Baggs State Recreation Area, 1200 South Crandon Boulevard, Key Biscayne, FL 33149; (305) 361-5811. Rising from open water more than 10 miles south of Cape Florida, the Fowey Rocks Lighthouse (1878) cannot be seen from land. The iron-skeleton tower marks a shoal named for the British frigate *Fowey,* lost here in 1748.

■ CARYSFORT REEF LIGHT ■
Key Largo (1852)

When completed in 1852, the 110-foot, iron-skeleton Carysfort Reef tower represented a completely new approach to lighthouse construction. Legendary contractor Winslow Lewis, who built so many of the nation's early masonry light towers, submitted a bid to erect this one, using familiar stone-construction techniques. Officials opted instead for a more radical plan put forward by the contractor's own nephew—and harshest critic—I. W. P. Lewis.

George Meade, the U.S. Army engineer who later led Union forces to victory at Gettysburg, supervised construction of the lighthouse I. W. P. Lewis envisioned. Built in open water directly over the reef, the tower stood—and still stands, a century and a half after it was built—on eight cast-iron legs arranged in an octagon some fifty feet wide. A screw pile, stabilized with massive iron discs four feet in diameter, anchors each leg to the sea bottom. Braced by iron girts and tie bars, the legs hold aloft a twenty-four-foot-wide platform supporting a two-story keeper's dwelling. The lantern rests on a second platform about one hundred feet above the water. Keepers climbed a staircase rising through a cylinder centered between the outer piles to reach the light.

Keepers formerly lived here year-round, but now the old lighthouse stands guard over the reef alone, as it has since 1960. Today batteries recharged by solar panels power the light. The flashing white and red beacon has a range of about fifteen miles.

Travel information: The tower is visible from CR–905 on Key Largo. To see it up close, however, you must charter a boat in Key Largo. Keep in mind that visitors are not allowed on the structure. The lighthouse is now part of John Pennekamp Coral Reef State Park; call (305) 451–1202.

■ ALLIGATOR REEF LIGHT ■
Matecumbe Key (1873)

Affectionately know as "Old Gator," the Alligator Reef Lighthouse is as tough as a reptile. Built during the early 1870s on a wave-swept shoal off Matecumbe Key, the 136-foot iron skeleton tower has withstood dozens of major hurricanes. Even the 1935 Labor Day superstorm that slammed the tower with a twenty-foot wall of water could not topple it.

Despite its playful moniker neither Old Gator nor the ship-killing reef on which it stands is named for the American alligator. Instead, the names honor the U.S. Navy schooner *Alligator*, sunk here in 1822. Over the years countless vessels have followed the U.S.S. *Alligator* to their doom on the reef's jagged coral. To stop or at least slow the losses, in 1870 the Lighthouse Board launched construction of a light tower here. Ironically, the project headquarters and workers' barracks were on nearby Indian Key, also inhabited by wreckers who made their living salvaging vessels caught by the reef.

Blows from a two-thousand-pound hammer drove twelve-inch iron pilings ten feet into the coral to support the tower. Iron discs help anchor the pilings to the coral. Completed in 1873 at the then phenomenal cost of $185,000, Old Gator still stands tall, its original fourth-order Fresnel lens focusing a white and red flashing light, now powered with batteries recharged by solar panels. The automated beacon has a range of about twelve miles.

Travel information: Driving the unique 126-mile Overseas Highway is a bit like motoring across the open ocean. Look to the southeast anywhere from Mile Marker 80, near the north end of Lower Matecumbe Key, to Mile Marker 77 to see the venerable Alligator Reef Lighthouse. To view or photograph the lighthouse at leisure, turn off the road at Mile Marker 79.

■ SOMBRERO KEY LIGHT ■
Marathon (1858)

Although scheduled for construction in 1854, storms and funding shortages delayed completion of the Sombrero Key Light-house until 1858. Army engineer George Meade, later to earn glory and fame as the Union commander at Gettysburg, saw the project through to its end. The tower he and his work crews built here cost the government $150,000, a considerable fortune at the time. But the tower proved well worth its hefty price, standing up to gales and hurricanes for more than 140 years.

Meade placed the 160-foot tower atop galvanized steel pilings, an innovation that may account for the lighthouse's extraordinary longevity. The station's original first-order Fresnel lens, which cost $20,000, produced a fixed, white light visible up to fifteen miles away. In 1931 the light was made to flash by fitting the lens with revolving opaque screens. In 1984 a modern optic powered by solar cells replaced the huge Fresnel.

> *Travel information:* You can view the lighthouse from Sombrero Beach State Park near the town of Marathon on Vaca Key. Turn left at Mile Marker 50. The station's old first-order Fresnel is on display in Key West. Contact the Key West Lighthouse Museum, 938 Whitehead Street, Key West, FL 33040; (305) 294–0012.

■ AMERICAN SHOAL LIGHT ■
Sugarloaf Key (1880)

The killer reef off Looe Key, about twenty miles northeast of Key West, has torn open the hulls of numerous ships—the exact number may never be known. Early attempts to stop the carnage included placing daymarks on Looe Key and erecting a tall, unlighted piling atop the shoal. But vessels caught in the tricky currents near the shoal often saw these markers too late, and at night, of course, they were of no use at all. Finally, in 1878, Congress appropriated $75,000 to place a lighthouse directly over the shoal.

Fabricated in a New Jersey shipyard, the 109-foot tower was shipped nearly 1,500 miles south and installed atop a massive underwater platform. The final cost of the station, including the tower, the octagonal keeper's dwelling resting on a platform about forty feet above the water, and the first-order Fresnel lens in the lantern room at the top, came to $125,000—$50,000 more than the original estimates. A reluctant Congress finally coughed up the extra funds, and the station's lamps shone out for the first time on July 15, 1880.

The Coast Guard automated the light in 1963, removing the original rotating, bivalve Fresnel lens. The modern optic currently in place is powered by batteries recharged daily by solar cells. Its flashing white and red light has a range of about thirteen miles.

Travel information: Near Overseas Highway Mile Marker 17 on Sugarloaf Key, turn left on Sugarloaf Boulevard (FL CR 939), then right on FL CR 939A. The lighthouse can be seen out in the ocean to the southeast of a bridge across a small inlet.

■ SAND KEY LIGHT ■
Near Key West (1827 and 1853)

On October 9, 1846, a hurricane devastated Havana and moved on the following day to blast the Florida Keys. Joshua Appleby, the old New England sea captain who kept the Sand Key Lighthouse not far from Key West, must have seen the swirling black clouds coming and known that he was in trouble. Mistakenly believing the hurricane season was over, Appleby had invited his daughter Eliza, her three-year-old son Thomas, and some friends to the island. No doubt the visit was a joy for the lonely keeper, but it ended tragically. By the time the storm clouds passed, the light tower and keeper's dwelling had disappeared. So, too, had Appleby and his visitors—their bodies were never recovered, and Sand Key had vanished.

Built in 1827, the sixty-five-foot brick tower on Sand Key weathered many harsh storms before succumbing to the 1846 hurricane. For nearly twenty years, its fourteen whale-oil lamps and twenty-one-inch Lewis reflector guided ships along safe channels south of the Keys. After Sand Key drowned, a lightship took up this duty until a new lighthouse was completed in 1853.

Designed by I. W. P. Lewis and built under the supervision of George Meade, the new iron-skeleton tower rose 105 feet above what was now open water. Perhaps with the 1846 disaster in mind, Meade gave the tower a solid underfooting of twelve

hefty steel pilings and heavily braced legs sloping inward toward the lantern. Fitted with a first-order Fresnel lens, its flashing light could warn mariners up to twenty miles away. The grand old Fresnel was removed when the station was automated just before the United States entered World War II in 1941. Nearly destroyed in a 1989 fire that started in the abandoned keeper's dwelling, the lighthouse recently underwent a $500,000 restoration.

Travel information: For information on boat charters from Key West or flying services offering overflights of Sand Key, contact the Key West Chamber of Commerce, 402 Wall Street, Key West FL 33040; (800) 648–6269.

■ KEY WEST LIGHT ■
Key West (1825 and 1847)

Once a stronghold for pirates, Key West became a thriving commercial center soon after the United States bought Florida and its Keys from the Spanish in 1819. After 1825 a sixty-five-foot brick lighthouse on Whitehead Point served the bustling Key West harbor, which attracted vast quantities of goods salvaged from shipwrecks in the Keys. Some people considered the notorious wreckers who did most of the salvaging little better than the pirates only recently expelled by the U.S. Navy.

The 1846 hurricane that swallowed up Sand Key swamped hundreds of vessels, generating plenty of business for the wreckers. But it also destroyed much of the town, along with its lighthouse. By 1847 a new tower stood on a more secure site farther from the water. A third-order Fresnel lens, placed in the lantern in 1872, improved the range of the beacon. So, too, did the twenty feet added to the height of the tower in 1892. The station was decommissioned in 1969 but was restored to active service in 1972 as a private aid to navigation. Presently, the lighthouse serves as one of many attractions in this sunny, water-besieged and margarita-soaked tourist mecca.

Travel information: The lighthouse and the Key West Lighthouse Museum (housed in the station's old keeper's bungalow) are located at the intersection of Truman Avenue (U.S. Highway 1) and Whitehead Street. Among the wide array of fascinating museum exhibits is a fourth-order Fresnel bull's-eye lens. Contact the Key West Lighthouse Museum, 938 Whitehead Street, Key West, FL 33040; (305) 294–0012.

■ GARDEN KEY LIGHT ■
Dry Tortugas (1826 and 1876)

About 120 miles west of the Florida peninsula, a scatter of small islands and reefs known as the Dry Tortugas rise out of the Gulf of Mexico. Unpredictable currents combine with a jumble of ship-killing shoals to make this one of the most dangerous places in all the world's oceans. To warn mariners the Lighthouse Service established a light station here in 1826, but not without considerable difficulty. Dramatizing the need for the light, one of the ships carrying materials for the seventy-foot brick tower wrecked on the very shoals the light was intended to guard.

By 1846 the tower's lantern barely peaked above Fort Jefferson, an impressive structure with walls fifty feet high, eight feet thick, and containing more than forty million bricks. Fort Jefferson's 450 smooth-bore cannons were capable of pummeling an entire enemy fleet but were never once fired in anger. Instead, the fort served as a prison,

its most notable inmate being Maryland physician Samuel Mudd, thrown into a stinking cell here for having—innocently enough—set the broken leg of Lincoln assassin John Wilkes Booth. President Grant pardoned Dr. Mudd in 1869 for his humanitarian efforts during a yellow fever epidemic.

A hurricane ruined the original Garden Key Lighthouse in 1873. Its replacement, completed three years later, consisted of a thirty-seven-foot cast-iron tower positioned atop the walls of the fort. Its fourth-order Fresnel lens, illuminated by kerosene lamps, gave the beacon a range of approximately sixteen miles. The light was decommissioned in 1912.

> *Travel information:* Garden Key and its lighthouse are part of Dry Tortugas National Park, encompassing nearly 65,000 acres of coral reef and churning surf, but only forty acres of dry land. Attractions include historic Fort Jefferson and a one-hundred-square-mile naturalist's paradise where ocean mammals, sharks, fish, and seabirds of every variety abound. Charter boats, ferries, and scheduled seaplane service are available from the Key West Chamber of Commerce, 402 Wall Street, Key West, FL 33040; (800) 648-6269. Contact Dry Tortugas National Park, P.O. Box 6208, Key West, FL 33041; (305) 242-7700.

■ DRY TORTUGAS LIGHT ■
Loggerhead Key (1858)

In 1836 the *America* ran aground in the Dry Tortugas. Instead of preventing the wreck, the weak navigational light on Garden Key may very well have lured the ship to its ruin. The controversy generated by the loss of the *America* persisted for decades, leading finally to funding of an entirely new Dry Tortugas light station. Built on Loggerhead Key for $35,000, the 157-foot tower was completed in 1858. Its considerable height and state-of-the-art second-order Fresnel lens gave the beacon a range of at least twenty miles, more than enough to keep ships away from the shoals.

Severely damaged by the same 1873 hurricane that destroyed the lighthouse on neighboring Garden Key, the tower was at first thought to be a complete loss. Masons sent to do emergency repairs, however, did their work so well that the tower still stands, survivor of at least a dozen additional major hurricanes.

Because of its remote location, in 1925 the station was outfitted with an automatic acetylene lamp to replace its full-time crew. A modern optic superseded the original clamshell Fresnel lens in 1986. It displays a flashing white light seen from up to twenty-five miles.

> *Travel information:* Loggerhead Key and its lighthouse are located within the 65,000-acre confines of Dry Tortugas National Park (see page 149). For advice on charter boats, ferries, and seaplanes providing access to the park, contact the Key West Chamber of Commerce, 402 Wall Street, Key West, FL 33040; (800) 648-6269.

■ SANIBEL ISLAND LIGHT ■
Sanibel Island (1884)

In 1883 a ship carrying iron to build the Sanibel Island Lighthouse struck a shoal and sank only a few miles short of its destination. Salvagers from Key West managed to pull most of the materials off the sandy sea bottom, and crews completed the tower in time to have it in service by August 1884. Afterward, its light guided ships in and out of the port of Punta Rassa, past the same shoals that sank the construction-supply ship.

An iron-skeleton structure designed to withstand hurricane winds, the tower stands on four legs braced by girts and tie bars. A central metal-walled cylinder provides access to the lantern via a winding staircase of 127 steps. Soaring one hundred feet above the low, sandy point, the lantern room at one time housed a third-order Fresnel lens displaying a flashing white beacon. The old, French-made glass lens eventually gave way to a modern plastic lens. Built on piles to protect them from storm-driven high waters, nearby keeper's cottages sport steeply sloped pyramidal roofs and wide wraparound verandas.

> *Travel information:* The lighthouse is open to visitors only by appointment; (941) 472-1100. From Fort Myers follow the Sanibel Causeway, Highway 867, and Lighthouse Road to the J. N. "Ding" Darling National Wildlife Refuge. The refuge's visitors center is located on One Wildlife

Drive, just off San-Cap Road. The original Sanibel Island third-order lens is now on display at the Sanibel Historical Museum; (941) 472–4648.

■ BOCA GRANDE REAR RANGE LIGHT ■
Boca Grande (1932)

To boost a hard-pressed Florida economy during the Great Depression, a range light system was established on Gasparilla Island to guide freighters carrying Florida phosphates to chemical plants along the Mississippi. A 105-foot steel-skeleton tower built in 1932 provided the rear-range light, whereas the older **Gasparilla Island Lighthouse,** located about a mile away in Port Boca Grande, served as the front range. With its peaked metal roof, the gangly Boca Grande Rear Range tower suggests the tinman in the *Wizard of Oz.* The tower's fixed white light, beaming from an aeromarine optic, remains in service.

Travel information: To reach Gasparilla Island from U.S. Highway 41, follow Florida Routes 776 and 771 to Placida. Then follow signs to the Boca Grande Causeway and toll bridge leading to Gasparilla Island. The lighthouse is located within the Gasparilla Island State Recreation Area; (941) 964–0375.

■ OLD PORT BOCA GRANDE (GASPARILLA ISLAND) LIGHT ■
Gasparilla Island (1890)

The Port Boca Grande Lighthouse balances on iron stilts above the erosive surf near the entrance to Charlotte Harbor, its square wooden tower and dwelling supported atop screw piles. Completed in 1890 at a cost of $35,000, the tower shot out its fixed

white beacon from a three-and-one-half-order Fresnel lens similar to those frequently used in the Great Lakes region. Red flashes warned mariners of nearby shoals.

From the first, erosion threatened the structure. By 1970 seawater lapped at supports that held up the lighthouse. Construction of a 265-foot granite jetty helped saved the historic building. So, too, did the Gasparilla Island Conservation Association, by raising funds to restore the lighthouse when the Coast Guard abandoned it in 1967. The station was relit and returned to service in 1986.

Travel information: The lighthouse is located on Gulf Boulevard at the far southern tip of the island. From Placida follow signs to the Boca Grande Causeway and toll bridge leading to Gasparilla Island. Meticulously restored during the 1980s, the old lighthouse was recently opened as a museum. Contact the Boca Grande Lighthouse Museum, P.O. Box 637, Boca Grande, FL 33921; (941) 964–0060.

■ EGMONT KEY LIGHT ■
St. Petersburg (1848 and 1858)

Courtesy Bob and Sandra Shanklin

In 1848 contractor Francis Gibbons completed a lighthouse on Egmont Key to serve the rapidly developing Tampa Bay area. Gibbons would later build the first lighthouses on the coasts of California, Oregon, and Washington State, many of which still stand. The lighthouse he built for $10,000 on Egmont Key—a small island named for an eighteenth-century British admiral—lasted only ten years. Repeatedly pounded by hurricanes so powerful they frightened one keeper into early retirement, it had to be torn down and rebuilt in 1858.

Masons reinforced the new eighty-seven-foot masonry tower with brick walls more than three feet thick. These stout walls have stood up to more than 140 years of hurricanes and gales. Located at the north end of the island, the structure still proudly stands. Its automated light remains active.

Travel information: Egmont Key and its lighthouse are accessible only by boat, but you can see and enjoy the signal from nearby Fort De Soto State Park. To reach the park follow Routes 682 and 679 south from St. Petersburg. Contact the Greater Tampa Chamber of Commerce, Tampa, FL 33601-0420; (813) 228-7777.

■ CEDAR KEYS LIGHT ■
Seahorse Key (1854)

Used in the manufacture of pencils, Cedar Keys hardwood attracted such an endless parade of lumber ships that the government established a light station in 1854. Built under the watchful eye of U.S. Army engineer George Meade, the lighthouse stands on Seahorse Key, about three miles southwest of Cedar Key, the largest island in the chain. Unlike his iron skeleton–type towers, Meade constructed this lighthouse as a one-story brick dwelling with a squat tower perched on its roof. The entire project cost a mere $12,000.

Although only twenty-eight feet high, the little Cedar Keys Lighthouse stands on a hill, placing the focal plane of its beacon some seventy-five feet above the water. The fixed white light from its fourth-order Fresnel lens was visible from fifteen miles away.

Courtesy Bob and Sandra Shanklin

During the last years of the nineteenth century, the economy of the Cedar Key area fell onto hard times, and the Cedar Keys Lighthouse was permanently darkened in 1915. Seahorse Key is now part of a wildlife refuge.

Travel information: Located in an environmentally sensitive wildlife refuge, Seahorse Key is closed to the public but can be seen from the water. For excursions contact the Cedar Key Chamber of Commerce, P.O. Box 610, Cedar Key, FL 32625; (352) 543–5600. Known for its great fishing and seafood, the Cedar Keys area can be reached from U.S. Highway 19 or I–75 via Florida Route 24 South.

■ ST. MARKS LIGHT ■
St. Marks (1831, 1840, and 1867)

The workmanship of the first St. Marks Lighthouse, built in 1831, proved so shoddy

that officials ordered it torn down lest it fall of its own accord. Rebuilt that same year, it lasted only until 1840, when erosion forced relocation of the station. A third St. Marks tower fell victim to a gunpowder explosion set off by Confederate raiders during the Civil War. The conical tower seen here today dates from 1867. Built atop a twelve-foot-deep limestone foundation, its four-foot-thick walls rise eighty-two feet into the Florida skies. Its automated light shines more than twenty miles out to sea.

Travel information: The St. Marks Lighthouse is located in a pristine coastal game refuge. Although the station is closed to the public, visitors are welcome to walk the grounds and enjoy the unmatched scenery. Follow Route 363 from Tallahassee to the St. Marks National Wildlife Refuge, then County Road 59 to the lighthouse.

■ CROOKED RIVER LIGHT ■
Carrabelle (1895)

On September 18, 1873, a major hurricane struck the Florida Panhandle, blasting the Dog Island Lighthouse, which had guided vessels into St. George Sound and along to Apalachicola since 1838. The storm swept away the tower and keeper's residence, but, miraculously, the keeper and his assistant survived. Perhaps wisely, the Lighthouse Board decided not to rebuild the exposed Dog Island station, and the area was left without a lighthouse for more than twenty years.

During the 1890s, lumber freighters flocked to the Crooked River just north of Dog Island to take on loads of hardwood. To guide them a lighthouse was built near the mouth of the river, this time on the more stable ground of the mainland. Its designers took into account the special geology and weather conditions of the Gulf Coast. Hurricane-force winds pass through the open iron skeleton, doing little damage. The 115-foot tower has stood now for more than a century, and its flashing light continues to serve mariners.

> *Travel information:* You can see the lighthouse from U.S. Highway 98, about a mile west of Carrabelle. The station is closed to the public, but the tall red-and-white tower soaring toward the sky is an inspiring sight.

■ CAPE ST. GEORGE LIGHT ■
St. George Island (1833 and 1852)

Rivers of cotton once flowed into Apalachicola on their way to distant ports in New England and Europe. To guide freighters into the bay, the government estab-

lished a light station on St. George Island in 1833. Well-known contractor Winslow Lewis built the seventy-foot brick lighthouse for $9,500, fitting it with one of his own patented lamp-and-reflector systems. As was the case with many Lewis lighthouses, the St. George Island beacon proved far less than adequate—its light reached only a few miles out to sea.

Bowled over by an 1851 hurricane that leveled several Florida light stations, the Cape St. George Lighthouse was rebuilt in 1852. Since then, the seventy-four-foot tower has successfully weathered dozens of major storms and even a Civil War cannonade by Confederates who tried but failed to destroy it. Seriously threatened by beach erosion, the Cape St. George tower is considered one of America's most endangered lighthouses. Restoration work completed in 1999 helped straighten the leaning tower, but it is still not out of danger.

Travel information: For more information on access to this scenic area, contact the Apalachicola Chamber of Commerce at (850) 653-8219.

■ CAPE SAN BLAS LIGHT ■
Cape San Blas (1847, 1856, 1859, and 1885)

The Cape San Blas Lighthouse stood for only four years before the 1851 hurricane that destroyed the Dog Island station knocked it down. Yellow fever delayed con-

struction of a replacement. Masons finally laid the last bricks of the new tower in 1856, just in time to see it toppled by another hurricane. A third tower, completed in 1859, served for less than two years before Confederate forces snuffed out its lamps, removing the third order Fresnel lens and setting fire to the tower. Renovated following the Civil War, the tower held out against repeated buffetings by gales and flood tides until 1882, when erosion cut the foundation away and it toppled into the Gulf.

A ship carrying the materials needed to rebuild this hard-luck lighthouse sank off Sanibel Island, and the tower was not completed until 1885. This time, however, the Lighthouse Board wisely chose an iron-skeleton design capable of withstanding hurricane winds. What is more, the tower is put together in such a way that it can be taken apart and reassembled elsewhere whenever threatened by the Gulf's bulldozerlike tides. This approach proved successful, and the tower has survived intact for more than a hundred years. Its third-order flashing Fresnel lens, intended to warn ships away from shoals off Cape San Blas, was discontinued in 1991.

Travel information: Follow Routes 30 and 30E to Cape San Blas. Located about half a mile from a U.S. Air Force radar station, the lighthouse is closed to the public.

■ ST. JOSEPH BAY LIGHT ■
Port St. Joe (1838 and 1903)

In 1838 delegates gathered in what was then the thriving Gulf port of St. Joseph to frame Florida's first state constitution. That same year the federal government acknowledged the town's growing importance by placing a lighthouse on the far tip of the St. Joseph peninsula to guide ships into port. Neither the town nor the lighthouse would last, however. Both sank in the flood tides of a titanic gale that hit the area in 1847.

From the ruins of the once-thriving community of St. Joseph, the village of Port

St. Joe emerged, but more than half a century passed before the government thought it merited a lighthouse. Finally, in 1903, a square wooden combination dwelling and tower was built on the mainland, directly across from St. Joseph Point. The lantern, situated atop the peaked roof of the main building, held a third-order Fresnel lens.

In 1960 the Coast Guard closed the St. Joseph Bay station, replacing its light with an automated beacon displayed from atop a steel tower resembling a broadcast antenna. The old lighthouse was sold off for use as a barn. Several years ago it was purchased and refurbished as a private residence.

Travel information: From Port St. Joe, drive northwestward for 10 miles to Beacon Hill. The existing steel tower rises just to the west of Beacon Road. The site of the original station is nearby.

■ PENSACOLA LIGHT ■
Pensacola (1824 and 1858)

Following the acquisition of Florida from Spain in 1819, President James Monroe ordered the U.S. Navy into the Gulf of Mexico to flush out pirates. With no base on the Gulf Coast, the U.S. fleet might as well have been patrolling foreign waters. Then the Navy found exactly what it needed at Pensacola in the Florida Panhandle—a deep-water port for its fighting ships. To this day, the U.S. Navy maintains a significant presence at Pensacola.

To guide Navy warships in and out of the new base, the Lighthouse Service established a station here in 1824. Winslow Lewis built the forty-five-foot tower on a sandy spit near the entrance to the harbor, fitting it with oil lamps and reflectors of his own design. Lewis billed the government a modest $5,725 for the entire project. Even so, the station was not worth its cost; for like many Lewis beacons, this one proved far less than adequate.

In 1858 a 160-foot-tall brick tower replaced the old Lewis lighthouse. It cost nearly $46,000, a bargain considering the tower has survived hurricanes, lightning strikes, and more than 140 years' worth of wear and tear, not to mention a fierce Union cannonade during the Civil War. Moreover, its impressive height and first-order Fresnel lens more than doubled the range of the old Lewis beacon to better than twenty-five miles. Now automated, the old light still guides Navy ships and Coast Guard cutters in and out of the harbor.

Travel information: Follow Navy Boulevard (Route 295) to the Pensacola Naval Air Station. The guard at the gate can provide a car pass and directions to the lighthouse. Exhibits at the nearby Naval Air Museum celebrate the history of the light station and the U.S. Navy's strong links to Pensacola. For additional information call (850) 453–8282 or (850) 675–5305.

▪ MOBILE POINT LIGHT ▪
Mobile (1822 and 1873)

A wall of barrier islands and a maze of shoals force ships entering Mobile Bay into the narrow channel that runs past Mobile Point. To guide vessels through this strategic passage, the Lighthouse Service established a light on the point. Completed in 1822 at a cost of $9,995, the station's forty-foot brick tower stood on the grounds of Fort Morgan. A soldier was paid an extra $15 per month to light its lamps each evening.

With a limited range of less than ten miles, the beacon gave scant warning of the dangerous shoals that lay up to nine miles south of the point. Hired to improve the light, Winslow Lewis installed a flashing lamp-and-reflector optic that he proudly claimed made the light visible from "thirty miles away." It did not. The Lighthouse Service finally solved the problem in 1838 by placing a lighthouse on remote Sand Island, several miles from the mainland.

Although bristling with cannon, Fort Morgan failed to stop the Union fleet of Admiral David Farragut in 1864, when he issued his famous order "Damn the torpedoes, full speed ahead!" and forced his way into Mobile Bay. During the ensuing battle Union gunners blasted the Mobile Point Lighthouse into a pile of rubble.

In 1873 the broken walls of the fort acquired a thirty-five-foot steel light tower. Its fourth-order Fresnel lens displayed a red light with a focal plane approximately fifty feet above high water. In 1966 this light was discontinued and replaced by a 125-foot, antennalike tower. Despite the untraditional—some might say ugly— looks of the present tower, its flashing white light efficiently guides ships in and out of Mobile Bay.

Travel information: From Mobile follow I-10 east to exit 44. Then follow Route 59 south to Gulf Shores and turn westward on Route 180. Signs lead the way to the Fort Morgan State Historic Site, which features fascinating Civil War displays and the old first-order Fresnel lens from the nearby **Sand Island Lighthouse.** The 1873 tower and present antenna-style tower, standing near each other beside the walls of the fort, offer a study in contrasting technologies. For information on Fort Morgan call (334) 540-7125. For other travel information call the Alabama Gulf Coast Visitors Bureau at (800) 745-7263.

■ MOBILE (MIDDLE) BAY LIGHT ■
Mobile (1885)

The Mobile Bay station consists of a hexagonal cottage perched atop iron pilings screwed securely into the muddy bottom of the bay, a style used frequently on the Chesapeake Bay. But Mobile Bay proved less

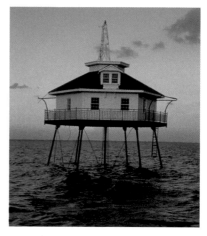

friendly to screw-pile construction techniques than the Chesapeake, and the structure was completed only with considerable difficulty. Storms repeatedly drove workers off the bay, and the soft mud swallowed up pilings almost as fast as they could be driven. Because of settling, the lighthouse ended up seven feet shorter than planned when finally completed in 1885. The signal, commissioned to mark a key turning point in a recently dredged, deep-water channel, served its purpose, however. Its red light guided ships through the bay for more than eighty years. Concerned Mobile citizens saved the lighthouse, deactivated in 1967, from the scrap heap.

> *Travel information:* Located in the middle of Mobile Bay, the restored lighthouse is a popular destination for day boaters. Contact the Mobile Visitors Bureau, One South Water Street, P.O. Box 204, Mobile, AL 36601; (800) 5MO–BILE.

■ SAND ISLAND LIGHT ■
Mobile (1838, 1859, and 1872)

Abandoned, isolated, and besieged by the waters of the Gulf, the Sand Island Lighthouse now serves only as a monument to its own often violent and tragic past. In 1859 a mighty 150-foot brick tower replaced a smaller lighthouse that had stood

here since 1838. In 1861 a Confederate raiding party stacked barrels of gunpowder inside the big tower and blew it up to prevent its use by Union forces. Ironically, the raiders were sent on their mission of destruction by General Thomas Leadbetter, who had designed and built the Sand Island Lighthouse only two years earlier.

Yellow fever decimated the crew sent to rebuild the tower in 1871. Nevertheless, they completed the task late the following year. Fitted with a first-order Fresnel lens, the new 132-foot tower displayed a white beacon with a range exceeding twenty miles.

During the late nineteenth century, Sand Island began to sink. It disappeared altogether after a 1906 hurricane, which also carried away the keeper's dwelling, the keeper, and his wife. An inspector sent to assess the damage sent the following poignant telegram to his superiors: "Sand Island Light out. Island washed away. Dwelling gone. Keepers not to be found."

Travel information: Deactivated in 1971, the Sand Island Lighthouse is closed to the public. It can be approached only by boat but can be seen from Fort Morgan State Historical Site, about 3 miles away. A museum at the fort houses Sand Island's first-order Fresnel lens. For Fort Morgan information call (334) 540-7125.

MISSISSIPPI

■ ROUND ISLAND LIGHT ■
Round Island (1833 and 1859)

A bank of threatening shoals lies just off Round Island, named by French explorers for its shape. To warn mariners of this danger and guide ships through Mississippi Sound to the bustling port of Pascagoula, the Lighthouse Service established a light station on Round Island in 1833. The entire station, including the tower,

keeper's dwelling, lamps, and reflectors, cost the government less than $6,000. The money was well spent, for the forty-five-foot brick tower survived hurricanes, flood tides, and even an invasion of freebooting adventurers bent on throwing the Spanish out of Cuba. The Cuban venture failed, and the lighthouse kept on shining.

Courtesy Bob and Sandra Shanklin

Tidal erosion finally undercut the tower during the 1850s, forcing construction of a new lighthouse on a higher and drier part of the island. Fifty feet tall and fitted with a fourth-order Fresnel lens, it served well until the Civil War darkened lights along the entire Gulf coast. In operation again by 1865, the light remained on duty for the next seventy-nine years. The Coast Guard discontinued it in 1944. Hurricane George destroyed what remained of the lighthouse in 1998 so it no longer stands. The Round Island Preservation Society hopes to rebuild the tower as part of a public park.

Travel information: You can reach Round Island only by boat. For information on charters and accessibility, contact the Pascagoula Chamber of Commerce, P.O. Box 480, Pascagoula, MS 39568-0480; (228) 762-3391. To reach the Round Island Preservation Society, write to P.O. Box 1034, Pascagoula, MS 39568, or call (228) 762-1574.

■ SHIP ISLAND LIGHT ■
Ship Island (1853, 1886, and 1972)

Before Jefferson Davis became president of the Confederacy, he lobbied fellow members of the U.S. Congress incessantly to secure federal facilities for Mississippi, his

home state. His pet project was a fort and naval base to be placed on Ship Island, about a dozen miles from Biloxi. Congress rejected funding the hugely expensive fort but mollified Davis by building the $12,000 Ship Island Lighthouse.

Completed in 1853, this handsome facility had a forty-five-foot brick tower and spacious keeper's dwelling. Initially, the lantern was fitted with an outmoded lamp-and-reflector lighting system, but this was updated with a state-of-the-art fourth-order Fresnel lens just three years later.

Eventually, Ship Island became home to a substantial military installation as well, but it was definitely not the one Davis had wanted. By 1861 Davis was the Confederate president. Late that year he learned that Union troops, backed by a powerful fleet of warships, had seized the island. For the remainder of the Civil War, the Ship Island beacon served the Union's Fort Massachusetts. The troops blackened the tower's north-facing windows so that the light would be of no use to Confederate raiders and blockade runners.

The Ship Island Lighthouse saw such hard service during the war and the years immediately after that it literally began to fall apart. Declared unsafe, it was pulled down in 1886 and replaced by a pyramidal wooden tower. Covered by protective weatherboarding, the frame structure survived until 1972, when it burned to the ground in a fire accidentally set by tourists. A steel-skeleton tower took its place, and its light still guides mariners. A replica of the original lighthouse was completed in 2000 by the Friends of the Gulf Islands National Seashore.

Travel information: Maintained by the National Park Service, the lighthouse and historic fort are all open throughout the year. Contact Gulf Islands National Seashore, 1801 Gulf Breeze Parkway, Gulf Breeze, FL 32561; (228) 875-9057.

■ BILOXI LIGHT ■
Biloxi (1848)

Often located on remote peninsulas or barrier islands, lighthouses are commonly far from the beaten path. Not so the Biloxi Lighthouse. Its white, forty-eight-foot tower stands like a giant traffic signal in the mid-dle of busy U.S. Highway 90.

A cast-iron shell sheathes the brick-and-mor-tar tower. The metal has protected the light from countless Gulf storms, including the infamous Hurricane Camille, which blasted Biloxi in 1968.

The even more destructive storm of the Civil War ravaged the Gulf coast a century earlier. The lighthouse survived, but following what Miss-issippians still call the "War Between the States," the Biloxi tower was painted black—some say as a token of mourning for President Abraham Lincoln. Ironically, the so-called memorial could be seen from the porch of Confederate President Jefferson Davis's former home. Maintained by the city of Biloxi, the tower's fourth-order Fresnel still shines today as a private aid to navigation.

> *Travel information:* The lighthouse is located on U.S. Highway 90 at Porter Avenue. Contact the Biloxi Recreation Department at (228) 435-6244.

LOUISIANA

■ CHANDELEUR ISLAND LIGHT ■
Chandeleur Island (1848, 1856, and 1896)

In January 1815 a British invasion fleet waited at Naso Roads, just inside Chandeleur Sound, while redcoats attacked New Orleans. Eventually, Andrew Jackson's frontier army drove the troops back to their ships.

To help friendly peacetime vessels take advantage of the same vast anchorage that once attracted the British war fleet, the government established a light station on the northern tip of Chandeleur Island in 1848. A seabreak of sand and shell protected its fifty-five-foot brick tower from gales. Even so, an 1852 hurricane swept over the wall and obliterated the lighthouse. The fifty-foot tower that replaced it in 1856 received a high-quality fourth-order Fresnel lens, enabling the light to effec-tively mark the dangerous, spreading shoals in Chandeleur Sound.

The destructive flood tide of an 1893 hurricane undercut the tower, forcing the Lighthouse Board to replace it once again, this time with a steel-skeleton structure better able to withstand high winds and water. Rising 102 feet above mean sea level, it held aloft a third-order clamshell-type Fresnel lens displaying a flashing white light. The Coast Guard automated the light in 1966, replacing the classic lens with a modern optic.

Courtesy Bob and Sandra Shanklin

Travel information: The still-active Chandeleur Lighthouse is part of a seven-thousand-acre wildlife refuge. The lighthouse and refuge can be reached only by boat. Call the U.S. Fish and Wildlife Service at (504) 646-7555.

■ TCHEFUNCTE RIVER LIGHT ■
Madisonville (1837 and 1867)

During the Battle of New Orleans in 1815, a ragtag flotilla of American gunboats gathered at Madisonville on Lake Pontchartrain before sailing off to be blasted to splinters by the heavy guns of the British invasion fleet. But defeated by Andrew Jackson on land, the British retreated, leaving Louisiana in relative peace and Madisonville to become a prosperous port.

In 1837 the Lighthouse Service made navigation on Pontchartrain easier and safer by establishing a light station near Madisonville. The lighthouse, a squat, thirty-eight-foot brick tower at the entrance of the Tchefuncte River, burned during the Civil War. Rebuilt in 1867 and automated during World War II, its light still guides vessels along Pontchartrain's northern shores.

Travel information: From I-12 take exit 59 and follow Route 22 to Madisonville. Follow signs to Fairview Riverside State Park and the lighthouse. An old fishing village, Madisonville is home to some of the best seafood restaurants in Louisiana. Contact the Madisonville Chamber of Commerce, P.O. Box 746, Madisonville, LA 70447; (504) 845-9824. For river cruises that pass the lighthouse, call (504) 845-2027 or (504) 845-3124.

■ PASS MANCHAC LIGHT ■
Ponchatoula (1839, 1842, 1846, 1859, and 1867)

The Pass Manchac Lighthouse marked the western reaches of Lake Ponchartrain, guiding vessels through the narrow passage that connects the enormous lake with the smaller, but still sizable Lake Maurepas. Vulnerable to storms, erosion, and Louisiana mud, which repeatedly swallowed its foundation, the tower was rebuilt many times.

The first tower lasted only three years. Its masons had used mud for mortar, which, not surprisingly, melted away in the rain. The tower literally fell to pieces. A second, better-quality structure succumbed to erosion during the 1840s, a third to the hungry mud in the 1850s, and a fourth to Union raiders during the Civil War.

The fifth Pass Manchac Lighthouse, completed in 1867 and fitted with a sparkling new fourth-order Fresnel lens, proved more fortunate and long-lived. A forty-foot brick tower built atop a stone foundation, it served for 120 years. Automated in 1952, it was finally retired in 1987.

> ***Travel information:*** Follow U.S. Highway 51 north from La Place toward Ponchatoula. The tower stands on the north side of Pass Manchac. The dwelling and other station buildings were removed long ago.

■ PORT PONTCHARTRAIN LIGHT ■
New Orleans (1839 and 1855)

A privately financed lighthouse marked Port Pontchartrain as early as 1832. The primitive device consisted of a square lantern hoisted between two fifty-foot poles. Under pressure from local business interests, Congress eventually funded an official lighthouse for the port. Completed in 1839 at a cost of only $4,400, its twenty-eight-foot, octagonal wooden tower displayed a flashing white beacon from its iron lantern. In 1855 the Lighthouse Board replaced the rotting structure with a forty-foot masonry tower equipped with a compact fifth-order Fresnel lens.

Many of the keepers who served here were women. Perhaps most notable of them was Margaret Norvell. She kept the light burning throughout the great hurricane of 1903, while playing host to some two hundred refugees.

Although inactive since 1929, the lighthouse still stands. Interestingly, the tower, at one time located half a mile from land, is now well inland. Over the years land-hungry New Orleans developers filled in large areas of the shallow lake, extending usable lands but leaving the little lighthouse high and dry.

Travel information: The lighthouse is now on private land and not open to the public. However, you may ask about the status of this light by calling the Lake Maurepas Society at (504) 542-6266 or the New Orleans Tourist Information Center at (504) 566-5011.

■ NEW CANAL LIGHT ■
New Orleans (1838, 1855, 1890s, and 1901)

The New Canal Lighthouse takes its name from a failed 1830s effort to link Lake Ponchartrain with downtown New Orleans by canal. A brick lighthouse marked the lake terminus of the canal, which was never completed. Rebuilt in 1855 and again during the 1890s, the lighthouse endured, despite the defunct canal.

The fifty-foot, square wooden tower that stands here today is said to date from 1901. The lantern and gallery rise through the second-story roof. Originally the lighthouse stood on piles in open water a quarter of a mile from shore, but landfill projects during the 1930s surrounded it with dry land. A fifth-order Fresnel lens formerly served here; now a modern optic provides the beacon.

Travel information: The lighthouse stands at the end of Lake Shore Boulevard, near a series of marinas. Seafood restaurants line the docks near the lighthouse— don't leave the area without trying some fresh crab or red snapper. For information on these and endless other delights in the Big Easy, call the New Orleans—that's "Nawlins" to local folks—Tourist Information Center at (504) 566-5011.

■ DELTA LIGHTS ■
Lower Mississippi Delta

Having negotiated the Great Lakes and nearly the entire length of the Mississippi, the French explorer La Salle reached the Gulf of Mexico in 1682. He placed a marker bearing his personal coat of arms at the mouth of the great river to help mariners recognize it among the maze of delta bayous and passes. Many years later navigational lights would guide vessels to the river. The first of these was built by the French in 1767 at a place called "La Balize," or seamark.

After the United States acquired Louisiana in 1803, President Thomas Jefferson ordered a lighthouse built on Frank's Island, near a key river entrance. Noted architect Benjamin Latrobe, who designed the Capitol Building in Washington, drew the plans. His design proved so grandiose and impractical that it was not completed until 1818. Its reluctant contractor, Winslow Lewis, warned officials that the $79,000 granite-and-marble structure could not stand for long in the delta mud. Sure enough, it fell down almost as soon as its last stones were cemented in place. Lewis then contracted to build a far more sensible eighty-two-foot masonry tower for the comparatively bargain price of $9,750. The **Frank's Island Lighthouse,** in service by 1823, guided mariners until 1856. Although its foundation has settled twenty feet into the mud, the original tower still stands.

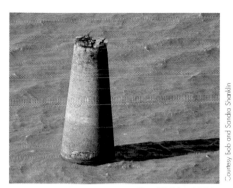

Frank's Island Light

Over the years the silt-laden Mississippi changes its primary outlets, opening new passages and filling in others. The Frank's Island Lighthouse ceased operations after the river began to favor the once-secondary Pass a l'Outre (meaning "Pass Beyond" or "the Way Out"). The Lighthouse Board constructed the **Pass a l'Outre Lighthouse,** an eighty-two-foot iron tower completed late in 1855, for the new river outlet. This light, in turn, was discontinued in 1930 after the Mississippi filled Pass a l'Outre with huge muddy lumps, making it almost impassable to ships. The structure still stands but has lost more than a quarter of its original height to the mud.

Pass a l'Outre Lighthouse

Light towers marked other Mississippi River outlets as well. These include the **South Pass Lighthouse** and **Southwest Pass Lighthouse,** both completed by Winslow Lewis in 1832, and the **Head of Passes Lighthouse,** first lit in 1836. All formerly served primary entrances to the river, and all survive to this day, though some have sunk down a bit in the muck.

The Coast Guard finally solved the sinking

South Pass Lighthouse

problem in 1965 with construction of the **Southwest Pass Jetty Light.** Built in open water atop large concrete supports, this modern light station resembles an offshore oil rig, a likeness that has earned it the nickname "Texas Tower." Its aeromarine beacon has a focal plane more than eighty feet above the Gulf waters and can be seen from up to twenty-four miles away.

Courtesy Bob and Sandra Shanklin

Southwest Pass Lighthouse

> *Travel information:* None of the lighthouses mentioned above can be reached by land and should be approached from the water only by highly experienced navigators. Contact the Eighth Coast Guard District, Hale Boggs Federal Building, 500 Camp Street, New Orleans, LA 70130.

■ SOUTHWEST REEF LIGHT ■
Berwick, Louisiana (1859)

Completed in 1859, the iron-clad Southwest Reef Lighthouse was built to withstand the fury of hurricanes blowing in from the Gulf. A storm of a very different type, however, put the station out of service little more than two years after it began operating. With the outbreak of the Civil War, local Confederate officials ordered removal of the lens, lamps, and even the lantern's window glass. Union troops recaptured these items late in the war, and by August 1865 the station's light once more sent out its signal.

The 125-foot tower stood on screw piles in open water, where its red light warned vessels away from a dangerous reef in the Atchafalaya Bay. The lighthouse served until 1916, when a dredging operation cut through the shoal. Afterward the old tower stood rusting in the bay for nearly three-quarters of a century. Then, during the 1980s, the southern Louisiana town of Berwick brought it ashore for use as the primary attraction of a city park.

Courtesy Bob and Sandra Shanklin

> *Travel information:* Berwick is on U.S. Highway 90, just west of Morgan City, Louisiana. The tower stands in Everett S. Berry Lighthouse Park, reached via Bellevue Front Street and Canton Street. The Berwick City Hall, about two blocks from the Lighthouse Park, displays a beautiful third-order Fresnel lens. Call (504) 384-8858.

Berwick also hopes to make the **Ship Shoal Light** (1859) a part of its

Ship Shoal Lighthouse

Timbalier Bay Lighthouse

Lighthouse Park. For the moment the abandoned iron-skeleton tower remains offshore several miles from Raccoon Point. To the east of Ship Shoal is another open-water light station, the still operational **Timbalier Bay Light** (1917). To the west, also in open water, is the inactive **Oyster Bay Light** (1904).

■ SABINE PASS LIGHT ■
Louisiana Point (1856)

The finlike concrete buttresses of this pre-Civil War structure give it a surprisingly modern appearance. Army engineer Danville Leadbetter, later a Confederate general, designed the fins to spread the tower's weight over the marshy ground and buttress it against hurricane winds. Leadbetter supervised construction of the lighthouse in 1856 and did such a good job that it still stands after more than 140 years.

The station received a fine third-order Fresnel lens at the time it entered service, but after only four years, Civil War fighting snuffed out its lamps. In fact, several sharp engagements between the Confederate and Union forces occurred within sight of the tower. The men in gray won most of these battles.

Relit following the war, the station served until the Coast Guard discontinued it in 1952. Plans to make the lighthouse part of a Louisiana state park eventually fizzled. The tower is now privately owned.

Travel information: Located on private land, the lighthouse is accessible only by boat. It can be seen, however, from the Texas side of the Sabine River. Contact the Port Arthur Visitors Bureau at (800) 235–7822. While in the area, be sure to visit Sea Rim State Park, just southwest of Sabine Pass. The park's scenery and wildlife offer a glimpse of Texas as it must have looked 150 years ago. Contact Sea Rim State Park, P.O. Box 1066, Sabine Pass, TX 77655; (409) 971–2559.

■ SABINE BANK LIGHT ■
Gulf of Mexico off Sabine Pass (1906)

Courtesy Bob and Sandra Shanklin

By the end of the nineteenth century, increasing numbers of deep-water freighters visited the docks at Port Arthur and other towns along the Sabine River. To reach the river entrance safely, however, ships had to steer clear of the Sabine Bank, a major shoal lurking below the surface about fifteen miles from shore.

To warn mariners lighthouse officials decided to place a navigational light directly over the shoal. A foundry in Detroit assembled a tanklike iron tower and shipped it to the Gulf, where it was placed atop a massive concrete caisson. Lamps inside the station's third-order Fresnel lens were first lit on March 15, 1906. An acetylene lighting system replaced the original Fresnel lens in 1923, when the light was automated. Today the old lighthouse still stands guard over the shoal, and its beacon remains in service.

Travel information: Because it remains an active aid to navigation, the Sabine Bank Lighthouse is off-limits to the public. Located in the open Gulf of Mexico about fifteen miles from the coast, it can be reached only by boat. (See preceding Travel information).

▪ BOLIVAR POINT LIGHT ▪
Galveston (1852 and 1872)

Built in 1852, Bolivar Point Lighthouse became a casualty of war ten years later. When the Civil War broke out, Confederate troops seized the lighthouse, pulled down the cast-iron tower, and reforged the metal. Then they fired the federals own back at them in the form of shot and shell.

Following the war, a yellow-fever epidemic delayed reconstruction of the structure, sorely needed to guide ships into Galveston Bay. So severe was the outbreak that the government placed the Texas coast under quarantine. Crews finally completed the new 117-foot tower in 1872, constructing it of cast-iron plates according to the original plans. A second-order Fresnel lens provided the beacon.

During the horrible Galveston hurricane and flood of 1900, dozens of storm refugees saved themselves by climbing the tower steps to avoid the rising waters. Many of those outside the tower were not so lucky. Thousands of Galveston residents drowned or had their necks literally broken by the wind.

Discontinued by the Coast Guard, the Bolivar Point Light has been dark now for more than half a century. Nonetheless, the historic tower, now privately owned, remains a favorite Texas landmark.

> *Travel information:* The lighthouse can be seen from Route 87 on the Bolivar Peninsula. To reach the peninsula take the free ferry from the north end of Galveston Island. The ferry also provides an excellent view of the tower.

▪ MATAGORDA ISLAND LIGHT ▪
Matagorda Island (1852 and 1873)

The Lighthouse Board established several lights along the Texas coast in 1852, including those at Matagorda Island near Port O'Connor and Bolivar Point near Galveston. Built in cast-iron sections much like the **Bolivar Point Lighthouse,** the Matagorda Island tower rose eighty feet above the island sands, placing the focal plane of its light more than ninety feet above the waters of Matagorda Bay. Nineteenth-century sailors had no trouble distinguishing it from other coastal towers since it was painted in red and white horizontal bands. Nowadays, however, the tower is black.

During the early 1860s Confederate soldiers removed the third-order Fresnel lens and buried it in the sand. They tried to blow up the tower with kegs of gunpowder but failed to topple it. The wounded structure remained precariously erect until well after the Civil War. Lighthouse Board workers finally dismantled it to keep it from falling over on its own. In 1873 they reassembled it on a new site and returned the old lens, retrieved from the sand, to its place of honor in the lantern. The original classic lens served the station—and ships entering Matagorda Bay—until 1977, when a modern optic replaced the Fresnel. The light remains operational, shining some twenty-five miles over the sea.

Matagorda Island Light

> *Travel information:* The lighthouse is accessible only by boat or ferry. For ferry schedules and reservations call (361) 983-2215. The **Halfmoon Reef Lighthouse** (1858), which once rested on pilings far out in Matagorda Bay, is now a well-loved landmark on Route 35 in Port Lavaca. Contact the Port Lavaca Chamber of Commerce, P.O. Box 528, Port Lavaca, TX 77979.

Halfmoon Reef Lighthouse

■ ARANSAS PASS (LYDIA ANN) LIGHT ■
Port Aransas (1857)

Breaking through an almost solid wall of barrier islands, Aransas Pass confronts navigators with rolling surf, uncharted shoals, and channels that seem to shift with every tide. Soon after Texas joined the Union in 1845, federal officials concluded that this strategic pass should be marked with a major navigational light, but no action was taken for more than a decade.

In 1855 the Lighthouse Board assigned the task of establishing the light station to Captain Danville Leadbetter, an Army engineer. Leadbetter built a fifty-foot octagonal brick tower and an adjacent wood-frame keeper's dwelling. The station's light, focused by a fourth-order Fresnel lens, began to shine late in 1857.

During the Civil War Leadbetter served as a Confederate general, and the lighthouse he had built at Aransas Pass became the target of both armies. Confederate raiders removed the lens and tried to blow up the tower. Union warships used it for target practice. Despite this abuse, however, the lighthouse survived the conflict, as did General Leadbetter.

Courtesy U.S. Coast Guard

Its lens restored, the lighthouse was back in operation by 1867, after which it served mariners more or less without interruption for more than eighty years. In 1952 the Coast Guard replaced the light with an automated beacon located on the opposite shore of Aransas Pass. Now privately owned, the historic station remains in prime condition, and its light still serves mariners. The light is shown on charts as the Lydia Ann Light, after the Lydia Ann Channel that runs close to the northeastern shore of the pass.

Travel information: The lighthouse is not open to the public, but both the tower and its light—visible from about 7 miles away—can be seen from boats in the nearby Lydia Ann Channel. The original Fresnel lens is on display in the Port Aransas Civic Center. Follow Route 35 north from Corpus Christi, then Route 361 toward Mustang Island. Contact the Port Aransas Tourist Bureau at P.O. Box 356, Port Aransas, TX 78373; (361) 749-6729.

■ POINT ISABEL LIGHT ■
South Padre Island (1852)

Built in 1852 on the site of an old army camp used by General Zachary Taylor and his troops during the Mexican War, the Point Isabel Lighthouse provided the backdrop for the last battle of America's Civil War. Northern forces used the tower as an observation post as the blue and gray armies fought the Battle of Palmito Ranch on

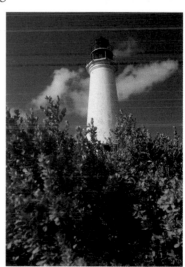

May 13, 1865. Ironically, the Southerners won the battle only to learn that they had already lost the war—Lee had surrendered at Appomattox the month before.

Permanently deactivated in 1905, the lighthouse now serves as the prime attraction of a state park. Even after nearly a century of disuse, the fifty-seven-foot brick tower remains in excellent condition along with its original third-order Fresnel lens.

Travel information: Follow Route 100 through Port Isabel to the Point Isabel State Historic Site. Contact the Port Isabel Lighthouse State Historical Park, 421 East Queen Isabella Boulevard, Port Isabel, TX 78578; (800) 792-1112.

WEST

East Brother Lighthouse

ALASKA
12 Lights

Anchorage •

Prince William Sound

Unimak Island •

Glacier Bay National Park

• Juneau

Cape Flattery •

• Dungeness

WASHINGTON
24 Lights

• Seattle
• Tacoma

Aberdeen •

Astoria •

Tillamook •

OREGON
9 Lights

Newport •

Coos Bay •

Crescent City •

Pacific Ocean

Eureka •

Mendocino •

San Francisco •

CALIFORNIA
38 Lights

Monterey •

San Luis Obispo •

Santa Barbara •

Los Angeles •

San Diego •

Kauai

Oahu

Molokai

Lanai

Maui

Hawaii
5 Lights

CALIFORNIA

▪ OLD POINT LOMA LIGHT ▪
San Diego (1855)

Hundreds of years ago, when California was still part of Spain's colonial empire, residents of San Diego built fires on lofty Point Loma to help royal supply ships reach harbor safely. Following acquisition of California by the United States in 1848, the government chose the point as the site for one of the West's first light-houses.

Built of locally quarried sandstone, the combination Cape Cod–style dwelling and forty-foot tower cost Uncle Sam a whopping $30,000. Despite its hefty price the structure was not constructed according to specifications. When its first-order Fresnel lens arrived by sailing ship from France, workers could not fit it into the lantern. Instead, they substituted a third-order lens.

Worse problems lay ahead for the lighthouse. Although the station's third-order lens was less powerful than the one intended for it, the 460-foot elevation of the light made it visible from distances of more than forty miles. That same extra-ordinary elevation, however, all too often placed the light above low-lying clouds and fog banks. In heavy weather mariners simply could not see it. So in 1891, only thirty-six years after its lamps were first lit, the Old Point Loma Light went dark. A skeleton tower, built at a lower, more practical elevation, took its place.

Travel information: Follow Route 209 to Cabrillo National Monument in San Diego. Having refitted it with a classic lens and furnished the dwelling much as it might have looked when its first keepers lived there, the Park Service maintains the Old Point Loma Lighthouse as a museum. Call (619) 557-5450.

■ POINT LOMA LIGHT ■
San Diego (1891)

The seventy-foot iron-skeleton tower of the Point Loma Lighthouse places its light eighty-eight feet above the Pacific. A white cylinder centered between the tower's braced iron legs allows access to the lantern room. The original third-order Fresnel lens placed here in 1891 still focuses its light. A horn at the base of the tower alerts vessels when fog shrouds the point.

Travel information: Follow Route 209 to Cabrillo National Monument in San Diego. An active Coast Guard facility, the station is closed to the public, but it can be enjoyed from the road leading to the monument's popular tidal pools.

■ LONG BEACH HARBOR LIGHT ■
Los Angeles (1949)

One could hardly imagine a less romantic edifice than the blocky, concrete structure marking the San Pedro Middle Breakwater in Los Angeles, but believe it or not, this is a lighthouse. Built half a century ago at a time when modernist architects thought in terms of the purely functional, it is indeed a radical departure from the old stone dwellings and towers built by Winslow Lewis or Francis Gibbons. Ultramodern even by present-day standards, it looks a bit like a space invader from a low-budget, 1950s science-fiction movie. No doubt that is why Los Angeles children know it as the "Robot Light."

Supported by six cylindrical columns made of cement cast into huge molds, the forty-two-foot-high rectangular tower is designed to withstand both earthquakes and high winds. When the light went into operation in 1949, its functions were monitored and controlled electronically from the nearby **Los Angeles Harbor Lighthouse.** Nowadays computers keep tabs on the light and relay commands to its airport-style beacon.

Travel information: The Long Beach Lighthouse cannot be reached easily from shore. Its light can be seen, however, from numerous points along the coast. A second Long Beach Lighthouse was completed in 2000 at Rainbow Harbor. A sixty-five-foot conical steel tower, it was built by the Lions Club and serves as a private aid to navigation.

■ LOS ANGELES HARBOR LIGHT ■
Los Angeles (1913)

Rising more than seventy feet above the Pacific, the Romanesque Los Angeles Harbor Lighthouse has anchored the far end of the San Pedro Harbor Breakwater since 1913. Despite gales, earthquakes, and even a brush with a U.S. Navy battleship, the old tower has remained solid and functional since its construction in 1913. Its distinctive vertical black stripes and flashing green light are a familiar sight to sailors entering the harbor and boaters enjoying the waters off Los Angeles.

Keepers lived full-time here until the station was automated in 1973. The Coast Guard replaced the original fourth-order Fresnel lens with a plastic optic when the facility was converted to solar power during the 1980s. The Los Angeles Maritime Museum in San Pedro now proudly displays the old, three-thousand-pound classic lens.

Travel information: Somewhat resembling a column from an ancient temple, the Los Angeles Harbor Lighthouse can be seen from Pacific Avenue and from the Point Fermin Park, where visitors can also enjoy the **Point Fermin Lighthouse.** The ferry to Santa Catalina passes by these lighthouses; call (800) 360-1212. Located at the lower end of Sixth Street in San Pedro, the Los Angeles Maritime Museum features informative lighthouse exhibits and is well worth a visit; call (310) 548-7618.

■ POINT FERMIN LIGHT ■
Los Angeles (1874)

No longer in operation, the Point Fermin Lighthouse remains a venerable landmark. Built in 1874 with highly durable redwood, its Victorian-era Italianate styling and decorative gingerbread make it an architectural delight. The fourth-order Fresnel lens that previously shone here was removed during World War II, when the structure was pressed into service as a coastal watchtower. Deactivated in 1942, the lighthouse is now the centerpiece of a Los Angeles city park.

Travel information: Now the home of a Los Angeles Parks Department employee, the lighthouse is closed to the public. Visitors can enjoy it from the park grounds, however. Located at the end of South Gaffey Street, on Paseo Del Mar, the park also offers an excellent place to view the **Los Angeles Harbor Lighthouse.**

■ POINT VICENTE LIGHT ■
Los Angeles (1926)

Situated on a cliff high above the blue Pacific and surrounded by graceful palms, the

sparkling-white Point Vicente tower fits everyone's romantic image of a Southern California lighthouse. In fact film crews have used it as the backdrop for countless movie and television scenes. Built in 1926 near the edge of a rocky cliff more than a hundred feet above the ocean, the sixty-seven-foot cylindrical tower is crowned by a handsome lantern with cross-hatched windows. A third-order Fresnel lens shines each night, producing a powerful 1.1-million-candlepower flash every twenty seconds. It can be seen from twenty miles at sea.

Naturally, this quintessential lighthouse has a resident ghost. The ladylike phantom, who appears only on foggy nights, is said to be the former lover of a sailor who died in a shipwreck on Point Vicente. Skeptics, on the other hand, say she is nothing more than an optical illusion created by stray refractions of the station's lens.

> *Travel information:* The lighthouse is located north of Marineland, off Palos Verdes Drive. A fine view of the light can be had from the grounds of the nearby Palos Verdes Interpretive Center. Exhibits recount the history of the lighthouse and explore the natural history of the Palos Verdes Peninsula. Call (310) 377-5370.

■ POINT HUENEME LIGHT ■
Oxnard (1874 and 1941)

An identical twin of the ornate **Point Fermin Lighthouse** once stood in Oxnard, northwest of Los Angeles, marking the heavily traveled Santa Barbara Channel.

Both structures consisted of a square, fifty-two-foot redwood tower rising through the roof of an Italianate residence. Not only did these stations look exactly alike, but they came to life on the same day, showing their lights for the first time on December 1, 1874. A matched pair of fourth-order Fresnel lenses focused their beacons. Their lights were not identical, however. The Point Hueneme station flashed white,

Point Hueneme as it once looked.

whereas the Point Fermin displayed alternate white and red flashes.

Also unlike its twin, the original Point Hueneme Lighthouse did not survive the ravages of time. Deteriorating from repeated battering by storms, it was sold to private owners in 1941 and eventually torn down. A somewhat less attractive, though effective, square fifty-foot concrete tower took its place.

> *Travel information:* Located on an active naval installation, the workaday Point Hueneme Light tower is off-limits to the public. Its light remains active and can be seen from many points along the nearby coast. The tower can be viewed by walking north along a path beginning near the Hueneme fishing pier.

■ ANACAPA ISLAND LIGHT ■
Anacapa Island (1912 and 1932)

From a distance Southern California's beautiful Channel Islands seem placid, but their jagged rocks have torn apart countless ships. The Spanish treasure ship *San Sebastion* wrecked here in 1784, dumping its shipment of gold doubloons into the

surf. In 1853 the steamer *Winfield Scott* slammed into Anacapa Island, stranding 250 passengers for several weeks without food or shelter.

Courtesy U.S. Coast Guard

Government officials had long recognized the crying need for a light to warn mariners of the dangers here, but until the twentieth century, few believed a lighthouse could be built on the island's rugged, almost perpendicular cliffs. In 1912 the project was finally attempted, and after considerable effort, a light station was established on Anacapa Island. Equipped with an automated acetylene lamp, its iron-skeleton tower stood near the spot where the *Winfield Scott* had run onto the rocks nearly sixty years earlier.

In 1932 the Lighthouse Service assigned resident keepers to the station and built a new, thirty-nine-foot masonry tower. Although not as tall, the tower looks much like the one at Point Vicente near Los Angeles. The height of the cliffs placed its light 275 feet above the ocean, from which elevation its third-order beacon could be seen from twenty-five miles away. Always difficult to supply, especially with fresh water, the station was automated in 1969. A modern lens replaced the original Fresnel in 1991.

> *Travel information:* The Anacapa Lighthouse is now part of Channel Islands National Park, one of the nation's foremost scenic wonders. Visits to Anacapa and other islands are available through park concessionaires in Ventura. Call (805) 658–5700. Also highly recommended is a stop at the park's Ventura visitors center, where the old Anacapa third-order Fresnel lens is now on display.

■ SANTA BARBARA LIGHT ■
Santa Barbara (1856 and 1926)

A simple white tower on a Coast Guard base just west of Santa Barbara now serves in place of the city's historic light-house, destroyed in a 1925 earth-quake. Among the first lighthouses in the West, the combination tower and dwelling was built by contractor George Nagle for a modest $8,000. Julia Williams, one of America's most famous lighthouse keepers, tended the Santa Barbara Light for more than forty years. It is said she spent only two nights away from the station during all that time.

Courtesy National Archives

Travel information: The existing automated light tower is closed to the public.

■ POINT CONCEPTION LIGHT ■
Point Conception (1856 and 1882)

At Point Conception ships headed along the California coast must change course, either northward toward San Francisco or eastward toward Los Angeles. Here colliding ocean currents generate some of the worst weather in America, causing experienced seamen to compare Point Conception to South America's notoriously stormy Cape Horn. And well they should. The crushed hulls of wrecked vessels—eighteenth-century Spanish sailing ships and more recent American steamers—litter the churning waters off this dramatic angle of land.

Aware of Point Conception's importance and nightmarish reputation, the U.S. government chose its isolated clifftops as the site for one of the West's earliest light stations. Built with great difficulty in 1854, the lighthouse was beset with problems from the start. Workmanship of the brick-and-mortar structure was shoddy, and the combination tower and dwelling began to fall apart almost as soon as it was finished. What was worse, the tower was too small for the first-order Fresnel lens assigned to it. Finally, the contractors had to tear the whole thing down and start over again. Then, when the keepers installed the big lens, they discovered that several key parts of the lighting apparatus were missing. New ones had to be ordered from France.

Courtesy Bob and Sandra Shanklin

Once the station finally became operational in 1856, it quickly became apparent that the tower had been built too high on the cliffs. Fog and low-lying clouds frequently obscured the light. Weakened by repeated gales and earthquakes, the building was finally abandoned in 1882 in favor of a better-constructed lighthouse built at a more practical elevation, about 130 feet above sea level. The two-foot-thick, fifty-two-foot-high brick-and-granite walls of the replacement structure have aged well. The lighthouse remains as solid as ever, and the station's original ten-foot-high first-order lens still flashes out its warning.

Travel information: Nearly impossible to approach from land or sea, the station is closed to the public.

■ POINT ARGUELLO ■
Point Arguello (1901 and 1934)

On the evening of September 8, 1923, seven destroyers slammed into fog-shrouded Point Arguello in one of the U.S. Navy's worst peacetime disasters. Tragically, the lives of twenty-three sailors were lost along with the fighting ships. Flotilla commander Edward Watson had misjudged his position and ordered his destroyers to turn eastward, thinking they were about to enter the Santa Barbara Channel. Instead, they each came to a grinding halt on solid rock. Had Captain Watson seen the Point Arguello Light that night, the ships and lives might not have been lost.

The Point Arguello Lighthouse no doubt prevented many such calamities, but on that particular night its light could not be seen because of the fog. Completed in 1901, the station's squat twenty-eight-foot tower stood on a cliff more than a hundred feet above the sea. In good weather its fixed white beacon, produced by a fourth-order Fresnel lens, could be seen from many miles out in the Pacific.

Isolated and difficult to supply, Point Arguello was among the first Pacific coast lights to be automated. Decommissioned in 1934, the lighthouse was razed and replaced by an aeromarine beacon on an iron-skeleton tower.

Travel information: As part of Vandenburg Air Force Base, Point Arguello is closed to the public. The best way to see the light is from the sea. Rail passengers riding past Point Arguello, however, may catch a glimpse of this remote and rather unglamorous light station.

Courtesy National Archives

■ SAN LUIS OBISPO LIGHT ■
San Luis Obispo (1890)

Although the lovely old Spanish town of San Luis Obispo had one of the best harbors in Southern California, it was among the last West Coast ports to receive a lighthouse. Regional political squabbling blocked congressional appropriations until the late 1880s, when funds finally became available.

Built on an isolated point on the west side of San Luis Obispo Bay, the station

was ready for service by June 1890. It consisted of a distinctly Victorian two-story residence with a square, forty-foot tower rising from one corner, and a fog-signal building with a ten-inch steam whistle. A fourth-order Fresnel lens produced the beacon, which had a focal plane 130 feet above sea level. Because there was no road leading to the point, Lighthouse Service supply steamers made regular calls at the San Luis Obispo station.

The light was automated in 1974, and two years later, the old lighthouse lost its job to a cylindrical structure built just to the east. The new, far less scenic tower boasts a pair of powerful, rotating airport-type beacons. The Fresnel lens that served so long in the lighthouse has been moved to a museum in town.

> **Travel information:** Since the lighthouse is located near the Diablo Canyon Nuclear Power Plant, it has long been off-limits to visitors. Local preservationists plan to restore it, however, and open it to the public. The station's Fresnel lens can now be seen at the San Luis Obispo County Historical Museum at 696 Monterey Street. Call (805) 543-0638.

■ PIEDRAS BLANCAS LIGHT ■
San Simeon (1875)

Automation transformed this once-handsome lighthouse into an ugly duckling. During a 1949 renovation its lovely old lantern was lopped off and a rotating, airport-style beacon set atop the decapitated tower to do the work of the original first-order Fresnel lens.

When completed in 1875, the cone-shaped brick tower stood ninety feet tall on a grassy knoll that boosted its light to an elevation of more than 140 feet. With its ornate gallery and crownlike lantern, the tower looked a bit like a giant, elegantly carved ivory chess rook. The unattractive modern beacon that now serves here is no less powerful and can be seen from up to eighteen miles at sea.

Travel information: The station is closed to the public but can be seen from Route 1. In the nearby town of Cambria, the station's restored first-order lens is housed in a handsome lanternlike structure. Lighthouse lovers traveling in California should not miss this unique opportunity to view a big classic lens up close.

The Piedras Blancas tower as it originally appeared.

■ POINT SUR LIGHT ■
Big Sur (1889)

At Big Sur the churning Pacific makes relentless war on a chain of coastal mountains. The same natural forces—weather and geology—responsible for this scenic spectacle have also made it a very dangerous place for ships. Countless seafaring vessels—and at least one dirigible—have been lost here. But since 1889, the powerful beacon of the Point Sur Lighthouse has warned mariners to keep away.

At one time it was thought impossible to build a light station on Big Sur's precipitous cliffs, but the Lighthouse Service took up the challenge during the late 1880s. Before construction could begin workers had to lay tracks for a special railroad to carry materials and supplies to the rugged sandstone mountain known as Point Sur. The project took two years of hard work and more than $100,000 to complete.

The station consisted of a forty-foot granite tower atop the cliffs and a collection of dwellings and other buildings nearer the water. Keepers found the lighthouse almost as hard to maintain as it had been to build. Every night they had to trudge up the 395 steps leading to the tower. The station was finally automated in 1972, eliminating the need for the long daily climb. At that time a rotating aerobeacon replaced the original first-order Fresnel lens.

In 1935 an unusual sea disaster took place just west of Point Sur and within sight of the lighthouse. Caught in a squall, the 780-foot dirigible U.S.S. *Macon* lost buoyancy and crashed into the Pacific, causing a loss of seventy-three lives.

> *Travel information:* The lighthouse can be seen from Route 1 along the way from Monterey to Big Sur. Guided tours are available on weekends. Call (831) 625–4419. The station's original first-order lens can now be seen at the Maritime Museum in Monterey; call (831) 373–2469.

■ POINT PINOS LIGHT ■
Pacific Grove (1855)

Now surrounded by a lush golf course, the West's oldest standing lighthouse is leased by the Coast Guard to a historical society, which uses it as a maritime museum. The forty-three-foot tower rises from the center of the keeper's dwelling. Both

the tower and dwelling were built during the 1850s by legendary lighthouse contractor Francis Gibbons. Originally granite, the structure was covered over with reinforced concrete following a severe shaking by the same earthquake that devastated San Francisco in 1906. The third-order Fresnel lens in place here since 1855 still shines.

Counted among the West's historic treasures, the old lighthouse has played host to many notables the likes of John Steinbeck and Robert Louis Stevenson. The station's first keeper, former gold-rush miner Charles Layton, died in a shootout with the notorious bandito Anastasio Garcia. Layton's wife then took over as keeper.

> *Travel information:* Located on Lighthouse Avenue between Sunset Drive and Asilomar Avenue in opulent Pacific Grove, the lighthouse is open to the public on Saturday and Sunday afternoons. Call the Pacific Grove Museum at (831) 648–5716 or (831) 648–3116.

■ SANTA CRUZ LIGHT ■
Santa Cruz (1869)

Established in 1869, the Santa Cruz Light guided lumber and lime freighters in and out of the harbor. Laura Heacox, daughter of the station's first keeper, tended this light for nearly half a century.

Its beacon was darkened during World War II, and the wood-and-brick lighthouse was torn down in

1948. The brick light tower seen here now was built in 1969 as a memorial to teenager Mark Abbott, who drowned in a nearby surfing accident. The building houses a surfing museum.

> *Travel information:* Follow West Cliff Drive to Lighthouse Point. The free museum is open every afternoon except on Tuesday. Call (831) 420-6289. In 2001 the Santa Cruz harbor received a new, privately-funded lighthouse. Its light is maintained by the U.S. Coast Guard.

■ PIGEON POINT LIGHT ■
Pescadero (1872)

The Pigeon Point Light, some fifty miles south of San Francisco, shines out toward the Pacific from an elevation of nearly 160 feet. Little more than forty feet of the height is provided by the point, the rest by the 115-foot brick tower. One of the tallest light towers on the Pacific coast, it was built in 1872 with brick shipped around Cape Horn from the east. The land, lighthouse, and huge first-order Fresnel lens cost the government approximately $20,000. An aeromarine beacon replaced the big glass lens in 1972. Pigeon Point takes its name from the Yankee clipper *Carrier Pigeon,* wrecked here in 1853.

> *Travel information:* Now open to the public as a hostelry, the station is located just off Route 1, south of Pescadero. The grounds are open all year. Call (415) 879-0633. To the south is the **Ano Nuevo Lighthouse** (1872), now part of a state nature preserve. Only ruins remain of the original station, deactivated in 1948.

■ POINT MONTARA LIGHT ■
Pacifica (1900)

In 1868 the steamer *Colorado* ran aground on a ledge near Point Montara. Four years later the freighter *Acuelo* wrecked just below the point, spilling into the sea a cargo of coal and iron worth at least $150,000. The latter disaster led to the placement of a fog signal on Point Montara in 1872. Nearly three decades would pass before the Point

Montara fog-signal station received a light. A simple pole light, set up in 1900, served until 1912, when it was replaced by a wooden tower.

The existing thirty-foot cast-iron tower was built at the edge of the rocky point in 1928. Its light shines out toward the Pacific from an elevation of seventy feet. The station's fourth-order Fresnel lens gave way to a modern optic in 1970.

> *Travel information:* Point Montara and its lighthouse are located off Highway 1 about 25 miles south of San Francisco. Most of the station buildings, including the keeper's Victorian-style quarters, are now used as a youth hostel. Visitors are welcome to walk the grounds. Call (650) 728–7177.

■ FORT POINT LIGHT ■
San Francisco (1855 and 1864)

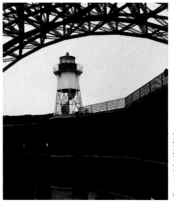

Courtesy John W. Weil

Completed in 1855, at about the same time as the original **Alcatraz Island Lighthouse,** the Fort Point Lighthouse stood empty for more than a year, waiting for its third-order Fresnel lens to arrive from France. This light had an important job to do, that of marking the channel through the Golden Gate and into San Francisco Bay, but the lens was never installed and the tower's lamps never lit. Before the station could be placed in operation, the lighthouse was torn down to make way for the massive brick walls of Fort Winfield Scott. The Fresnel lens originally intended for Fort Point was given instead to **Point Pinos Lighthouse** on Monterey Bay, where it still shines after more than 140 years.

While the three-story fortress was under construction, workers built a wooden light tower outside its walls. By 1864 storm-driven Pacific waves threatened to sweep it away and undermine the foundations of the fort. To make way for a protective seawall, the Fort Point Lighthouse had to be torn down for a second time. It was replaced by a twenty-seven-foot iron-skeleton tower, perched atop the walls of the fort. The additional height made the light, focused by a rather modest fifth-order lens, easier for approaching seamen to spot.

The station served its purpose for more than seven decades until construction of the Golden Gate Bridge made the old lighthouse obsolete and it was discontinued in 1934. Towering 740 feet above the sea, the bridge itself is a mammoth lighthouse. Mariners can see its lights and recognize the distinctive inverted arches of its supporting cables from many miles at sea. Completed in 1937, the bridge is one of the world's most recognizable landmarks and seamarks.

> *Travel information:* Follow Lincoln Boulevard and Long Avenue to Fort Point National Historical Site. Open daily except on major holidays, the old fort, with its tiny lighthouse, offers wonderful views of San Francisco and the Golden Gate Bridge. Call (415) 556–1693. Less scenic, although still operational, is the blocky, concrete **Lime Point Light** (1900), on the

opposite side of the Golden Gate Strait. It can be viewed from behind a fence at the end of Sausalito's Fort Baker Road. The sun powers the **Mile Rocks Light** (1901), just outside the Golden Gate and well to the west of Fort Point.

■ ALCATRAZ ISLAND LIGHT ■
San Francisco (1854 and 1909)

Courtesy U.S. Coast Guard

Derived from *alcatraces*, the Spanish word for pelican, the name Alcatraz now has a cold and forbidding ring to it, and no wonder. For years Alcatraz Island in San Francisco Bay was the unhappy home of Al Capone and many other notorious criminals. Here they served "hard time" at a federal penitentiary made escape-proof by high concrete walls and the shark-infested waters of the bay.

In contrast mariners and lighthouse lovers have warm feelings toward the island, for it is home to the oldest major navigational light on the West Coast. Francis Gibbons built the island's original lighthouse, a Cape Cod–style dwelling with a short tower peeking just above its roof. Focused by a third-order Fresnel lens, its light first shone on the evening of June 1, 1854. At that time gold-hungry miners were still arriving by sea, and the Alcatraz Island Light guided them and their ships into San Francisco Bay and on toward their destiny—only a handful would ever find the riches they sought.

The great San Francisco earthquake of 1906 caused keeper B. F. Leeds to believe he was witnessing "the end of the world." Not so, but the shaking did end the career of the little Gibbons lighthouse. The severely damaged structure was soon replaced by an eighty-four-foot reinforced-concrete tower and adjacent bay-style dwelling. The height of the octagonal tower allowed its light to be seen above the high walls of the military prison then under construction.

For more than fifty years, the light station would share its rugged roost with prisons, both military and civilian. As a result, keepers here endured many sleepless days as well as nights during major breakouts and riots. The worst incident came in 1946, when inmates took over the prison, holding police and U.S. Marines at bay for nearly two days. Both the lighthouse and its keeper survived the battle. Ironically, the light was automated in 1963, not long before the doors of the federal penitentiary, first opened in 1934, slammed shut for the last time. The two-story keeper's residence was burned during a protracted demonstration by young Native Americans in 1969.

Travel information: Alcatraz Island is part of the Golden Gate Recreation Area; call (415) 705-1042. Tours of the island, prison, and lighthouse are offered at Pier 41 in the Fisherman's Wharf district; call (415) 705-5555 or (405) 773-1188. A museum on the island displays the fourth-order Fresnel lens formerly used here; the station now employs a modern optic.

■ YERBA BUENA LIGHT ■
San Francisco (1874)

This lighthouse at one time guided dozens of passenger ferries passing back and forth each day between San Francisco and Oakland. The Bay Bridge, opened in 1939, now carries most cross-bay traffic, but the light on Yerba Buena Island still shines. Nowadays it mostly serves pleasure craft and the U.S. Coast Guard base, which takes up the entire 140-acre island.

The original fourth-order Fresnel lens crowns the station's two-story octagonal tower. It displays a fixed white light. A Coast Guard Admiral now lives in the old keeper's dwelling.

Travel information: Located on an active Coast Guard station, the lighthouse is not open to the public. Its light can be seen from the water, from a variety of points along the shore, and from the Bay Bridge linking Oakland to San Francisco.

■ BLUNTS REEF LIGHTSHIP WAL-605 ■
Oakland (1950)

Lightship *WAL-605* rode at anchor for nearly ten years at Blunts Reef, off Eureka. Launched in 1950 at a shipyard in East Boothbay, Maine, the *WAL-605* was assigned originally to Overfalls Station, near Cape May, New Jersey. In 1960 it was sent west for service at Blunts Reef. During its last years on active duty with the Coast Guard—it was retired in 1975—the *WAL-605* served as a relief lightship at San Francisco Station or wherever it might be needed.

Sold as surplus property by the Coast Guard, the *WAL-605* later functioned as a historical museum and even as a fishing boat. Currently it is owned by the nonprofit Lighthouse Society in Oakland, which is doing lighthouse lovers, students of maritime history, and the nation an enormous favor by restoring the old ship.

The *WAL-605* has a steel hull 108 feet long, with a thirty-foot beam. The mushroom anchor, which so often held it firmly on station, weighs seven thousand pounds. The lightship is berthed on the Oakland waterfront.

Travel information: The Lighthouse Society is restoring this fine old vessel for use as a floating museum in the San Francisco Bay area. Call (415) 362-7255. The society can also provide a wealth of facts and information on lighthouses and lightships throughout the United States and Canada and on general lighthouse history. You may want to join. Write to United States Lighthouse Society, 244 Kearney Street, Fifth Floor, San Francisco, CA 94108.

■ EAST BROTHER LIGHT ■
Richmond (1874)

Built in 1874, the classically Victorian East Brother Lighthouse now serves as both a navigational light, guiding vessels into San Pablo Bay, and as a popular bed-and-breakfast inn. Located on a small island just off San Pablo Point, the lighthouse marks the channel through the narrow and often treacherous San Pablo Straits that link the Sacramento River estuary to the open San Francisco Bay.

Unable to buy property on the mainland at an acceptable price, the government resorted to building the station on tiny East Brother Island. Construction crews had to blast away much of the one-third-acre island in order to level the site. There was hardly room on what remained to squeeze the combination two-story tower and dwelling and separate fog-signal building.

In 1967 the Coast Guard decided to automate the station, place its light on a pole, and tear down the old buildings. Local preservationists managed to save the structure and, over time, restore the station to its original Victorian charm. The fifth-order light is still in operation.

Carquinez Strait Lighthouse

Courtesy Bob and Sandra Shanklin

Travel information: For overnight reservations at the East Brother Lighthouse B&B, call (510) 233-2385. Day visits are also encouraged.

To the north, at 2000 Glenn Cove Drive in Vallejo, is the **Carquinez Strait Lighthouse** (1910), which once marked the western reaches of the San Pablo Bay. Located off Route 780, this retired lighthouse is now privately owned, but visitors are welcome to walk the grounds.

■ POINT BONITA LIGHT ■

San Francisco (1855 and 1877)

Seamen approaching San Francisco from the west often scan the horizon looking for the bright beacon of Point Bonita Lighthouse. It points the way to the Golden Gate and the bay while warning mariners to keep well away from Point Bonita and its deadly rocks.

Built in 1855 on a high ledge more than three hundred feet above the sea, the original station had a fifty-six-foot brick tower and a detached, Cape Cod–style dwelling. Officials considered this lighthouse so important that they assigned it an exceptionally powerful second-order Fresnel lens. The light could be seen from up to twenty miles at sea, except in a heavy fog, which could make it completely invisible.

Since low-lying clouds frequently masked the beacon, the station needed an effective fog signal. Originally it was equipped only with a surplus army cannon fired off with an ear-splitting roar by the keepers whenever fog rolled in, which it did nearly every day. The cannon was eventually replaced by a 1,500-pound bell.

In time officials decided to build another lighthouse down closer to the water, where its beacon would be more effective. Construction got under way in 1872, but fitting the new station onto the only available site—a frightfully narrow ledge about 120 feet above the waves—was no simple matter. To bring materials to the site, a landing platform, derrick, and incline railway had to be built and a tunnel blasted through more than one hundred feet of solid rock. It took more than five years to complete the thirty-three-foot tower and associated structures. Equipped with the Fresnel lens from the original lighthouse and a pair of steam-driven fog sirens, the station was, at last, ready for service by the winter of 1877.

The lighthouse survived the earthquake that leveled much of San Francisco in 1906. During the 1940s, however, a landslide destroyed the land bridge that connected the tower and fog-signal building. The Coast Guard first replaced it with a wooden bridge, then with the attractive suspension bridge that still serves the station. In 1981 the Point Bonita Light became the last of California's lighthouses to be automated.

> ***Travel information:*** Now part of the Golden Gate National Recreation Area, this extraordinarily scenic lighthouse is located off Highway 101, just north of San Francisco. From San Francisco, cross the Golden Gate Bridge, take the Alexander Avenue exit, and follow Conzelman Road to the lighthouse. The winding road to Point Bonita provides spectacular views of the city and the coast. You should bring sensible shoes, since reaching the lighthouse requires a hike of more than a mile. Call (415) 556–0560.

■ POINT REYES LIGHT ■
Point Reyes National Seashore (1870)

In 1885 Point Reyes keeper E. G. Chamberlain wrote the following: "Solitude, where are your charms . . . better dwell in the midst of alarms than in this horrible place." It is not hard to understand keeper Chamberlain's melancholy when one considers that Point Reyes is socked in by fog more than 110 days a year. Keepers lived and worked on this isolated and frequently shrouded point for more than a century and

must at times have thought they were on another planet. Established in 1870, the station was not automated until 1975, much to the relief of the no doubt lonely, wind-battered keeper.

Considered one of the West's most dangerous navigational obstacles, Point Reyes sweeps more than fifteen miles southwestward from the mostly southeastward-trending Northern California coast. With its fog, wind, and tricky currents, the mostly low-lying point has been tearing open the hulls of ships since the sixteenth century.

Clinging to a cliff more than 250 feet above the sea, the Point Reyes Lighthouse warns ships with its extraordinarily powerful first-order beacon. Its flashing light is still focused by the station's original two-ton Fresnel lens. The huge lens dominates the sixteen-sided brick tower, which, despite its lofty elevation, is only forty feet tall.

> *Travel information:* The lighthouse is located in Point Reyes National Seashore, off Route 1 northwest of San Francisco. Visitors should stop first at the Bear Valley Visitors Center near the entrance. Call (415) 669-1534.

■ FARALLON ISLANDS LIGHT ■
South Farallon Island (1855)

A toiling construction crew, consisting of failed gold-rush prospectors and a mule named Paddy, built the first lighthouse here in 1853. Then, almost immediately, they tore it down and started work on another. Like several other early western lighthouses, the original structure had to be demolished when it proved too small to house its bulky Fresnel lens. The second tower was ready and its enormous first-order lens installed by January 1, 1856.

Early keepers at this station were caught in the middle of a bizarre "Egg War." Freebooting poachers made large profits stealing eggs from the millions of seabirds nesting on South Farallon and other nearby islands. So large and lucrative were their hauls that greedy poachers fought with one another—first with fists, then with pistols—for gathering rights. When people started getting shot, California lawmen stepped in and drove off the poachers.

One of the nation's most isolated lighthouses, the South Farallon Island station was automated in 1972. At the same time the big first-order Fresnel was exchanged for a modern aerobeacon.

Courtesy National Archives

Travel information: Located some 23 miles west of San Francisco, the rugged, pristine islands are now part of the Farallon National Wildlife Refuge; call (510) 792–0200. The light station is off-limits to the public. However, some Oceanic Society wildlife cruises provide views of the station; call (800) 326–7491.

■ POINT ARENA LIGHT ■
Point Arena (1870 and 1908)

Like much of the California coastline, Point Arena turns a hospitable face to travelers who come by land but bares its teeth to mariners. Jagged, saw-toothed rocks rise from the waves just offshore. Two and a half miles to the west, predatory Point Arena Rock rises from the sea, waiting to tear open the hulls of ships. Since 1870 the powerful flashing beacon of the Point Arena Lighthouse has warned vessels of these dangers.

The point's rugged topography was created by movement of the San Andreas Fault, which lies beneath the lighthouse. The legendary fault slipped and growled in 1906, flattening much of San Francisco and, not surprisingly, devastating the Point Arena Light station. Fatally cracked by the shaking, the original brick tower had to be replaced. To buttress the new, 115-foot tower against future quakes, builders gave it walls of reinforced concrete. A first-order Fresnel lens focused the powerful flashing beacon until 1972, when it was replaced by a modern optic.

Travel information: Take Lighthouse Road north from the town of Point Arena. The lighthouse and a museum located in the old fog-signal building are open to the public daily. Write Lighthouse Keepers Association, P.O. Box 11, Point Arena, CA 95468; call (877) 725-4448.

■ POINT CABRILLO LIGHT ■
Mendocino (1909)

A small clapboard fog-signal building and attached octagonal wooden light tower have guarded lonely Point Cabrillo since 1909. The original third-order Fresnel lens still serves mariners, flashing white six times each minute. The light has a focal plane about fifty feet above sea level and can be seen from up to fifteen miles at sea. The fog signal that at one time blasted from the back of the main building is now sounded by an offshore buoy.

Courtesy Nancy A. Fizzo

> *Travel information:* Located near Russian Gulf State Park off Route 1 north of Mendocino, the lighthouse is open to the public on a limited basis. The glorious old frame building can be viewed or photographed from Highway 1 or from Cabrillo Drive.

■ PUNTA GORDA LIGHT ■
Petrolia (1912)

A rounded, nearly treeless cape thrusting eight hundred feet above the sea, Punta Gorda rises above the Northern California coast like a fist waiting to smash vessels that venture too close to its jagged rocks. Eight ships were lost near Punta Gorda between 1899 and 1907. The last of these, the *Columbia*, took eighty-seven people down with her.

Prompted by these disasters, Congress funded a light station in 1908, but building the new lighthouse was not easy. Materials had to be landed well to the north of the site and then dragged down the beach on horse-drawn sleds. Nonetheless, by 1912, the tower's

Courtesy U.S. Coast Guard

fourth-order Fresnel lens began to cast its flashing light toward the sea.

Since it was as difficult to maintain as it had been to build, the lighthouse was abandoned by the Coast Guard as soon as it became practical to do so. The station was closed permanently in 1951. All that remains of it is a single-story concrete watch room with a spiral staircase leading to an iron lantern room overhead. Resting on a bluff forty-eight feet above the surf, the entire structure stands only twenty-seven feet high.

Travel information: From Highway 101 in Northern California, take

Highway 211 to Ferndale, then Mattole Road to Petrolia. Keep in mind this road is steep and winding, and that it may be difficult for some vehicles. The lighthouse can be reached from Petrolia via Lighthouse Road and a three-mile trail.

■ CAPE MENDOCINO LIGHT ■
Capetown (1868 and 1909)

California's westernmost point is also one of its most imposing headlands. Cape Mendocino's soaring 1,400-foot cliffs drop almost vertically into the Pacific. Although the cape was among the West's best-known seamarks and most-feared navigational obstacles, no light was placed here until the late 1860s.

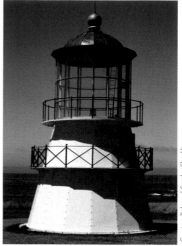

Courtesy Bob and Sandra Shanklin

Establishing a lighthouse on the cape proved a daunting challenge. The first ship bringing supplies to the construction site wrecked on the merciless rocks to the south. When a second ship finally delivered the necessary materials, they had to be hoisted hundreds of feet up the cliffs with ropes. Laborers were forced to endure weeks of rain and fog and to camp out in howling winds. Despite the difficulties workers eventually completed a two-story brick dwelling and barn and erected a sixteen-sided iron tower that had been prefabricated by machinists in San Francisco.

Focused by a first-order Fresnel lens, the light first shone on the night of December 1, 1868. With a focal plane more than four hundred feet above the Pacific, the light could be seen from more than twenty-five miles at sea. During the 1970s, the historic lighthouse was deactiviated and its job taken over by an automated light on a pole located farther up the cliffs. The original tower was dismantled and reassambled in Mal Coombs Park in Shelter Cove.

> **Travel information:** Near Garberville on U.S. Highway 101, take the Redway exit and drive west, following the signs to Shelter Cove. The lighthouse is located in Mal Coombs Park off Machi Road.

■ HUMBOLT HARBOR/TABLE BLUFF LIGHTS ■
Humbolt Bay (1856 and 1892)

Completed in 1856, at a time when much of the U.S. Pacific coast was still a wilderness, the Humbolt Harbor Lighthouse was among the first light stations in the West. Built at a cost of $15,000, it consisted of a Cape Cod–style dwelling with a twenty-one-foot tower rising through the middle section of its roof. The lantern room held a fourth-order Fresnel lens.

Built on a sandy foundation, the lighthouse was threatened by nature almost from the beginning. Wracked by earthquakes, storms, and beach erosion, the structure began to deteriorate. In 1885 a cyclone tore away its roof and drove floating logs against its walls. The building was repaired, but soon its masonry began to crack and fall apart. It eventually collapsed into a jumble of masonry on the beach.

By 1892 a new lighthouse, built high atop nearby Table Bluff, was ready for service. A Victorian-style structure with an attached, square tower, it was given the same fourth-order lens that had once shone from the tower of the Humbolt Harbor Lighthouse. Although the Table Bluff tower was only thirty-five feet tall, its elevation placed the light almost 190 feet above the bay. The light could be seen from up to twenty miles away.

After more than eighty years of service, the Table Bluff Lighthouse was decommissioned in 1975 and turned over to a private foundation. The tower of the lighthouse was cut into two parts and trucked to Woodley Island, near Eureka, where it was reassembled and repaired.

Travel information: The Table Bluff tower is on display at Woodley Island in the Eureka Inner Harbor area. Follow U.S. Highway 101 into Eureka, turn toward the water on Route 255, and follow signs to the lighthouse. The nearby Humbolt Bay Maritime Museum contains the original Table Bluff fourth-order Fresnel lens; call (707) 444-9440. Nothing remains of the old Humbolt Harbor Lighthouse except, perhaps, for a few chunks of stone on the beach.

■ TRINIDAD HEAD LIGHT ■
Trinidad (1871)

Set on a jagged cliff face almost two hundred feet above the Pacific surf, this little lighthouse has aided commercial fishermen and other mariners seeking the shelter of Trinidad Harbor for more than a century. Built in 1871 to guide schooners carrying lumber to San Francisco, the light helped close a gap of darkness between Crescent City and Humbolt Bay to the south. Although the station's fourth-order lens was small for a coastal light, the elevation of the tower, which was perched on a high cliff, made its beacon visible from up to twenty miles at sea. When the light was automated in 1947, its classic lens was replaced by an airport-style beacon.

Travel information: Take the Trinidad exit from U.S. Highway 101. Now automated, the Trinidad Head Lighthouse is closed to the public. Hiking trails lead to an overlook with a view of the old lighthouse, but less energetic visitors have another attractive option. For the benefit of tourists who constantly ask the locals how to get to the lighthouse, a replica of the tower has been built in the town. It is a near-perfect match for the original and now houses the antique Fresnel lens that served for so many years at the Trinidad Head station.

■ BATTERY POINT (CRESCENT CITY) LIGHT ■
Crescent City (1856)

Pressed by Northern California lumber interests during the 1850s, Congress designated Crescent City as a site for a lighthouse. Like many other early western light stations, this one consisted of a simple Cape Cod–style dwelling with a tower rising through the center of its roof. Beginning in 1856, the beacon focused by its fourth-order Fresnel lens guided freighters into the city's bustling harbor, then out again, bearing loads of redwood bound for San Francisco.

Captain John Jeffrey and his wife, Nellie, took over keeper's duties at the Battery Point Lighthouse in 1875. They became near-permanent fixtures of the station. In all, they spent thirty-nine years in the lighthouse and raised four children there.

The thick stone walls of the lighthouse, built for a mere $15,000, outlasted several generations of keepers. They still stand, little changed from the station's earliest days. Except for a stroke of luck, however, the station's last night might have been that of March 27, 1964. The earthquake that hit Alaska on that date sent five titanic tidal waves hurtling toward the coast of Northern California, where they stormed ashore shortly after midnight. Keepers Clarence and Peggy Coons saw them coming but could do little but say their prayers. Fortunately, the enormous waves struck at such an extreme angle that the lighthouse and its keepers were spared.

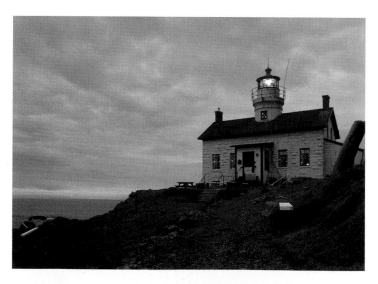

Although discontinued in 1965, the light was reestablished in 1982 as a private aid to navigation. The building now serves as a history museum.

Travel information: The lighthouse and museum are located at Battery Point on the west side of the Crescent City harbor. Write to the Del Norte County Historical Society, 577 H Street, Crescent City, CA 95531 or call (707) 464–3089 (lighthouse) or (707) 464–3922 (museum).

■ ST. GEORGE REEF LIGHT ■
Crescent City (1892)

Built on an exposed rock constantly pounded by the Pacific, the St. George Reef Light station cost the U.S. government $704,633, making it the most expensive lighthouse in the nation's history. Mariners who long dreaded this deadly obstacle certainly thought the money was well spent. Over the centuries this notorious reef has ruined numerous ships including the side-wheeler *Brother Jonathan*, wrecked here in 1865 with a loss of more than two hundred lives.

The hulking and costly stone tower was erected on a giant elliptical base of granite and concrete. Rising more than 140 feet above the waves, the tower held a first-order Fresnel lens, displaying an alternating red and white flashing light.

Because of the station's isolated and dangerous location, families were never housed here. The all-male crews who lived on the rock for months at a time found the tower damp and cold. Most keepers considered the St. George Reef station an unpleasant and undesirable posting. Mercifully, the light was discontinued in 1975 and replaced by a large buoy. The original lighthouse is now being restored.

Travel information: The abandoned but spectacular lighthouse can be seen from the end of Crescent City's Washington Boulevard. The station's 18-foot-high first-order Fresnel lens is on display in the Del Norte County Historical Society Museum on Sixth Street in Crescent City. Call (707) 464–3922.

Courtesy National Archives

OREGON

■ CAPE BLANCO LIGHT ■
Port Orford (1870)

Cape Blanco and its light station take their names from the precipitous white cliffs that drop almost vertically down to the beaches nearly two hundred feet below the lighthouse. Oldest and southernmost of Oregon's major beacons, the light shines from atop a fifty-nine-foot conical tower erected in 1870. The considerable height of the cliffs raises the focal plane of the light to a lofty 245 feet above mean sea level. Focused by a second-order Fresnel lens, the light can be seen from up to twenty-two miles at sea. Unfortunately, vandals ravaged the classic lens in 1992, doing more than $500,000 in damage.

Courtesy John W. Weil

> *Travel information:* The lighthouse is located near Cape Blanco State Park, off U.S. Highway 101 a few miles north of Port Orford. Visitors are welcome to walk the grounds.

■ COQUILLE RIVER LIGHT ■
Bandon (1895)

Now an attraction of Bullards Beach State Park, this little lighthouse stood empty and ignored for nearly half a century—longer than it served as an active light station. Gutted by fire after the Coast Guard abandoned the structure in 1939, it was nearly destroyed by wind, weather, and vandals. Its story has a happy ending, however, as the old lighthouse has now been lovingly restored by the state.

When it was built in 1895, the forty-foot brick lighthouse tower was covered in a protective layer of stucco and was painted white. Given a fourth-order lens, it served for more than four decades before it was discontinued and replaced by a series of buoys and a small jetty light.

To the delight of Bullards Beach visitors, the park has placed a light in the tower.

Interestingly, since it is not an official coastal beacon, the light is blacked out on the ocean side.

> *Travel information:* Bullards Beach State Park and its lighthouse are located off U.S. Highway 101 near Bandon. The Lighthouse Inn in Bandon offers a fine view of the tower. For Bullards Beach Park information, call (541) 347–2209.

■ CAPE ARAGO LIGHT ■
Charleston (1866, 1908, and 1934)

The prosperous lumber ports on Coos Bay have been served by several lighthouses. The first, completed in 1866, was established on a small, strategically placed island just north of the prominent headland known as Cape Arago. An iron tower, it stood for more than four decades before erosion forced the Lighthouse Board to replace it. A wooden structure built farther back from the rapidly weathering cliffs, it served for nearly thirty years before it, too, threatened to tumble into the Pacific.

One of the more recently completed of the West's lighthouses, the existing reinforced-concrete tower has proven more durable than its predecessors. The forty-foot, octagonal concrete tower rises through the roof of a rectangular fog-signal building. The light was originally focused by a fourth-order Fresnel lens, but a solar-powered modern optic now shines from the lantern room at the top of the tower, about 100 feet above the Pacific.

> *Travel information:* Cape Arago and its lighthouse are located about 2 miles south of Charleston near the entrance to Coos Bay. Turn west off U.S. Highway 101 at the town of Coos Bay. The lighthouse is not open to the public.

■ UMPQUA RIVER LIGHT ■
Winchester Bay (1857 and 1894)

The conical, plaster-covered masonry tower rises just above the treetops of a state park named in its honor. At night the flashing light, alternating red and white, can be seen from twenty-one miles away. The existing tower dates from 1894, but a lighthouse stood here as early as 1857.

Erected under the constant threat of attack by Indians, the first Umpqua River tower stood for only four years. Floods quickly undercut its foundation, and in 1861 it collapsed into the river. Nothing was done to revive the station until the

1890s. Completed in 1894, the present sixty-five-foot tower was crowned with a powerful, first-order Fresnel lens. The huge lens remains in place and is one of the few first-order Fresnels still in use. The site, well above the river, raises the focal plane of the light 165 feet above the sea.

> *Travel information:* The light can be seen and enjoyed from the adjacent Umpqua River Lighthouse State Park, located off U.S. Highway 101 just south of Winchester Bay. A fine visitors center with museum occupies the former Umpqua River Coast Guard station; call (541) 271-4631.

■ HECETA HEAD LIGHT ■
Florence (1894)

Before 1894 there was no light to guide ships along the ninety-mile stretch of coast between Cape Foulweather and Cape Arago. The crews of ships plying these waters were left to find their way in the dark. But in the spring of that year, a fifty-six-foot-tall white masonry tower was completed high up on the Heceta Head cliffs, and a bright light began to shine from its lantern.

To build the lighthouse in this remote location took nearly two years and $180,000—a fantastic sum at the time. Construction materials had to be brought in by ship to the nearby Suislaw River and then hauled by mule-drawn wagon to the construction site.

The new lighthouse was fitted with an exquisite first-order Fresnel lens with 640 individual prisms. Originally, the light came from a five-wick coal-oil lamp. A weighted cable powered the gears that turned the lamp, causing the light to flash. Although the old lamp has given way to a million-candlepower electric bulb, the original classic lens still shines. Its beam flashes seaward from an elevation of more than two hundred feet and can be seen from a distance of up to twenty-one miles.

> *Travel information:* One of the most scenic light stations in the West, Heceta Head Lighthouse is popular with photographers. It stands on a craggy point about 11 miles north of Florence. The station is now owned by the U.S. Forest Service and operated as an interpretive center and bed-and-breakfast inn; call (541) 547-3696. To reach the lighthouse turn off U.S. Highway 101 at Devils Elbow State Park.

■ YAQUINA BAY LIGHT ■
Newport (1871)

Built on the crest of a hill near the entrance to Yaquina Bay, the lamps in the little red lantern atop this wood-frame lighthouse first burned in November 1871. Less than three years later they were permanently snuffed out. Due to an extraordinary bureaucratic bungle, a second lighthouse was mistakenly erected nearby, rendering the Yaquina Bay Light superfluous.

People might have supposed at the time that the abandoned, two-story lighthouse would soon be demolished, but not so. The building was eventually put to use as a crew station for the U.S. Lifesaving Service. Later it was carefully restored and became an attractive historical museum.

Travel information: The Yaquina Bay Lighthouse is located near the north end of the Yaquina Bay Bridge in Yaquina Bay State Park. Filled with nineteenth-century furnishings and artifacts, the building now serves as a museum; call (541) 574-3116.

■ YAQUINA HEAD LIGHT ■
Newport (1873)

One of the most beautiful lighthouses in America, the Yaquina Head Light is a magnet for photographers and tourists, who can see it from U.S. Highway 101, the Pacific Coast Highway. The magnificent outcropping of rock on which the tower stands is a more literal magnet. At its core is a rich vein of magnetized iron, which sends the compasses of passing ships into a crazy spin. For this reason and others, this headland is a formidable threat to shipping and, over the years, has claimed many fine vessels.

Interestingly, the ninety-three-foot conical tower built atop the cliffs here had been intended for Cape Foulweather, miles to the north. Construction crews, however, mistakenly landed their materials on Yaquina Head and built the tower there instead. Lighthouse officials detected the mistake soon after the station was completed in 1873. Rather than tear down the expensive masonry towers, they left it in service and deactivated the redundant **Yaquina Bay Lighthouse.**

A huge, twelve-foot-high classic lens has graced the lantern room for more than a century. It still shines today, casting seaward a beam visible from nineteen miles away.

Travel information: Located about 4 miles north of Newport on U.S. Highway 101, the station is open to the public when weather permits. Call (541) 574-3100.

■ CAPE MEARES LIGHT ■
Tillamook (1890)

As with the **Yaquina Head Light** well to the south, the lighthouse that now stands on Cape Meares was built in the wrong place. Originally intended for Cape Lookout, the station ended up on Cape Meares because of a mapmaker's error. The two names had been reversed on U.S. Coast Survey charts, and dismayed officials did not discover the mistake until the station was almost complete. Rather than incur the cost of building an entirely new facility on Cape Lookout, the Lighthouse Service decided to leave well enough alone.

Only thirty-eight feet tall, the octagonal iron tower stood at the edge of a cliff, placing the focal plane of its light 215 feet above the breakers. A huge first-order Fresnel lens, for many years illuminated by a coal-oil lamp, made the light visible from twenty-one miles at sea.

Deactivated in 1963, the old lighthouse is now a popular tourist attraction. Much to their discredit, vandals have damaged the magnificent lens on more than one occasion.

> *Travel information:* Located in Cape Meares State Park, the lighthouse can be reached via Three Capes Loop Road, off U.S. Highway 101 at Tillamook. Call (503) 842–3182 or (800) 551–6949.

■ LIGHTSHIP *COLUMBIA* ■
Astoria (1951)

Among the last of America's lightships, the 128-foot *Columbia* was launched in Maine in 1951. For nearly three decades she rode the waves on station eight miles off the dangerous Columbia River bar. Retired in 1979, she has since served as the prime attraction of the Columbia River Maritime Museum in Astoria.

Travel information: The lightship is moored near the Columbia River Maritime Museum at 1792 Marine Drive in Astoria. For hours and tours call (503) 325-2323.

WASHINGTON

■ CAPE DISAPPOINTMENT LIGHT ■
Ilwaco (1856)

This cape received its melancholy name from fur trader John Meares, who mistook the headland for another landfall farther south—the one now named for him—and sailed away in disappointment. The captains of many other ships have encountered another, more bitter form of disappointment at this cape. Countless vessels have foundered here and on the nearby Columbia River bar.

Federal surveyors recommended as early as 1848 that a lighthouse be erected on

the cape, but eight years went by before one was finally completed. Constructing a station on the isolated cape proved far more difficult and expensive than anyone had imagined. During the fall of 1853, the bark *Oriole* foundered on the Columbia River bar while attempting to deliver materials for the tower. It took almost a year to bring in a second shipment. Once it arrived, downpours and deep mud further delayed the project. Finally, in 1856, the fifty-three-foot conical tower was finished, and the oil lamps inside its first-order Fresnel lens were lit on October 15 of that year.

In 1898 the Cape Disappointment Lighthouse lost its classic first-order lens and much of its status to the recently completed light station on nearby North Head. A fourth-order Fresnel optic replaced the original lens and remains in operation. It displays alternating red and white flashes.

For many years the station's closest neighbor was Fort Canby. Bristling with artillery, the fort controlled access to the Columbia. The concussion of its huge guns sometimes shattered windows in the tower.

Travel information: From Ilwaco follow signs for Cape Disappointment and Fort Canby State Park. Visitors can reach the lighthouse via a short hike from a well-marked parking area. The park's Lewis and Clark Interpretive Center offers exhibits that celebrate the famous explorers and their visit to the cape nearly two centuries ago. Call (360) 642-3078.

■ NORTH HEAD LIGHT ■
Ilwaco (1898)

Built in 1898 for $25,000, the North Head Light station was established to warn ships approaching the Columbia River from the north. The Columbia's extensive bar is very dangerous and has claimed many vessels.

The white tower is sixty-five feet tall and stands at the edge of a cliff almost 130 feet high. Originally fitted with a first-order classic lens removed from the nearby **Cape Disappointment Lighthouse,** it received a less powerful fourth-order lens in 1930. Nowadays, a rotating aeromarine beacon serves here.

Courtesy John W. Weil

North Head is said to be the windiest spot in the nation. Winds blast across the narrow peninsula at speeds that have been clocked at 150 miles per hour. Trees, chimneys, and fences have been flattened by these gale force winds. In 1932 a wild duck, blown off course by the wind, smashed into the lantern, shattering a window and chipping the glass prisms of the lens. The damaged equipment was repaired, but the unfortunate duck was beyond help.

> *Travel information:* From the town of Ilwaco off U.S. Highway 101, follow the signs to Cape Disappointment and Fort Canby State Park. Markers point the way to the lighthouse. The park's Lewis and Clark Interpretive Center houses the enormous first-order classic lens that served at Cape Disappointment from 1856 to 1898 and North Head from 1898 until 1932. Call (360) 642-3078.

■ GRAYS HARBOR LIGHT ■
Westport (1898)

Towering more than one hundred feet from base to lantern, the octagonal Grays Harbor Lighthouse is one of the tallest on the Pacific coast. The light, still focused by the station's original third-order Fresnel lens, serves as a major coastal light and guides vessels to the harbor and fishing town of Westport. The lens has three bull's-eyes, about eight inches in diameter, emitting white and red flashes. The light is visible from about twenty-one miles away.

> *Travel information:* The lighthouse is closed to the public except on holiday weekends during summer, but it can be viewed anytime from

Ocean Avenue in the delightful seaside town of Westport, or from the Westport Maritime Museum; (360) 268-0078. Photographers are especially fond of this tower, which rises like an empress above a lush forest of conifers.

■ DESTRUCTION ISLAND LIGHT ■
Destruction Island (1891)

During the eighteenth century an Indian war party killed several seamen who had gone ashore here to fill casks with fresh water. Afterward, this wilderness landfall would always be known as Destruction Island, and the name proved an apt one.

Over the years the boulder-strewn island, often hidden under heavy blankets of fog, was to exact a heavy toll in ships and lives.

As early as 1855 the Lighthouse Board saw the need for a powerful navigational light to warn ships away from Destruction Island. Building a lighthouse on this remote and extraordinarily rugged offshore site, however, was a daunting task. Although Congress set aside $45,000 for the project, it was deemed impractical, and the money was spent elsewhere.

Spurred on by a sharp increase in shipping along the Washington coast and the lengthening list of wrecks on the island's jagged rocks, work on the lighthouse finally got under way in 1888. Materials had to be brought ashore in small boats from a tender anchored in a cove near the construction site, and the tower, dwelling, and outbuildings took nearly three years to build. At last the steam-driven fog signal began to sound in November 1891, and one month later, keepers lit the lamps inside the station's first-order Fresnel lens. Although the Destruction Island station was automated in 1963—much to the relief of its lonely Coast Guard keepers—its classic lens remains in operation.

Travel information: Destruction Island Lighthouse is off-limits to the public, but it can be seen from a parking area along U.S. Highway 101, about a mile south of Ruby Beach.

■ CAPE FLATTERY LIGHT ■
Cape Flattery (1857)

Situated at the far northwestern corner of the United States (not counting Alaska), the Cape Flattery Light beams out into the Pacific from barren Tatoosh Island at the entrance of the Strait of Juan de Fuca. Thirty miles across the stormy strait is Canada's Vancouver Island.

Not only is this the most northwesterly lighthouse in the lower forty-eight states, it is also one of the nation's most isolated light stations. The sixty-five-foot stone tower and Cape Cod–style dwelling stand as a testament to the hardiness of lighthouse keepers and their families who lived here for more than a century.

Among the West's first great navigational sentinels, this lighthouse was completed and placed in operation in 1857. The stone

Courtesy U.S. Coast Guard

tower rose directly out of the keeper's dwelling so that station personnel could climb its steps and keep the light burning without braving the harsh weather. Tatoosh Island is a hundred feet high, which elevates the light's focal plane to 165 feet above the ocean.

The original first-order Fresnel lens had been intended for Old Point Loma, but it was brought to Cape Flattery instead, because the Point Loma tower proved too small to hold the lens's enormous frame. Automated in 1977, the station now employs a modern rotating optic.

> *Travel information:* Inaccessible from the land, the station can be seen from the water or from a trail on the Makah Reservation at the end of Route 112. The trail requires several steep climbs and moderate physical exertion.

■ NEW DUNGENESS LIGHT ■
Dungeness (1857)

The lighthouse that stands near the tip of the eight-mile-long Dungeness Spit is the same one built there in 1857, but nowadays the tower is only about half as tall as it was 145 years ago. Suffering from structural weakness, the original structure was in danger of collapse by the late 1920s. To save it engineers decided to take some of the strain off its walls by lopping thirty-seven feet off the top.

During its early years the light guided not only ships and fishing vessels but canoes paddled by Indian warriors prepared to do battle on the spit. Traditionally, tribes living on opposite sides of the Strait of Juan de Fuca would meet on the spit to settle their differences. After the lighthouse was built, they continued the practice, but now their meeting place was much easier to find. Apparently happy to have a light to guide

Courtesy National Archives

them to their dark and bloody work, the war parties never molested the keepers—only one another.

The lighthouse and the spit on which it stands took their name from Dungeness Point in England, coincidentally famed for *its* magnificent lighthouse. Like its British namesake, Dungeness Spit is a ship killer. The list of vessels wrecked on its sands is nearly endless. The New Dungeness Light, originally focused by a classic Fresnel lens, slowed the pace of the wrecks but did not stop them. The beacon, now provided by a modern optic, remains in operation.

Travel information: The lighthouse is accessible only by boat or by means of an 8-mile hike along highly scenic Dungeness Spit, a wildlife refuge. Take U.S. Highway 101 west of Sequim; then turn north and follow the signs to the Dungeness Wildlife Area. For more information contact the New Dungeness chapter of the U.S. Lighthouse Society at P.O. Box 1283, Sequim, WA 98382; (360) 683-9166. Lodging is available at the lighthouse, where guests serve as "keepers" and help maintain the property.

To the west of New Dungeness, near Port Angeles, the **Ediz Hook Light** (1865, 1908, and 1946) beams from a sixty-three-foot tower atop a hangar on a Coast Guard air station. Two earlier, more conventional lighthouses once stood on Ediz Hook, and their dwellings are now used as residences. The station is closed to the public.

Still farther west is the **Slip Point Light** (1905), located at the east end of Clallam Bay. During the 1950s the original lighthouse was torn down and replaced by a fifty-foot tower with an automated light. This station, too, is closed to the public.

Near the far eastern end of the Strait of Juan de Fuca is Smith Island, where a Cape Cod–style lighthouse stood for a century. Undercut by erosion, the **Smith Island Lighthouse** (1858) collapsed during the late 1950s. It was replaced by a modest light mounted on a steel tower. The station is closed to the public.

■ POINT WILSON LIGHT ■
Port Townsend (1879 and 1914)

Traditionally, sailing ships approached Port Townsend along the eastern shore of Admiralty Inlet. The **Admiralty Head Light,** established in 1861 on Whidbey Island, guided them into port. But steam-powered vessels, with their deeper drafts, favored the inlet's western side. As sail gave way to steam, shippers and citizens of Port Townsend lobbied for a light to mark the western shore.

Eventually, the Lighthouse Board responded, and on December 15, 1879, keeper David Littlefield lit the new station's lamps for the first time. A fourth-order Fresnel lens focused the light, visible from any point along a sweeping 270 degrees of horizon.

In time erosion threatened to undercut the tower, and in 1914 a forty-six-foot, octagonal masonry tower replaced the original wooden lighthouse. Set a safe distance from water's edge, the 1914 lighthouse still stands. The station's classic fourth-order lens remains in use.

Travel information: The lighthouse is located in Fort Warden State Park, at the far northeastern end of the Olympic Peninsula. Take Route 20 to Port Townsend and then follow signs to the park, open all year during daylight hours. Contact Fort Warden State Park, 200 Battery Way, Port Townsend, WA 98368; (360) 344-4400.

On an island a few miles southeast of Point Wilson is the **Marrowstone Point Lighthouse** (1888). Nearby is Fort Flager, once an army base and now a state park. From Route 20 south of Port Townsend, follow the signs to Hadlook, Fort Flager State Park, and the lighthouse.

■ POINT NO POINT LIGHT ■
Hansville (1880)

The pilots of ships moving up from Puget Sound into Admiralty Inlet often notice a prominent headland sweeping up from the southwest. They may think they are seeing Foulweather Bluff at the far end of Washington's long central peninsula, but they are mistaken. This land feature is the appropriately named Point No Point.

A key navigational light has shone from Point No Point since 1880. Built on a forty-acre tract acquired by the Lighthouse Service for just $1,800, the Point No Point Light station is a near twin of its sister lighthouse on West Point, near Seattle. Both stations consist of a rectangular fog-signal building with a squat tower barely peeking through its roof and separate keeper's dwellings. The lanterns of the Point No Point tower still hold the original bull's-eye-type fourth-order Fresnel lens. The bull's-eye lens focuses the light into a series of flashes, which can be seen from about fifteen miles away.

Over the years the Point No Point Lighthouse saved many ships from disaster. One that it could not save was the small passenger liner *Admiral Sampson*, which sank off the point in 1914 after colliding with a second liner, the *Princess Victoria*. Eleven passengers and crew went down with the *Sampson*, including Captain Zimro Moore.

Travel information: From Port Gamble follow Highway 104 south and then Highway 305 east. Then turn north onto Hansville Road Northeast and follow it for approximately 10 miles to the town of Hansville. Signs show the way to the lighthouse. Call Kitsap County Parks and Recreation at (360) 337-4595.

■ POINT ROBINSON LIGHT ■
Tacoma (1887 and 1915)

Pilots of vessels plying the Puget Sound waters between Seattle and Tacoma keep a sharp eye out for the Point Robinson Light. Located on the eastern end of Maury Island, the light marks a key safe channel in this narrow but heavily trafficked waterway.

A fog signal was placed on the point in 1885 to protect ships against running aground on the island. Particularly threatening was a low, sandy spit extending several hundred yards out into Puget Sound. Lighthouse officials soon concluded that the fog signal alone was inadequate, and in 1887 a modest lantern and lens were added to the station.

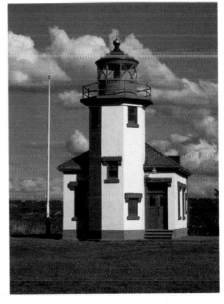

As shipping increased in the lower Puget Sound, the station's importance grew. In 1915 a full-fledged lighthouse was established here. It consisted of a pair of keeper's dwellings and a thirty-eight-foot concrete tower and lantern room containing a fifth-order Fresnel lens. The cylindrical tower and fog-signal building stand approximately 150 yards out on the spit.

With its peaceful, scenic location and proximity to Tacoma and Seattle, Robinson Point Lighthouse was once a very popular duty station for keepers and their families. Nowadays, the light is automated and does its job without the help of resident keepers.

> *Travel information:* The lighthouse is located in Point Robinson Park on the northeast corner of Maury Island, just across from the larger and more populous Vachon Island in Puget Sound. The station is open to the public from noon until 4:00 P.M. on weekends.
>
> Other lights in the lower Puget Sound include the **Dofflemyer Point Lighthouse** (1887 and 1934) near Olympia, Washington's capital city, and **Browns Point Lighthouse** (1887), near Tacoma. The thirty-foot concrete tower on Dofflemyer Point is closed to the public. Its near twin at Browns Point is located in a public park, open year-round during daylight hours. Take Route 509 north from Tacoma, turn left on Le-Lou-Wa, and follow signs to Browns Point. Call King County Parks at (206) 463-9602.

■ ALKI POINT LIGHT ■
Seattle (1887 and 1913)

Thrusting far out into the blue waters of Puget Sound, wedge-shaped Point Alki makes a notable impression on mariners who must swing their ships wide to avoid it. Perhaps hoping it would develop into a burgeoning commercial center, early settlers called the point "New York," but it was not destined to become a West Coast Manhattan. Overshadowed by bustling Seattle only a few miles to the northeast,

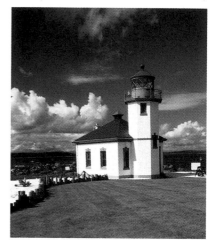

the point languished, almost completely ignored by commercial interests. Disappointed landowners took to calling it Point "Alki," after a Chinook Indian word meaning "by-and-by" or "all in good time."

Point Alki was of obvious importance to shipping, however, both as a daymark showing the way to Seattle and a threat in fog and at night. Even so, no light was displayed here until the 1880s, when landowner Hans Martin Hanson hung up a small lantern as a humanitarian gesture. In 1887 the U.S. Lighthouse Service improved the light, installing a small lantern and lens. Hanson was paid $15 per month to keep the lamp burning.

With shipping traffic between Seattle and Tacoma to the south on the increase, the government eventually decided to build a full-fledged lighthouse on Point Alki. Buying land from Manson's heirs for $10,000, the Lighthouse Service built an octagonal, thirty-seven-foot-tall masonry tower, attached fog-signal building, and nearby keeper's dwelling. Originally, the station employed a fourth-order Fresnel lens, but now a modern optic serves here, flashing white every two seconds.

> ***Travel information:*** Alki Lighthouse is located just to the south of the public beach at Alki. To reach the beach and lighthouse from Seattle, follow I–5 south, then the West Seattle Freeway to the Harbor Avenue exit. Turn right on Harbor Avenue and follow it (Harbor Avenue eventually becomes Beach Drive) along the water to the lighthouse. An active Coast Guard facility, the lighthouse is not regularly open to the public.

■ WEST POINT LIGHT ■
Seattle (1881)

Rising twenty-three feet above a low, sandy peninsula at the north entrance to Elliot Bay, West Point Lighthouse has welcomed ships to Seattle for more than a hundred years. Situated five miles from the city's thriving business core, the old lighthouse stands at the foot of Magnolia Bluff in Discovery Park.

The little lighthouse was built in 1881 at a cost to taxpayers of $25,000, a rather princely sum in those days. Fitted with a complex fourth-order Fresnel lens with twelve separate bull's eyes, it began operation in November 1881. According to a Coast Guard estimate, its flashing light has put in more than 400,000 hours of service. The beacon can be seen from fifteen miles away.

Travel information: A popular attraction of Seattle's Discovery Park, the lighthouse is located about a mile and a half from the entrance. A pleasant way to enjoy an exterior view of the lighthouse is with a relaxing stroll along West Point Beach. The park offers weekend tours of the lighthouse. Call (206) 386-4236.

■ MUKILTEO LIGHT ■
Mukilteo (1906)

Centuries ago, Indian tribes often gathered at the place we now call Mukilteo, a Native American word meaning "good spot for camping." In the early 1900s, the Lighthouse Service decided that Mukilteo was also a good location for a navigational light to guide vessels headed for Everett. Completed in 1906, the Victorian-style structure was fitted with a fourth-order Fresnels lens and equipped with a

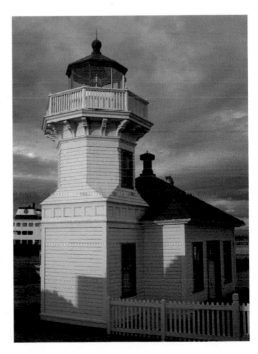

Daboll trumpet to warn ships plowing blindly through fog or heavy weather.

In 1960 the Coast Guard planned to replace the station's Fresnel lens with an aeromarine beacon. Residents of Mukilteo and other nearby communities protested, however, and the old Fresnel remains in operation to this day, flashing white every five seconds.

Travel information: The lighthouse contains a photographic exhibit on the lights of the Puget Sound. Located near the Whidbey Island ferry landing, the wood-frame structure is open to the public during the afternoon and on weekends.

■ ADMIRALTY HEAD LIGHT ■
Whidbey Island (1860 and 1903)

Completed during the months just prior to the Civil War, the ancestor of the Admiralty Head Lighthouse was among the West's earliest navigational markers. The frame structure was built atop a knob called Red Bluff. Its tower rose forty-one feet from base to lantern, and it had a fourth-order Fresnel lens. The station's fixed

white light, which could be seen from about sixteen miles away, welcomed Puget Sound marine traffic into Admiralty Inlet.

During the Spanish American War, the U.S. Army built a fort on Red Bluff to protect the entrance to the inlet. To make room for Fort Casey, the old lighthouse was demolished. The present Spanish-style structure was ready for service in 1903. Its brick tower rose only a few feet higher than the attached two-story residence, but the elevation of Admiralty Head placed its light more than 120 feet above the water.

As it turned out, the new lighthouse had a relatively short active life. It was discontinued in 1927, after which it became a residence for officers posted to Fort Casey. Nowadays, the carefully restored lighthouse serves as a museum.

> *Travel information:* The lighthouse is part of Fort Casey State Park, not far from the Keystone/Port Townsend ferry slip and a few miles from the historic island town of Coupeville. The park is open year-round, but visitors may tour the lighthouse only in summer. Call (360) 679–7391.

■ LIGHTS OF THE SAN JUAN ISLANDS ■
Turn Point Light (1893); Patos Island Light (1908);
Lime Kiln Light (1914); Burrows Island Light (1906);
Cattle Point Light (1935)

Pleasure boaters, yachtsmen, and ferry pilots who frequent the San Juans, an unspoiled chain of 172 islands in the straits between Washington State and Canada, know that navigation here can be difficult and dangerous. A tangle of narrow passages separates the islands, some of which are large enough for several towns and harbors, whereas others are no more than a scrap of exposed rock.

Courtesy Bob and Sandra Shanklin

Turn Point Light

(above) Patos Island Light, (right) Lime Kiln Light

Burrows Island Light

Cattle Point Light

Several lighthouses mark the way for mariners. Built in 1893, **Turn Point Lighthouse** shines from a squat, sixteen-foot concrete tower on the northwest end of Stuart Island. The thirty-eight-foot wooden tower of **Patos Island Lighthouse,** completed in 1908, stands on the western side of a scenic, 260-acre islet in the northern part of the chain. The octagonal tower of **Lime Kiln Lighthouse** dates from 1914 and marks the key shipping channel through Haro Strait. Built in 1906, the thirty-four-foot wood-frame **Burrows Island Lighthouse,** marking the southern entrance to Rosario Strait, has served well for more than ninety years. **Cattle Point Lighthouse** marks the southern end of San Juan Island.

Travel information: Access to the San Juan Islands and their lighthouses is by boat or ferry. For information and schedules contact the Washington State Ferry Service at (206) 464–6400.

ALASKA

■ LINCOLN ROCK LIGHT ■
Clarence Strait (1903)

Few light stations proved as difficult to establish and maintain as the one on Lincoln Rock, a tiny, barren island near the western end of the Clarence Strait some fifty-four miles northwest of Ketchikan, Alaska. Funded in 1902, the project got off to a shaky start when the con-

struction contractor lost a small steamer, a barge, and a large load of lumber in a gale. No doubt financially strapped, the contractor tried to recoup his losses by using substandard materials and was eventually fired by the Lighthouse Service.

Purchasing its own materials, the Lighthouse Service hired laborers and completed the station in time for an official lighting on December 1, 1903. A short, square tower pushed through the roof of the two-story wooden keeper's dwelling. The lantern room contained a fourth-order Fresnel lens, which displayed a fixed white light.

Much of the tiny island is submerged at high tide, so the lighthouse was built atop a concrete pier to protect it from the waves. As it turned out, however, the building was much more exposed than was at first thought. Large storm-driven waves often broke over the pier, smashing into the side of the dwelling. By 1909 the lighthouse had been so badly damaged by wave action that it had to be abandoned. It was never completely rebuilt.

In 1911 a manned fog-signal station went into service about a quarter of a mile from the old pier. An automated acetylene light took the place of the original beacon. The Lincoln Rock Station was permanently discontinued in 1968.

> *Travel information:* The site of the Lincoln Rock Lighthouse is not accessible to the public. To the south of Lincoln Rock is **Guard Islands Lighthouse** (1904). The square wooden structure displays a fixed white light that marks the entrance to Tongass Narrows, a few miles north of Ketchican.

Courtesy U.S. Coast Guard

■ CAPE DECISION LIGHT ■

Cape Decision (1932)

The appropriately named Cape Decision, located on the far southeastern end of Kuiu Island about sixty miles from the old Russian settlement of Sitka, presents mariners with a difficult choice. Here they must choose between several likely routes. Here, too, they face an assortment of dangers including strong tides, hidden rocks, and unpredictable weather as well as the ubiquitous coastal fog.

During the early twentieth century, seamen near the cape had to rely for guidance on an unwatched acetylene light that shone from one of the nearby Spanish Islands, but most mariners considered it woefully inadequate. Their pleas for a better, more powerful light fell on deaf ears in the tight-fisted Congress of the 1920s. Finally, only a few months before the Stock Market Crash of 1929 and the beginning of the Great Depression, Congress relented and approved partial funding for a lighthouse on Cape Decision.

The isolation of the site, funding shortages during the early years of the Depression, and the cape's notoriously foul weather all hindered progress. After three years of start-and-stop construction, the lighthouse was finally completed in 1932 at a total cost of $158,000 and placed in service on March 15 of that year.

The station's square, forty-foot tower rises from the flat roof of the main reinforced-concrete building. Its flashing, 350,000-candlepower light reaches out to mariners from an elevation of ninety-six feet. During the fogs and heavy weathers that frequently blanket the cape, an especially powerful fog signal warns vessels away from nearby rocks. A radio beacon helps guide ships in from the open Pacific. Automated in 1974, the Cape Decision Light was formerly fully staffed around the clock by keepers and assistants. After a year of service, station crewmen received a ninety-day leave.

In 1997 the U.S. Coast Guard leased the structure to the Cape Decision Lighthouse Society, which is refurbishing the station. The society hopes to open the lighthouse to overnight guests in the near future.

> ***Travel information:*** The Cape Decision Lighthouse is accessible only by boat or float plane. Call (907) 747–7803 for the up-to-date status of the station. The old Cape Decision third-order Fresnel lens is now on display at the Clausen Museum in Petersburg; call (907) 772–3598.

■ FIVE FINGER ISLANDS LIGHT ■
Five Finger Islands (1902 and 1935)

One of Alaska's first two official lighthouses, the Five Finger Islands Light station was established just after the turn of the twentieth century to guide ships through the Inside Passage to Juneau. Located on a craggy island in the northern section of Frederick Sound north of Petersburg, its beacon first shone on March 1, 1902, the same night the **Sentinel Island Light** was placed in service.

A two-story combination dwelling and tower, the original Five Finger Islands Lighthouse displayed a fixed white light focused by a fourth-order Fresnel lens. The lantern room peeked through the roof of the structure, its light shining from a point sixty-eight feet above high water. A wooden structure, the lighthouse served for more than thirty years before it burned to the ground in December 1933.

The government moved quickly to restore this vital Inside Passage light station, and a new lighthouse was completed and in operation by late in 1935. This one was built to last and, to this day, continues to guide ships, ferries, and fishing boats plying the waters of the passage. Standing on a hefty concrete pier, the forty-foot-square main building is built of reinforced concrete. It serves as a platform for the sixty-eight-foot tower, which places the station's light more than eighty feet above the water.

The Five Finger Islands station remained fully staffed longer than any Alaskan lighthouse. For months at a time, the keepers shared the building with boilers, batteries, and a jumble of other equipment. The last full-time keepers left the station in 1984, bringing to a close a unique era in lighthouse history.

> *Travel information:* The light can be seen from the decks of the ferries that travel the extraordinarily scenic Inside Passage. Otherwise, like most other Alaskan lighthouses, it is accessible only by boat or float plane. The Juneau Lighthouse Society now leases the station and hopes to open it to visitors by 2003. For current status write to the society at 10945 Glacier Highway, Juneau, AK 99801.

■ SENTINEL ISLAND LIGHT ■
Frederick Sound (1902 and 1935)

Among Alaska's earliest light stations, the Sentinel Island Lighthouse was established in 1902 to guide vessels into the Lynn Canal, northwest of Juneau. The residence, where keepers lived a rustic and solitary existence for a year or more at a time, was torn down after the light was automated in 1966. The station remains in operation but needs little human assistance. Solar panels help charge the batteries that supply electric power for the light and fog signal.

Courtesy U.S. Coast Guard

Travel information: Accessible only by boat, the lighthouse has been leased by the Gastineau Channel Historical Society. Limited overnight accommodations are occasionally available. Contact the society at 1001 Basin Road, Juneau, AK 88901; (907) 586-5338.

■ POINT RETREAT LIGHT ■
Northern end of Admiralty Island (1904)

Located at the northern tip of Admiralty Island, Point Retreat Lighthouse marks a watery crossroads where key shipping channels converge to link Alaska's capital city of Juneau with the Inside Passage and the Pacific. The station was established in 1904, and until it was automated in 1973, its light was focused by a giant clamshell Fresnel lens. The beacon still shines from atop the relatively short twenty-five-foot tower, but nowadays it is provided by a solar-powered modern optic. The Coast Guard has leased the station buildings and other property to the Alaska Lighthouse Association. The organization has undertaken a complete restoration of the lighthouse and hopes to open it to the public as a maritime museum.

Courtesy Bob and Sandra Shanklin

Travel information: The station is accessible only by air or boat. Contact the Alaska Lighthouse Association at 2116-B Second Street, Juneau, AK 99801 or over the Internet at info@aklighthouse.org.

■ CAPE SPENCER LIGHT ■
Cape Spencer (1925)

The keepers of Cape Spencer Lighthouse must have thought they were living at the end of the Earth. Located on a barren, rocky island at the entrance to Cross Sound

on the northern end of the Alaska Panhandle, this duty station placed keepers a half-day round-trip journey from mail or services of any kind. The nearest town, Juneau, was more than seventy miles away.

As early as 1906 commercial maritime interests had pressed the Lighthouse Service for a light to mark the cape and the route through Icy Strait, which was often followed by vessels trying to avoid the stormy Outside Passage. At that time, however, service resources were stretched to the limit, and it was not until 1913 that a small, automated acetylene beacon was placed on the cape.

Construction of a fully operational light station began in 1923 atop a precipitous, exposed rock just off the tip of the cape. The isolation and ruggedness of the site drove the cost of the facility to more than $175,000. Completed in 1925, it consisted of a fourteen-foot-wide square tower rising twenty-five feet above the flat roof of a reinforced-concrete fog-signal building, which also served as a residence for the keepers.

The lantern displays a flashing white light with a focal plane 105 feet above the water. The station's exceptionally powerful radio beacon, often received by ships as far as two hundred miles from shore, also guides vessels. The Cape Spencer Light has been automated since 1974. The tower and other station property are now managed and maintained by Glacier Bay National Park.

> **Travel information:** The Cape Spencer Lighthouse can be reached only by boat or helicopter. Often it can be seen from a distance by passengers on cruise ships visiting Glacier Bay National Park. Planes offering scenic tours of Glacier Bay operate out of Juneau during warmer-weather months and occasionally fly near the lighthouse. Contact Glacier Bay National Park at P.O. Box 140, Gustavas, AK 99826; (907) 697–2230. The station's original third-order lens is now on display at the Alaska State Museum in Juneau; (907) 465–2901.

■ ELDRED ROCK LIGHT ■
Haines (1906)

This unusual octagonal lighthouse stands on Eldred Rock, south of Haines and Skagway at the northwestern end of the Alaska Panhandle. The fifty-six-foot tower rises through the roof of the dwelling. The elevation of Eldred Rock places the focal plane of the light more than ninety feet above the water. The light guides ships along the strategic Lynn Canal.

In 1898, eight years before the light went into service, the steamer *Clara Nevada* wrecked and burned not far from Eldred Rock. Lost with the vessel were $100,000 in gold dust and more than a hundred passengers, most of them miners returning from the Klondike.

The Coast Guard has leased the lighthouse to the Sheldon Museum and Cultural Center in Haines. The museum hopes to make Eldred Park and its historic lighthouse more accessible to the public.

Travel information: The light station can be reached only by boat or helicopter. Contact the Sheldon Museum and Cultural Center, P.O. Box 269, Haines, AK 99827; (907) 766-2366. The station's original fourth-order Fresnel lens is on display at the museum.

■ CAPE ST. ELIAS LIGHT ■
Cape St. Elias (1916)

The monumentlike, 1,700-foot peak soaring above the rock-strewn beaches of Cape St. Elias makes this one of the most spectacular landfalls in all of North America. It is also among the most dangerous. As if to warn against the threat, mysterious colored lights are said to play along the shores here. Some especially imaginative mariners say a sea monster lurks in the bays and inlets near the mountain.

Funds for a lighthouse to guide ships through the perilous waters off Cape St. Elias were not approved until 1913. One year earlier, the lighthouse tender *Armeria* had wrecked while on route to place a buoy here. By the fall of 1916, the embarrassed Lighthouse Service had completed a permanent light station on the cape. It consisted of a fifty-five-foot-tall reinforced-concrete tower rising from the corner of a fog-signal building, a two-story keeper's dwelling, a boathouse, and storage buildings.

So isolated was the station that supply ships arrived only once a year. Usually, only men served here, and some keepers considered this the "worst lighthouse posting in America." The storms that blew in off the cape were often so powerful that rocks, kelp, and small fish were thrown up into the lantern room. The mountain behind the station posed other dangers as, occasionally, huge boulders came tumbling down its precipitous slopes and crashing through the trees. No doubt, few of the keepers who had served at Cape St. Elias were sorry to hear that the station was decommissioned in 1974 and replaced by an automated light.

Despite its considerable power the light at Cape St. Elias has never been particularly effective. The beacon is often obscured by fog, and the relatively low eighty-five-foot elevation of its focal plane limited its range to only about fifteen miles. To help guide mariners a radio beacon was installed here in 1927. The station has been leased to a local organization called the Cape St. Elias Lighthouse Keepers. The old keeper's house and other buildings are being restored.

Travel information: The lighthouse is accessible only by boat or helicopter. Contact the Cape St. Elias Lighthouse Keepers at their e-mail address: jbocci@alaskalighthouse.org.

■ CAPE HINCHINBROOK LIGHT ■
Hinchinbrook Island (1910 and 1934)

Hinchinbrook Island and its southwestward thrusting cape have been recognized as key seamarks for as long as oceangoing vessels have visited Alaska—Russian ships started coming here in the 1740s. The Lighthouse Service considered placing a light on the cape as early as 1900 but could not coax the necessary $125,000 from a reluctant Congress until 1909.

Courtesy U. S. Coast Guard

In April 1909 contractor A. B. Lewis of Seattle brought a crew of forty men to Hinchinbrook Island, hoping to complete the station that same year. But as was often the case with construction projects in Alaska, the weather played havoc with the schedule. Rain and wind halted work at Cape Hinchinbrook for weeks at a time. An especially powerful storm washed away a scow loaded with supplies valued at $12,000. Not until the following fall were the tower and other structures in place. The station's lamps were first lit on November 15, 1910.

The light and fog signal were housed in an octagonal concrete building more than fifty feet in diameter. Equipped with a third-order Fresnel lens of an advanced design said to provide the same power as a first-order lens, the lantern stood atop the two-story roof. Shining from an elevation of almost two hundred feet, its light could be seen from as far as twenty-five miles at sea.

The lighthouse was of such advanced design and so solidly built that some thought it to be "indestructible." Not so. In 1927 and again in 1928, earthquakes rocked the station, cracking concrete walls, breaking up the foundation, and threatening to dump the entire structure into the Pacific.

Alarmed by the damage, the Lighthouse Service decided to build another light tower on Cape Hinchinbrook, this time on a more stable foundation of solid rock. Completed in 1934, the reinforced-concrete structure rises sixty-seven feet above the cliff and displays a powerful light supplied by the station's original third-order lens. Along with several other Alaskan lights, this one was automated in 1974.

Travel information: The lighthouse is inaccessible to the public. It can sometimes be seen, however, from the deck of cruise ships, ferries, and other vessels entering or exiting Prince William Sound. The station's original third-order lens can be seen at the Valdez Museum at 217 Egan Drive in Valdez. Call (907) 835-2764.

■ SCOTCH CAP LIGHT ■
Unimak Island (1903, 1940, and 1950)

The original Scotch Cap Lighthouse was an octagonal wooden structure located on the side of a cliff about ninety feet above the sea. Built for a total of $76,571 by a team of thirty workers brought from Seattle, the tower and other station facilities took more than a year to complete. Placed in operation on July 15, 1903, it displayed a flashing white light produced by a third-order Fresnel lens.

Courtesy U.S. Coast Guard

In 1940 the old wooden lighthouse was replaced by a reinforced-concrete structure. Ironically, it was this new, much sturdier building that was smashed and swept away by the great tsunami of 1946. Several keepers lost their lives in the disaster.

A replacement facility was ready for duty by 1950. Built far up on the cliff to keep it safe from future tidal waves, the new lighthouse bore little resemblance to its predecessors. A rugged, rectangular concrete building, it looks more like a storage building than a lighthouse. A rotating aeromarine beacon shines from atop its flat roof 116 feet above the sea. Since the facility is fully automated, no personnel are stationed at Scotch Cap today.

Travel information: Located in one of the most remote and inhospitable places on the planet, the Scotch Cap station is, of course, inaccessible to the public.

■ CAPE SARICHEF LIGHT ■
Unimak Island (1904 and 1950)

Clinging to what the Aleuts sometimes describe as the "Roof of Hell," on bleak Unimak Island in the Aleutians, Cape Sarichef Lighthouse is the most westerly lighthouse in North America. Automated since 1950, the station was established in 1904 to guide ships through Unimak Pass, which links the Pacific Ocean with the Bering Sea.

Courtesy U.S. Coast Guard

The original lighthouse had a thirty-five-foot octagonal tower, which rose through the roof of a fog-signal building. Its third-order Fresnel lens displayed a fixed light with a focal plane more than 125 feet above the sea.

In 1950 the lighthouse was replaced by a concrete structure built higher on the cliffs to protect it from tsunamis like the one that destroyed the nearby Scotch Cap station. The light was deactivated in 1979.

Travel information: The station is inaccessible to the public.

HAWAII

■ MAKAPUU POINT LIGHT ■
East of Honolulu (1909)

The huge, twelve-foot-high Fresnel at Makapuu is the largest lighthouse lens in the United States. Ironically, it is housed in a relatively small tower only thirty-five feet tall, but what the station lacks in stature it more than makes up in the power of its beacon—visible from more than twenty-eight miles at sea. Unlike the tower itself, the station's surroundings are Olympian in scale. When the Makapuu Lighthouse was built in the early twentieth century, workers had to blast a site from a solid wall of lava several hundred feet high. Perched on an artificial ledge more than 300 feet above the waves, the stone and steel tower still serves mariners.

Courtesy Bob and Sandra Shanklin

Travel information: Located off Highway 72 in the easternmost corner of Oahu, the lighthouse can be reached only by means of a strenuous uphill climb. Bring your hiking shoes.

■ DIAMOND HEAD LIGHT ■
Honolulu (1899 and 1917)

Certainly among Hawaii's most important navigational aids, the Diamond Head Light guides vessels headed toward the busy mid-Pacific port of Honolulu. Built in 1899, the lighthouse had to be completely rebuilt after severe cracks appeared in its foundation. The new tower, completed in 1917, was given reinforced-concrete walls

and fitted with the station's original third-order Fresnel lens. Essentially unchanged in more than eighty years, the lighthouse remains in operation, its automated beacon shining out over the ocean from an elevation of 147 feet. Nowadays, the station dwelling serves as residence for the commander of the U.S. Coast Guard 14th District.

Travel information: Located southeast of Waikiki, the station is part of an active Coast Guard base and is not open to the public.

■ LAHAINA LIGHT ■
Lahaina on Maui (1840 and 1916)

Having unified the islands through conquest during the 1790s, Hawaii's King Kamehameha I established his royal capital at Lahaina. Its harbor became an

important port of call for diplomats, merchants, and missionaries who came here to ask favors of Kamehameha and his descendants. Beginning in 1840, Lahaina's harbor was marked by a lighthouse, perhaps the first in all of what is now the western United States. Unfortunately, nothing is left of that early lighthouse, which was replaced in 1916 by the existing concrete tower. The simple, pyramidal structure still guides vessels in and out of the harbor with a modest beacon.

Travel information: The tower is located just off Front Street near the center of Lahaina. Call (808) 667-9193.

■ KALAUPAPA LIGHT ■
Kalaupapa Peninsula on Molokai (1908)

Once the site of a notorious leper colony, the Kalaupapa Peninsula on Molokai is backed by the highest sea cliffs in the world—some soaring more than 2,000 feet above the waves. To help mariners keep their distance from these rugged shores, the government established a light-house on Kalaupapa Point in 1908. The exceptional remoteness of the peninsula made getting materials and construction crews to this faraway site unusually difficult and expensive. Building the station cost $60,000, but it has proven invaluable to mariners and their vessels. The 138-foot tower is the tallest on the Pacific.

Courtesy Bob and Sandra Shanklin

Travel information: Reaching the remote Kalaupapa Peninsula is not much easier today than it was a century ago. Since there is no direct road access, visitors climb down from the cliffs on foot or ride down on the backs of sure-footed mules, but these options are not recommended for the faint of heart. Some flights are available. Contact Kalaupapa National Historical Park, Kalaupapa, HI 96742. For tours call (808) 567–6171.

■ KILAUEA POINT LIGHTHOUSE ■
Kilauea Point on Kauai (1913)

Established in 1913, the Kilauea Point Lighthouse guided several generations of mariners, its beacon focused by one of the largest clamshell lenses in the world. A light here still marks the far northwestern edge of the Hawaiian chain, but it no longer emanates from the lighthouse or the giant Fresnel that still graces the fifty-two-foot tower. Instead it shines from a much smaller structure nearby. The old lighthouse and lens are now a key attraction of the Kilauea Point National Wildlife Refuge, a natural wonderland alive with frigatebirds, albatrosses, and other seabirds.

Travel information: Kilauea Point National Wildlife Refuge and its lighthouse are located about 10 miles northwest of Anahola off Highway 56 on Kauai. Call (808) 828–1413.

(Facing page) *Kilauea Point Light* Courtesy Bob and Sandra Shanklin

GREAT LAKES

Seul Choix Lighthouse

CANADA

Kingston •

Oswego •

Rochester •

Buffalo •

NEW YORK
12 Lights

PENNSYLVANIA
2 Lights

Toronto •

Erie •

*Lake
Ontario*

*Lake
Erie*

Cleveland •

OHIO
9 Lights

Toledo •

Sault Ste. Marie •

*Lake
Huron*

Port
Huron •

Presque
Isle •

Mackinaw
City •

MICHIGAN
Lower Peninsula
32 Lights

INDIANA
2 Lights

Grand Marais •

Muskegeon •

Michigan
City •

Sturgeon
Bay •

*Lake
Michigan*

Marquette •

MICHIGAN
Upper Peninsula
14 Lights

Chicago •

ILLINOIS
3 Lights

*Lake
Superior*

Bay Field •

Milwaukee •

WISCONSIN
34 Lights

CANADA

MICHIGAN
Isle Royale
4 Lights

Thunder
Bay •

Duluth •

MINNESOTA
6 Lights

NEW YORK

■ ROCK ISLAND LIGHT ■
Rock Island (1847)

From the mid-1800s until after World War II, ships coming up the St. Lawrence River from the Atlantic used

the Rock Island Lighthouse to help them navigate their way safely to Lake Ontario. Built in 1847 as one of six lighthouses commissioned to help ships negotiate this important passage, the Rock Island signal actually sits just off the island—a stone walkway connects the concrete foundation to the land. When the station was deactivated following World War II, its sixth-order Fresnel lens was removed.

> *Travel information:* You can see the lighthouse from Thousand Island Park on Wellesley Island or from Fisher's Landing, a community not far from the Thousand Island Bridge. There is no public transportation to Rock Island, but enough private boats make the trip to warrant summer visiting hours. For the schedule call (315) 654-2522.

■ TIBBETTS POINT LIGHT ■
Cape Vincent (1827 and 1854)

Lighthouses are nearly always strategically located, but this is especially true of Tibbetts Point Lighthouse. Its beacon marks the entrance to the St. Lawrence River and the beginning of the last leg of any journey from the Great Lakes to the Atlantic.

Originally, the stone tower stood fifty-nine feet high and employed a whale-oil lamp and reflector beacon. A major renovation in 1854 raised the tower's height by ten feet, and the addition of a fourth-order Fresnel lens (still in use) dramatically improved the light's performance. A steam-powered fog signal was added in 1896. Automated in 1981, the station now serves as a youth hostel and is a popular destination for photographers and history buffs.

> **Travel information:** From Watertown follow Highway 12F and then Highway 12E to Cape Vincent. Turn left onto Broadway and drive 2.5 miles to the lighthouse. The grounds are open daily, whereas the hostel operates mid-May to mid-October. For hostel reservations call (315) 654–3450.

To the southwest, near Sackets Harbor, is the seventy-three-foot tower of the **Stony Point Lighthouse** (1837). From New York Route 3, follow Military Road and then Lighthouse Road to Stony Point.

■ SELKIRK LIGHT (POINT ONTARIO) ■
Selkirk (Pulaski) (1838)

One of the more fascinating and historic structures on the Great Lakes, the Selkirk Lighthouse guided Lake Ontario sailors from 1838 until 1859. Taken out of service shortly before the Civil War, it remained dark for more than 130 years, but it is once again guiding mariners.

Produced by a fourteen-inch parabolic reflector-and-oil-lamp system, the original beacon could be seen from fourteen miles out in the lake. A sixth-order Fresnel lens replaced the outmoded reflector system shortly before the shrinking local economy caused lighthouse officials to snuff out the light.

The unique two-story fieldstone tower and dwelling would later be used as a hotel. At present the building, recognized for both its architectural and historic significance, is privately owned. Although not open to the public, it is sometimes rented out to overnight visitors. The light has been restored and serves as a private aid to navigation.

> **Travel information:** Take Route 3 to Port Ontario; then follow Lake Road to its end. The lighthouse stands near the mouth of the Salmon River. Contact Selkirk Lighthouse, 6 Lake Road Extension, P.O. Box 228, Pulaski, NY 13142; (315) 298–6688.

■ OSWEGO WEST PIERHEAD LIGHT ■
Oswego (1822, 1836, and 1934)

Several lighthouses have served Oswego. The first, a simple stone tower and keeper's dwelling completed in 1822, stood beside strategic Fort Ontario on the east bank of the Oswego River. But the booming shipping and fishing port of Oswego soon outgrew this modest beacon, and in 1836 a new tower was erected at the end of a long pier on the west side of the harbor. Its light, focused by a fine third-order Fresnel lens, could be seen from at least fifteen miles out in Lake Ontario.

The hearts of Lake Ontario sailors and Oswego old-timers were saddened when the Oswego Lighthouse was pulled down by wreckers in 1930, some ninety-four years after its lamps first burned. But the city's harbor would not go unmarked for long. By 1934 a new pier light was in service. It beamed from a square metal tower attached to a small dwelling at the far end of a long stone breakwater. Colored red by tinted windows, its light still shines.

Travel information: The public is not allowed to visit the lighthouse, but its white walls and red roof are visible from several places in Oswego, including Bretbeck Park. To reach the park from Route 104, turn toward the lake on West First Street, then left onto Van Buren, then right onto Lake Street. The park is just beyond Wright's Landing. While in the area, take time to visit historic Fort Ontario, where the keeper's residence of the original 1822 lighthouse can still be seen.

■ SODUS POINT LIGHT ■
Sodus Point (1825 and 1871)

In the early 1800s ship captains and residents of Sodus Point petitioned Congress for a light to mark the entrance of Sodus Bay. In 1825 Congress allocated funds, and a rough split-stone tower and dwelling went up. By the end of the Civil War, however, these structures were in a sad state of disrepair.

In 1871 a new forty-five-foot square stone tower took over the job of warning sailors. The new station served until 1903, when its light was extinguished and the still-operating **Sodus Point Pierhead Lighthouse** took over. The original 1871 structure remains, however. It now houses a maritime museum run by the Sodus Bay Historical Society. Visitors climbing the tower stairs can examine the three-and-a-half-order Fresnel lens (a type often seen on the Great Lakes) and catch a spectacular view of Sodus Bay and the lake beyond. The 1901 lighthouse, a simple square tower that resembles a chess rook, stands at the end of a nearby concrete pier.

> *Travel information:* Take Route 104, then Route 14 north to the village of Sodus Point and turn left onto Ontario Street (at the fire hall). The Old Sodus Lighthouse is open weekends, July to mid-October. For hours call (315) 483-4936.

■ CHARLOTTE-GENESEE LIGHT ■
Rochester (1822)

In 1822, the same year the **Oswego Lighthouse** went up near Fort Ontario, the Genesee beacon was first seen by sailors on Lake Ontario. It shone from atop a forty-foot octagonal limestone tower on a bluff overlooking the juncture of the Genesee River and the lake. David Denman, the first keeper, lived in an adjacent small limestone cottage and tended the station's old lamp-and-reflector system (ten Argand lamps and a set of reflectors to concentrate the light).

A more powerful and efficient fourth-order Fresnel lens replaced the reflectors in 1852. That same year, a second, smaller lighthouse was built on a nearby pier.

In 1884 the Genesee Lighthouse was discontinued, leaving the pier light to guard the shore alone. Having deteriorated over the years, the old lighthouse was slated to be torn down in 1965. To save it students at nearby Charlotte High School circulated petitions and, in time, convinced the government to hand the building over to the Charlotte-Genesee Lighthouse Historical Society. Today the handsomely restored station is counted among the Great Lakes' most historic structures.

Braddock Point Lighthouse

Travel information: In Rochester take Seaway Trail (Lakeshore Boulevard); then follow Lake Avenue north to Holy Cross Church, or take the Lake Ontario State Parkway to Lake Avenue. The lighthouse parking lot is behind the church. Grounds are open daily, and the Charlotte-Genesee Lighthouse Historical Society opens the tower and dwelling to the public on weekends. Write to Charlotte-Genesee Lighthouse Museum, 70 Lighthouse Street, Rochester, NY 14612 or call (716) 621–6179.

To the west of Rochester near the Lake Ontario State Parkway is the site of the **Braddock Point Lighthouse** (1890s). Much of the tower is gone, and the Victorian-style dwelling is now a private residence. What remains of the old station is best viewed from the water off the point.

■ THIRTY MILE POINT LIGHT ■
Somerset (1876)

This light station marks a noted headland some thirty miles east of the Niagara River. Built in 1875 at the top of Golden Hill above Thirty Mile Point, the station was constructed of squared-off gray stones shipped in from Chaumont Bay, near the St. Lawrence River. The station cost the government $90,000, but in time it proved well worth this hefty price, as it served without interruption for more than eighty years.

The beacon, produced by a classic Fresnel lens, had a focal plane seventy-eight feet above Lake Ontario and could be seen from eighteen miles out in the lake. Originally, oil or kerosene powered the lamp, but in 1885 the government installed an electric bulb—one of the first ever used in a lighthouse. Lighthouse officials were impressed with the results and noted that, with its newfangled electric bulb, Thirty Mile Point now had the strongest light on Lake Ontario and the fourth strongest on the Great Lakes.

The lighthouse served the area until 1959, when a slender steel tower with an automated signal took over its duties. The stately old lighthouse is now part of Golden Hill State Park. Self-guided tours of the well-preserved structure are a popular attraction at this historically rich site.

Travel information: To reach Golden Hill State Park, take Route 18 to Route 269 north; then turn west on Lower Lake Road. The park offers campsites, picnic tables, a marina, and an engaging nature trail in addition to the self-guided lighthouse tour. Call (716) 795–3885.

■ FORT NIAGARA LIGHT ■
Youngstown (1781, 1823, and 1872)

Around 1781 the British built a stone light tower atop Fort Niagara, which they had captured in 1759, near the end of the French and Indian War. The fort was a natural place for a navigational light, as it overlooked the strategic juncture of the Niagara River and Lake Ontario and marked the site of overland portages around Niagara Falls. Following the American Revolution, the U.S. Army took possession of the fort, but by 1796 had quit using the lighthouse. The tower was dismantled sometime between 1803 and 1806.

In 1823 a light once again shone from Fort Niagara, this time from a wooden tower. The light did not signal a revival of the old fort's commercial significance, however, for within two years the Erie Canal began diverting most of the river's east-west traffic away from the old Niagara Portage. When Canada opened its Welland Canal in 1829, Buffalo, on Lake Erie, became overnight a booming commercial center, whereas Fort Niagara settled into the life of a minor trading port.

In 1872 a new fifty-foot octagonal stone tower was completed on the lake shoreline just south of the fort, and the signal at Fort Niagara was extinguished. This new tower had eleven feet added to its height in 1900, enabling its beacon to shine out some twenty-five miles over Lake Ontario. The refurbished tower included a watch room, complete with a built-in desk for the keeper. A lamp-oil shed sat at the tower's base. This new tower served lake vessels until the 1990s. The deactivated lighthouse is one of many exhibits in Old Fort Niagara State Park, where it placidly watches over the park's numerous military reenactments.

> *Travel information:* From Niagara, New York, take the Robert Moses Parkway to the Old Fort Niagara State Park entrance. Once inside the park, follow signs to the lighthouse. Visitors should set aside plenty of time to enjoy this historic site, which is a gold mine for history buffs. Living-history exhibits and military reenactments are part of the park's summer offerings. The fort is open mid-April through Labor Day. The lighthouse is open weekends in June, then daily through Labor Day. Call (716) 745-7611.

■ BUFFALO MAIN LIGHT ■
Buffalo (1818 and 1833)

In 1805 the U.S. government designated the then village of Buffalo a port of entry and made plans to build a lighthouse there. Political squabbling delayed construction, and when British troops burned Buffalo during the War of 1812, it began to look as if the lighthouse might never be built. Buffalo recovered, however, and in 1818 the tower was finally completed.

With the opening of the Erie Canal in 1825, Buffalo became one of the fastest growing cities in America and its port one of the busiest in the world. In 1833 a new octagonal limestone tower signaled Buffalo's growing importance as a commercial center. This tower stood at the end of a 1,400-foot-long pier, its beam shining lakeward from a lantern some sixty-eight feet above the lake.

A new breakwater station went up in 1872. Built at the far end of a four-thousand-foot-long breakwater, the tower boasted a fourth-order fixed red light. The old 1833 tower stood empty and neglected for many years, but during the early 1960s, citizens began raising money to restore it. In 1987 the beacon was relit to help celebrate Buffalo's first International Friendship Festival.

Travel information: The Buffalo Main Lighthouse is on the grounds of a Coast Guard station; however, since 1985 it has been leased to the Buffalo Lighthouse Association. Nearby is the rather extraordinary **Buffalo Bottle Light** (early 1900s), which looks like a cross between a buoy and light tower. Take I-190 to the Church Street exit; then turn right at the first traffic signal onto Lower Terrace. Follow signs to the Erie Basin Marina and Buffalo Main Lighthouse. The lighthouse is best viewed, however, from the Naval and Serviceman's Park, across the river in downtown Buffalo. Call (716) 947-9126.

■ DUNKIRK (POINT GRATIOT) LIGHT ■
Point Gratiot (1829 and 1875)

The original 1829 Point Gratiot Lighthouse was the work of Buffalo contractor Jesse Peck. Like most lighthouses at the time, its lamps were fueled by whale oil. Several attempts were made to convert the station to natural gas, but the innovative experiments failed. The light was nonetheless powerful. Fitted with a third-order Fresnel lens in 1857, it produced a fifteen-thousand-candlepower beam visible from seventeen miles offshore.

After almost half a century of service, this lighthouse was replaced by the existing sixty-one-foot tower. The tower stands on a twenty-foot-high bluff. Unfortunately, its guiding light could not always prevent wrecks, and several vessels have sunk within sight of the tower. In 1893 the *Dean Richmond* sank nearby, along with a cargo of bagged meal and flour, copper sheets, $50,000 worth of pig zinc, and $141,000 in gold and silver bullion. In 1897 the *Idaho* went down with a load of merchandise intended to be sold as Christmas presents. Afterward, large slabs of chocolate washed up on shore.

Currently the light station at Point Gratiot serves not only as an active navigation station, but also as a military memorial, and the seven-room keeper's home now houses one of the best lighthouse museums on the Great Lakes. The station's original third-order Fresnel lens remains in use.

> ***Travel information:*** The lighthouse complex is in Dunkirk, just off Route 5, which parallels the lakeshore northwest of the New York State Thruway (I-90). The complex is open daily from April through November and at other times upon request. Call ahead to find out about special events such as War of 1812 reenactments, craft shows, and lighthouse moonlight cruises: (716) 366-5050.

■ BARCELONA LIGHT ■
Barcelona (1829)

The Barcelona Lighthouse's claim to fame is its distinction as the first public building in the United States—and perhaps the only lighthouse in the world—to be illuminated by gas. The structure stands near a gas-emitting spring, so the experiment in using this alternative fuel source was a natural.

The lighthouse, built in 1829 on a bluff in Portland Harbor, as it was then called, had conventional oil lamps and a fourteen-inch reflector. Three years after it began operating, residents of this community made an astonishing discovery: a pool of water that would, on occasion, catch fire. This "burning spring" produced natural gas, which was soon piped to the tower and put to work guiding ships. The gas, burned in a specially designed lamp, produced a flame so intense that sailors on Lake Erie sometimes reported that the whole lighthouse seemed on fire.

Sometime after 1838 the gas ran out and the Barcelona keeper had to replace the tower's original oil lamps.

In 1859 the lighthouse achieved another distinction, this one embarrassing. Government inspectors discovered that the station had been a mistake from the first. The light had been built to guide vessels into Barcelona's harbor, but Barcelona, as it turned out, had no harbor. The light was immediately discontinued.

Despite its short career the lighthouse survived and still stands today. Now a private residence, the forty-foot conical tower and its keeper's cottage are so attractive that they are often depicted on postcards. The lantern was removed long ago, but a wooden framework at the top suggests the tower's original function.

Travel information: Located just off I-90 on East Lake Road (Route 5) in Barcelona, the lighthouse is a private residence not open to the public. The structure can be seen from the public right-of-way, but visitors are asked to please not trespass on the private property.

PENNSYLVANIA

■ PRESQUE ISLE LIGHT ■
Erie (1819, 1867, and 1873)

In French *presque isle* means "almost an island." A port town that grew up on the shore of Lake Erie apparently used the term to refer to their long, narrow peninsula. The peninsula came close to also being "almost Pennsylvania," for, originally, Pennsylvania had no shore frontage on Lake Erie. Recognizing the strategic importance of access to the new country's inland seas, the state bought a forty-five-mile stretch of beaches and inlets immediately after the Revolutionary War. Included in the purchase was a fine harbor at a place that later would become Erie, Pennsylvania.

Here, during the War of 1812, Lieutenant Oliver Hazard Perry built the fleet of American warships that defeated the British in the famous Battle of Lake Erie. A few years later, the government acknowledged Erie's strategic importance and growth as a port by erecting one of the first Great Lakes lighthouses here. Built in 1819 with large blocks of sandstone, on the sandy lakeshore across from Presque Isle, the **Erie Land Lighthouse** operated until the late 1890s.

In 1873 a brick lighthouse was built at the

end of Presque Isle, a seven-mile-long finger of sand stretching into the lake. The lantern at the top of its sixty-eight-foot tower held a fourth-order Fresnel lens, which displayed a fixed white light. This light station is still active, but these days the Fresnel is gone, replaced by an automated airport-style beacon.

Erie Land Lighthouse

Travel information: The current Presque Isle Lighthouse is in Presque Isle State Park; call (814) 833-7424. From I-79 take Pennsylvania Alternate Route 5 west. At the fourth streetlight turn right onto Route 832 (Peninsula Drive) and continue north to the park entrance. The lighthouse is located about 3 miles from the entrance. The restored Erie Land Lighthouse is in Dunn Park. To reach the park follow Lake Road East about half a mile beyond East Avenue, and then turn toward Lake Erie onto Lighthouse Street. The Erie North Pierhead Lighthouse (1858) still marks Erie's historic harbor. It is located in Presque Isle State Park.

OHIO

▪ ASHTABULA LIGHT ▪
Ashtabula (1916)

The squat Ashtabula Light sits on the end of a long breakwater, where it marks the entrance to the harbor at Ashtabula, Ohio. Lighthouses have guided ships from this location since 1835. The current light has been in operation since 1916. Nearby is the Great Lakes Marine and U.S. Coast Guard Memorial Museum.

Travel information: Visitors can view the lighthouse from Point Park, near the intersection of Walnut and Hulbert Streets, in the Ashtabula waterfront district. The museum, open weekends and holiday afternoons June through October, is across from the park. For more information call (440) 964-6847.

■ FAIRPORT HARBOR LIGHT ■
Fairport (1825, 1871, and 1925)

The original Fairport Harbor Light began its long career of welcoming immigrants to the American Midwest in 1825, the same year the Erie Canal opened. Fairport served as an important refueling and supply port for passenger and freight steamers bound westward from Buffalo, New York.

The original 1825 brick tower at Fairport was thirty feet high, had supporting walls three feet thick at ground level, and was capped with an octagonal iron lantern. Its two-story keeper's house had spacious rooms, each with plastered walls, three windows, and a fireplace.

But by mid-century the tower and keeper's cottage were badly deteriorated, and in 1869 Congress appropriated $30,000 to replace them. Four years later a new sandstone tower, fitted with a third-order Fresnel lens, was ready to begin operating. The lighthouse served until 1925, when a combination light and foghorn station took over. The federal government planned to raze the old lighthouse, but local citizens launched a campaign to save the historic structure. In 1941 Fairport leased the lighthouse from the Coast Guard. Presently the Fairport Harbor Historical Society maintains the lighthouse and keeper's dwelling as a marine museum.

> *Travel information:* The lighthouse and museum—noted for its collection of artifacts from the early days of the Lighthouse Service—are at the northwest corner of Second and High Streets in the village of Fairport Harbor. From U.S. Highway 20 at Painesville, follow either Route 283 or Route 535 to the village. The museum is open from 1:00 to 6:00 P.M. on Wednesday, Saturday, Sunday, and legal holidays from Memorial Day through Labor Day. Call (440) 354-4825. Across the harbor is the still-active **Fairport West Breakwater Lighthouse** (1925).

■ WEST PIERHEAD LIGHT ■
Cleveland (circa 1910)

A pair of lighthouses, the West Pierhead Light and the **East Pierhead Light,** mark either side of Cleveland's harbor. Both date from about 1910. The west light marks the entrance to the navigable Cuyahoga River as well as the entrance to the inner harbor. Its thirty-foot brick tower and connected steel foghorn building are painted white with green trim. At night floodlights make the light station a landmark attraction of the harborscape.

The West Pierhead beacon, visible from ten miles away, passes through a fourth-order Fresnel lens and has a focal plane sixty-three feet above the lake surface. The station's foghorn was originally operated by steam. The deep-throated horn, the story goes, sounded so animal-like that the horn

became known locally as "the cow." Despite its peculiar sound the horn was effective. On foggy nights its warning could be heard up to twelve miles out.

The East Pierhead Light stands about half a mile across the harbor from its counterpart. The small tower sits on a circular platform protected by a low wall of steel and stone, which marks the tip of an extensive breakwater that forms the Cleveland inner harbor and helps protect the shoreline from storm-driven waves.

Travel information: From I-90 in downtown Cleveland, take the Ohio Highway 2 exit, drive west about 1 mile to the Ninth Street exit, and turn right. Then follow Ninth Street for about two blocks and park in the lot beside the harbor. You can see both lighthouses from many points along the waterfront, but harbor cruises may offer the best views.

■ LORAIN LIGHT ■
Lorain (1837 and 1917)

The original navigational light at Lorain, Ohio, was a lantern hung from the end of a pole on the Lake Erie shoreline, but by 1837 a full-fledged lighthouse had taken over. The new light, however, was not much of an improvement. The tower, built at the end of a pier, was wooden, and its lamps burned soot-producing lard oil. In contrast the present light tower is a monument to lighthouse technology. Its 1917 builders, the Army Corps of Engineers, used hundreds of tons of concrete and fill to form a foundation massive enough to resist Lake Erie's awesome storm waves. They constructed concrete-and-steel walls ten inches thick to protect keepers from gale-force winds.

Interestingly, although built like a fortress, the structure has the appearance of an old-fashioned, two-story town home. The chimney, rising from one end of its red-tiled pitched roof, gives the building a domestic air. But the short, square tower, which protruded a few feet from one corner of the roof, and the small, cast-iron lantern room perched atop it made clear that this was no ordinary residence, as indeed it wasn't. For almost half a century, a rotating fourth-order Fresnel lens flashed its light from the lantern room's diamond-shaped windows every ten seconds. Mariners could see the beam fifteen miles out on the lake.

By 1965 times had caught up with the Lorain Lighthouse. A small, fully

Courtesy David Kramer

automated light tower at the tip of a recently constructed breakwater took over navigational duties, and the old building was scheduled for demolition. Lorain citizens began mobilizing to save their town's landmark. Eventually, a five-year struggle with government officials to save the lighthouse ended in success. Saving the old tower was no easy—or inexpensive—task, however. Five hundred cubic yards of grout and $850,000 were required to keep it from falling into the lake.

Travel information: From U.S. Highway 6, turn north onto Oberlin Avenue and drive approximately 3 blocks to the parking area at the municipal pier. The lighthouse can be viewed from the north end of the parking area and from several other points along the Lake Erie shore.

■ VERMILION LIGHT ■
Vermilion (1877 and 1991)

The perky red, white, and black lighthouse that visitors see at Vermilion today has never been a commissioned light station. Rather, this is a 1991 replica of the 1877 Vermilion Lighthouse. The original had a long record of service—it operated until

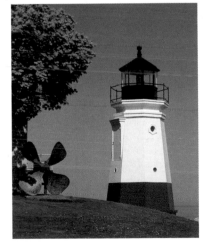

1929. But its many years of pounding by Lake Erie storms left both tower and foundation in such a state of deterioration that the Lighthouse Service was afraid the structure would collapse. Rather than risk this, they had the structure demolished.

Sixty years later, construction of the replica began. At present this monument to local history is one of the featured exhibits of the Inland Seas Maritime Museum in Vermilion.

Travel information: The lighthouse and museum are at the end of Main Street, about 3 blocks north of U.S. Highway 6 in Vermilion. For more information contact the Inland Seas Maritime Museum, P.O. Box 435, Vermilion, OH 44089; call (440) 967-3467.

■ MARBLEHEAD LIGHT ■
Bay Point (1821)

Marblehead is home to the oldest active light tower on the Great Lakes. Its beacon has faithfully served mariners since the station began operating in 1821. The old stone tower has changed very little over the last one hundred eighty years, although ten feet were added to the height of the original fifty-five-foot tower in the late

nineteenth century. The station's fourth-order Fresnel lens still displays a flashing green light over Lake Erie, as it has for years and years.

The lighthouse has stood silent witness to a lot of history; for instance, a nearly successful attempt by Confederate partisans to rescue prisoners of war on nearby Johnson Island. The would-be rescuers commandeered a passenger steamer and headed toward the island only to encounter the mighty Union gunboat *Michigan,* which guarded the approach. No match for the *Michigan*'s heavy cannon, the Confederates' first and only Great Lakes warship fled for Canadian waters, where it was scuttled.

The lighthouse still watches over history from its strategic location at the entrance to Sandusky Bay. Although it remains an active light station, its keeper's dwelling has been converted to a museum run by the Ottawa County Historical Society.

> **Travel information:** From U.S. Highway 2 at Port Clinton, take Route 163 to Marblehead. A convenient parking area offers a good view of the light. Contact the Marblehead Lighthouse State Park at (419) 797–4530.

■ TOLEDO HARBOR LIGHT ■
Toledo (1904)

Toledo's century-old light station is surely one of the architectural wonders of the Great Lakes. With its chocolate-colored brick walls, Romanesque arches, and bulging round-edge roof, it has been described as a cross between a Victorian

palace and a Russian Orthodox church. Its outward appearance belies the solidness of its construction. The station sits on a massive concrete-and-stone crib that rises almost twenty feet above the water, and its three-story, thick brick walls are topped with a light tower, which pushes it even higher.

The lighthouse was situated

Courtesy David Kramer

well offshore in 1904 to mark a channel the Army Corps of Engineers dredged from Lake Erie into the Maumee River. This channel opened Toledo's harbor to an influx of deep-water freighter traffic. Together, channel and lighthouse helped the city capture its share of Great Lakes commerce.

Some say that the lighthouse is haunted, whereas others maintain that the U.S. Coast Guard began rumors of a ghost to discourage vandals. Another source of ghost stories may be the mannequin that occupies the still-active lighthouse. This fully uniformed inhabitant took up residence in 1965, when the light became automated and the last keeper came ashore for good. The station's original 3.5-order Fresnel lens remains in use.

Travel information: The only way to get a good look at the Toledo Harbor Lighthouse is from a boat. The active station is off-limits to visitors, but its distinctive red and white flashing light is visible from many points along the Toledo shoreline.

MICHIGAN
LOWER PENINSULA

■ LIGHTSHIP *HURON* ■
Port Huron (1921)

Commissioned in 1921 as *Lightship No. 103*, the vessel know today as the *Huron* was used as a relief ship for Lake Michigan's Twelfth Lighthouse District. The *103* would replace lightships temporarily out of service while under repair. After fourteen years of filling in for others, the *103* took over a station of its own at Gray's Reef, Michigan. Later it served at Manitou Shoals on northern Lake Michigan, then in 1935 at Corsica Shoals in Lake Huron. Here its beacon helped guide traffic in and out of the narrow dredged channel that allowed large vessels to navigate the St. Clair River and lower Lake Huron.

The ninety-seven-foot lightship came equipped with a fifty-two-and-a-half-foot lantern mast and a five-thousand-pound mushroom anchor. It originally was steam powered, but in 1949 it received a diesel engine, radar, and a radio beacon.

The *Huron* was the last lightship to serve on the Great Lakes.

When it was finally decommissioned in 1970, the city of Port Huron bought the ship. Two years later *Lightship 103* began a new era of service, this time as a museum and National Historic Landmark.

Travel information: The lightship rests in Pine Grove Park in Port Huron. From I-94 drive south onto Pine Grove Street (M-25), turn left onto Prospect Street, and follow it 1 block to the parking area. The lightship and museum are open from 1:00 to 4:30 P.M. Wednesday through Sunday in July and August and weekends in May, June, and September. Call (810) 982-0891.

■ FORT GRATIOT LIGHT ■
Port Huron (1825 and 1829)

In addition to the *Huron*, the last lightship to serve the Great Lakes, Port Huron can also boast Michigan's oldest light station. The Fort Gratiot Light station dates

from 1825, well before Michigan became a state in 1837. After almost one and three-quarters centuries of service, the station still marks the Lake Huron entrance to the St. Clair River.

The original tower did not last long. The materials and workmanship were so shoddy that the tower collapsed within four years. A new tower went up in 1829, this one more sturdily constructed, with thick, conical walls of stone overlaid with brick. It still stands and remains in operation. Automated in 1933, its eighty-two-foot height gives the beacon a focal plane eighty-six feet above Lake Michigan. The white tower, redbrick keeper's cottage, and fog-whistle house are an active Coast Guard facility and rarely open to the public. In deference to its historic significance, however, visitors are allowed on the grounds a few times a year so that they can view Michigan's oldest lighthouse up close and personal.

Travel information: From I-94 take Pine Grove Street (M-25) north. Turn right onto Garfield Street and follow it to Gratiot Avenue. Parking is available in the area. For tours call (810) 982-3659 or ask at the nearby Huron Lightship Museum (see above Travel information).

■ PORT SANILAC LIGHT ■
Port Sanilac (1886)

Once a vital link in a 300-mile chain of navigational lights guiding vessels along Michigan's eastern shores, the Port Sanilac beacon was the first light mariners saw as they exited the St. Clair River and steamed northward into Lake Huron. Although its importance as a navigational aid has diminished with time, the light remains in operation. The fourth-order Fresnel lens atop the sixty-nine-foot octagonal tower remains in use. The station's unusual step-sided brick keeper's dwelling is now a private residence.

Travel information: Now a private home, the lighthouse is not open to the public. However, it can be viewed from the end of a breakwater off Cherry Street in Port Sanilac.

■ POINTE AUX BARQUES LIGHT ■
Port Austin (1848 and 1857)

This lighthouse is located on a strategic headland near the spot where Saginaw Bay opens into Lake Huron. French traders called the place Pointe Aux Barques or "Point

of Little Boats," because of the many canoes that used to gather here during fur-trading season. A town grew up here and, after Michigan became part of the United States, grew into a prime shipping port.

In 1848 the federal government approved $5,000 to build a lighthouse at Pointe Aux Barques. It proved far less than adequate, and nine years later, it was replaced by the eighty-nine-foot conical brick tower that still stands here. Originally fitted with a state-of-the-art third-order Fresnel lens, the station now employs an automated optic. Its powerful flashing white light is visible from eighteen miles out on Lake Huron. The beautiful old classic lens that once served here can now be seen at the Grice Museum in Port Austin.

Travel information: To reach the lighthouse take M-25 to Lighthouse Road. The county park, where the lighthouse stands, is about 10 miles east of Port Austin and 6 miles north of Port Hope. The park offers camping and picnicking facilities. The museum and gift shop are open weekends from noon to 4:00 P.M. Memorial Day through Labor Day. Located less than a mile northwest of the lighthouse, the Huron City Museum offers exhibits depicting nineteenth-century life and times. Museum hours are 10:00 A.M. to 5:00 P.M. daily, except Tuesday, July through Labor Day. The museum can be reached from M-25 via Huron City Road. Call (989) 428-4749.

■ TAWAS POINT LIGHT ■
Tawas City (1853 and 1876)

Built in 1853 to mark the northern entrance to Saginaw Bay, the first Tawas Point Lighthouse served for only twenty years. By the 1870s the rapidly shifting shoreline had placed the light more than a mile from the water, rendering it useless. The Lighthouse Board appealed to Congress for funds to build a new structure, and in

1876 a sixty-seven-foot tower, fitted with a rotating fourth-order Fresnel lens, began operating on a site closer to the bay. Its light can still be seen.

The Tawas Point Lighthouse now serves as the residence for a high-ranking Coast Guard officer and sits on the grounds of Tawas Point State Park. Tours of the tower are available during summer.

Travel information: Take U.S. Highway 23 to about 1½ miles west of Tawas City; then turn right onto Tawas Beach Road, which will take you to Tawas Point State Park; call (517) 362-5041. Drive to the beach parking area at the end of the road. Follow the walking path to the lighthouse. The tower is open to the public in June, and the Coast Guard offers tours during most summer months. Call (989) 362-4429.

■ STURGEON POINT LIGHT ■
Alcona (1870)

Not far from Sturgeon Point on Lake Huron, a potentially deadly reef lies in wait for unwary vessels. Built in 1870 to warn mariners to steer clear of this dangerous obstacle, the Sturgeon Point Light has prevented countless accidents. Even so, many vessels have wrecked practically in the shadow of its sixty-eight-foot tower.

On the station grounds sits a big rudder salvaged from the wooden steamer *Marine City,* which burned near here in an 1880 disaster just off Sturgeon Point. Also lost nearby were the 233-ton schooner *Venus* in 1887, the three-masted schooner *Ispeming* in 1903, the *Clifton* in a 1924 gale, and many other vessels.

The Alcona County Historical Society owns the station, and the old keeper's residence houses museum exhibits. The light, automated since 1939, remains active. Occasionally visitors are allowed to climb the tower's eighty-five steps to the lantern room, where the station's three-and-a-half-order lens sits ready to beam its warning out across the lake.

Travel information: To reach the lighthouse take U.S. Highway 23 north from Harrisville; then follow Lakeshore Drive and Point Road to Sturgeon Point. The parking lot is less than a mile down the road. The museum is open daily from Memorial Day to Labor Day. During the fall-color season, the museum is open weekends. For hours call (989) 724-5107.

■ MIDDLE ISLAND LIGHT ■
North of Alpena (1905)

Established in 1905, the Middle Island Light station was automated and abandoned by the Coast Guard years ago. However, thanks to a hardworking group of lighthouse preservationists, this handsome seventy-one-foot island tower north of Alpena is being restored to tip-top condition. Known as the Middle Island Light Keepers Association, the group hopes to open the station to guests as a bed-and-breakfast inn.

Travel information: The lighthouse is accessible only by boat. Contact the Middle Island Light Keepers Association, 5671 Rockport Road, Alpena, MI 49707; (989) 595-2821. The same group helps sponsor and organize the Great Lakes Lighthouse Festival held each October in Alpena. Across the Thunder Bay River from Alpena is the spindly-legged, red metal tower of the **Alpena Lighthouse** (1914), known affectionately to some locals as "Sputnik."

■ NEW PRESQUE ISLE LIGHT ■
Presque Isle (1871)

A treasure trove of lighthouses awaits visitors at Presque Isle, home to no less than four light towers. The oldest, a thirty-foot stone-and-brick structure now known as **Old Presque Isle Lighthouse,** served the peninsula from 1840 to 1871. During the Civil War a pair of range lights were built to mark the channel for vessels

bound in and out of the harbor. In addition, President Abraham Lincoln authorized construction of a new, higher light tower at the main light station. The New Presque Isle Lighthouse took several years to complete and finally went into service in 1871. The 113-foot tower, one of the highest on the Great Lakes, still holds its original third-order Fresnel lens. Its beacon is visible from up to twenty-five miles away.

The Old and New Presque Isle Light towers and the two peninsula range lights now stand in neighborly proximity. The New Presque Isle Light sits amid a scenic one-hundred-acre park maintained by the Presque Isle Township. All four lighthouses are easily accessible and together give visitors an unusually complete look at the history of a light station.

Old Presque Isle Lighthouse

Travel information: From Presque Isle, follow Grand Lake Road past the intersection of Highway 638, or from U.S. Highway 23 take Highway 638 to Grand Lake Road and turn left. The Old Presque Isle Lighthouse and Museum are just over half a mile to the north. The front- and rear-range light towers stand nearby. From the museum, continue north about 1 mile on Grand Lake Road to New Presque Isle Lighthouse, where you'll find a second museum and gift shop; call (989) 595-9917. For the Old Presque Isle Lighthouse Museum, call (989) 595-2787.

■ FORTY MILE POINT LIGHT ■
Rogers City (1897)

One of the last dark stretches facing ships navigating the Great Lakes was finally lit when the Forty Mile Point Lighthouse beacon began to flash in 1897. Shining from a square brick tower equipped with a fourth-order Fresnel lens, the light guided vessels passing between Cheboygan and Presque Isle.

The architecturally interesting dwelling features two gables, one on either side of the light tower. A brick oil house and fog-signal building complete the station. Although well maintained, the tower, dwelling, and other structures are not open to the public at this time. Nonetheless, the site is well worth a visit. The grounds and buildings are lovely, and the beach below the lighthouse features the hulk of a wooden ship that wrecked here long ago.

Travel information: Drive about 6 miles north of Rogers City on U.S. Highway 23. Look for a sign pointing the way to Presque Isle County Lighthouse Park. Turn right onto an otherwise unmarked road and follow it to the lighthouse (do not take Forty Mile Point Road).

■ MICHIGAN REEF LIGHTS ■

Northwestern Lake Huron

During the late nineteenth century, the growth of shipping on the Great Lakes focused attention on the dangers of the Straits of Mackinac, the link connecting Lake Huron to Lake Michigan. Here Huron narrows to a mere few miles in width, forcing ships to run a gauntlet of treacherous shallows and killer reefs. Some believed this stretch of water to be the most dangerous in all the Great Lakes. To make navigation safer the government marked the most threatening obstacles with lighthouses, some of them built in open water directly over the shoals. They were all part of the network of markers that evolved to help vessels maneuver safely through these waters.

After the submerged claws of Spectacle Reef hooked a pair of large schooners in 1867, Congress approved funds to mark the shoal with a lighthouse. The job took $406,000 and two hundred men working nearly four years, but by 1874 the

Courtesy U.S. Coast Guard

Spectacle Reef Lighthouse

Courtesy U.S. Coast Guard

Poe Reef Lighthouse

Courtesy National Archives

Detour Reef Lighthouse

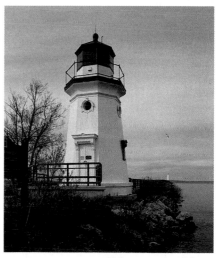

Cheboygan Crib Lighthouse

Spectacle Reef Lighthouse was at last complete. Its beacon, now solar-powered, still warns ships.

The **Round Island Lighthouse** (1895), near Mackinac Island, has been partially restored and reactivated. The **Poe Reef Lighthouse** (1929), remains in operation, as does the **Detour Reef Lighthouse** (1931), now undergoing extensive restoration. All are now automated. These reef lighthouses are not open to the public, and most are difficult to view from land.

Round Island Lighthouse

The **Cheboygan Crib Lighthouse** (1910), at one time located offshore on a concrete-and-stone crib, was decommissioned when its foundation settled into the lake. The town of Cheboygan salvaged the structure and gave it a new home at the end of a short pier in a park.

> *Travel information:* Michigan's reef lighthouses are off-limits to the public. The exception is Cheboygan Crib Lighthouse, located in a city park at the end of Huron Street, off U.S. Highway 23 in Cheboygen. Nearby is the **Cheboygan River Front Range Lighthouse** (1880).

■ OLD MACKINAC POINT LIGHT ■
Mackinaw City (1892)

In 1957 a bridge over Mackinac Straits opened, making the Old Mackinac Point Light obsolete. Vessels began taking bearings from the long string of bridge lights, and the beacon at the top of the forty-foot-tall, turn-of-the-century station was soon turned off. Within three years the building had been converted into a maritime museum.

The original Mackinaw City station opened in 1890 as a fog-signal station. It was, obviously, much needed. During one amazingly foggy two-week stretch, hard-working stokers burned fifty-two cords of wood to keep its boilers filled with steam.

By late 1892 a lighthouse was ready to supplement the fog signal, and the forty-foot tower, equipped with a fourth-order lens, began a stint of service that ended only after the 1957 bridge opened up. Today the buff-colored station, with its bright red roof, is part of a historical park run by the Mackinac Island State Park Commission.

> *Travel information:* Take I-75 to exit 336. From this exit follow Nicolet Avenue through Mackinaw City and turn right onto Huron Avenue. The Old Mackinac Point Lighthouse parking area is about two blocks down Huron

Avenue. The lighthouse sits in a park that overlooks the Mackinac Bridge. Picnic tables and lovely surroundings will tempt you to make this a leisurely stop. The lighthouse is being restored and when the work is complete, the station's fourth-order Fresnel lens will be returned to the tower. For a status report call (906) 847-3328.

■ SOUTH MANITOU ISLAND LIGHT ■
South Manitou Island (1839 and 1872)

Among the most impressive structures on the Great Lakes is the white conical tower of South Manitou Island Lighthouse. Soaring 104 feet into the skies over Lake Michigan, its stark white walls now seem a natural part of the pristine island that surrounds them. The tower and keeper's dwelling have been empty since 1958, when the Coast Guard decommissioned the station. Handsomely restored by the U.S. Park Service, they are now part of the Sleeping Bear Dunes National Lakeshore.

Built in 1872 to replace an early structure, this grand lighthouse once marked the Manitou Passage for ships navigating the tricky Mackinac Straits. Its powerful light, seen from a distance of eighteen miles, was produced by a third-order Fresnel lens.

Travel information: To reach the South Manitou Island Lighthouse, take the ferry from Leland, on the mainland. For schedules and prices call (231) 256-9061. Passengers can get a good view of the **North Manitou Island Shoal Light-house** (1935) during the passage. The South Manitou Light-house is a short hike from the ferry slip. The Sleeping Bear Dunes National Lake-shore offices can be reached at (231) 326-5134.

■ BEAVER ISLAND LIGHT ■
Beaver Island (1858)

Well north of the Manitou Islands is historic Beaver Island, where radical Mormon James Jesse Strang at one time reigned as a self-styled king. He had already been deposed by 1858, when the island became the home of the forty-six-foot-high, yellow-brick Beaver Island Lighthouse and its attached two-story keeper's dwelling.

The Beaver Island station was once a popular destination for picnickers, who rode sleighs over the winter ice from Charlevoix, on the mainland. Occasionally, even cars made the trip. In 1929 three Model T Fords set out for the island only to get lost in the fog. The resident keeper finally guided them to safety with the station's fog bell. The Coast Guard kept the light in operation until 1970. At present the building serves a different use: It is now an environmental education center for Charlevoix County public schools.

> *Travel information:* A ferry from Charlevoix provides access to Beaver Island. The three-hour ride can be expensive. For schedules and prices call (231) 547–2311.

■ ST. HELENA ISLAND LIGHT ■
St. Helena Island (1873)

Established in 1873, the St. Helena Light served ships passing through the Mackinac Straits. Automated in 1922, the seventy-one-foot brick tower and attached dwelling suffered greatly from neglect and vandalism. It might have fallen into ruin, but believing it deserved a better fate, the Great Lakes Lighthouse Keepers Association has begun the formidable task of repairing and caring for the structure. Michigan Boy Scouts can earn Eagle Scout badges by helping with restoration work.

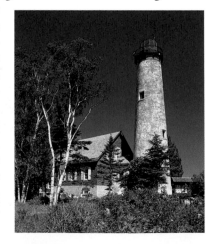

> *Travel information:* St. Helena Island can be reached by boat from St. Ignace. For information on the lighthouse restoration project, write to Great Lakes Lighthouse Keepers Association, P.O. Box 580, Allen Park, MI 48101, or call (313) 662–1200.

■ CHARLEVOIX SOUTH PIERHEAD LIGHT ■
Charlevoix (1885 and 1948)

A narrow, mile long channel links the pristine waters of Lake Charlevoix to Lake Michigan. Ferries, Coast Guard patrol boats, and other vessels are guided in and out of the channel by the red flash of the Charlevoix Lighthouse beacon. Established in 1885, this light has served mariners for more than a century. The existing metal structure replaced an earlier wooden tower in 1948.

Travel information: Charlevoix is located on U.S. Highway 31 about 50 miles north of Traverse City. A parking area off Grant Street provides a good view of the lighthouse.

■ OLD MISSION POINT LIGHT ■
Near Traverse City (1879)

Interestingly, this light station is located on the forty-fifth parallel, exactly halfway between the North Pole and the equator. Most of the mariners who depended on this light, however, were more likely interested in the fact that the Mission Point beacon marked the far end of the slender—and sometimes dangerous—peninsula that divides Traverse Bay. Established in 1879, the station was deactivated in 1933. Nowadays, the combination wooden tower and dwelling serve as the central attraction of a local park.

Travel information: From Traverse City follow M–37 north to its end. A small historical park surrounds the lighthouse.

■ GRAND TRAVERSE LIGHT ■
North Port (1853)

Built in 1853 on strategic Cat Head Point, this lighthouse commanded the entrance to Grand Traverse Bay, guiding ships with a beacon produced by a relatively small fourth-order Fresnel lens. The light beamed out into the lake from atop a square tower that rose just above the roofline of a large, two-story brick dwelling. After serving mariners for almost one and a quarter centuries, the old lighthouse was retired in 1972, its duties taken over by a nearby skeleton tower. The structure currently houses an excellent lighthouse museum. Among its exhibits is a fourth-order Fresnel lens.

Travel information: The lighthouse is located in Leelanau State Park, at the end of a long peninsula pointing northward into Lake Michigan. From Traverse City follow M–22 to Northport and then CR–201 to the park. Contact the Grand Traverse Lighthouse Museum at (231) 386–7195.

■ POINT BETSIE LIGHT ■
Frankfort (1858)

Built in 1858 to mark a key turning place for ships moving in or out of the strategic Manitou Passage, the Point Betsie Lighthouse has long been considered among the most important navigational aids on the Great Lakes. The original thirty-seven-foot tower and attached two-story dwelling still stand, and the light still shines each night.

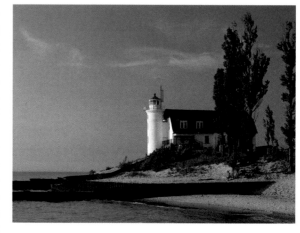

The Point Betsie Lighthouse was among the last light stations on the Great Lakes to be automated. Resident keepers operated the light until 1983, when electronic machinery took over the job.

Travel information: Used as a private residence, the lighthouse is not open to the public but can be viewed from Point Betsie Road, off M–22 about 5 miles north of Frankfort.

■ BIG SABLE POINT LIGHT ■
Ludington (1867)

The construction of the 107-foot Big Sable Point Lighthouse in 1867 helped fill one of the last dark stretches along the western Michigan shore. The light, produced by a third-order Fresnel lens, helped coast-hugging vessels avoid the point and reach Ludington safely. So did the station's powerful foghorn, which proved quite a bit more efficient than its predecessor. Previously, local citizens had warned ships away from the point by firing up an old steam engine and giving a blast on its whistle.

Wind and weather hammered away at the tower's brick walls, and by the 1920s the lighthouse was in danger of collapse. To protect it officials had the tower encased in a shell of riveted iron plates. Painted in broad white and black bands, the Big Sable Point tower is one of the most distinctive structures on the Great Lakes. Now part of Ludington State Park, the station remains in operation.

Travel information: From U.S. Highway 10 in Ludington, turn right onto Lakeshore Drive and follow it for approximately 6 miles to Ludington State Park. The lighthouse can be reached via a half-mile walk up the beach from the parking lot. Also in the area is the **Ludington Pierhead Light,** which can be reached by following Ludington Avenue to Stearns Park. Built early in the twentieth century, it stands on a concrete base that looks something like the bow of a ship.

■ LITTLE SABLE POINT LIGHT ■
Mears (1874)

When completed in 1874, the tower at Little Sable Point was nearly a twin of its sister lighthouse at Big Sable Point. Both towers stood 107 feet tall, both were constructed of brick, and both were fitted with third-order Fresnel lenses. But unlike its neighbor, which was eventually covered in steel plates, the Little Sable tower still looks much the way it did more than one and a quarter centuries ago.

The keeper's dwelling was demolished when the station was automated during the 1950s, leaving the tower to stand a solitary vigil. One of the loveliest lighthouses on the lakes, its redbrick walls offer a handsome contrast to the white dunes of Silver Lake State Park. The station's original Fresnel lens remains in use.

Travel information: From U.S. Highway 31 near Mears, turn west on Shelby Road and follow the signs to Silver Lake State Park. For the nearby **White River Lighthouse** (1875), turn west off U.S. Highway 31 on White Lake Road, and then follow South Shore Road and Murray Road. Discontinued in 1941, the combination tower and dwelling houses the delightful Great Lakes Marine Museum. Inside, visitors will find on display the station's original fourth-order Fresnel lens. Call (231) 894–8265.

Courtesy John W. Weil

White River Lighthouse

■ MUSKEGON SOUTH PIER LIGHT ■
Muskegon (1903)

The eastern shores of Lake Michigan are marked by several of the most beautiful and distinctive pier lighthouses in America. Located on often lengthy stone or concrete piers that place them well out in the lake, these towers guide vessels in and out of harbors and warn them away from the piers and other dangerous obstacles. Many of the Michigan pier lighthouses were built during a flurry of construction in the early 1900s.

As is the case with several of these offshore towers, the Muskegon South Pier Lighthouse is painted bright red for better daytime visibility. Built in 1903, the tower is forty-eight feet high, and its lantern holds a fourth-order Fresnel lens. The tower and its light guide vessels through the passage that links Muskegon Lake with the open waters of Lake Michigan.

Travel information: In Muskegon take Sherman Boulevard to Beach Street and follow it to Pere Marquette Park. The pier and lighthouse are located just north of the park, which offers excellent swimming and picnicking.

■ GRAND HAVEN PIER LIGHTS ■
Grand Haven (1895)

Among the most striking of Michigan's pier lighthouses are those that mark the entrance to Grand Haven River,

which offers one of the state's best deep-water harbors. Known as the Grand Haven South Pierhead Inner Light and Pier Light, they stand several hundred feet apart on a long stone pier. The inner tower, which was built in 1895, consists of a fifty-one-foot steel cylinder topped by a small lantern. The squat pierhead tower was originally the station's fog-signal building and was moved to its present location when the pier was extended in 1905. A tiny lantern nestles on the roof. The towers have been sheathed in iron to protect them from the lake's destructive, storm-driven waves.

Travel information: From U.S. Highway 31 in Grand Haven, follow Franklin Avenue and South Harbor Drive to Grand Haven State Park. The pier is open to the public and attracts droves of fishermen. The park also offers picnicking and swimming.

To the south are the **Holland Harbor (Black Lake) Lighthouse** (1936) and **South Haven South Pier Lighthouse** (1903). Both are painted bright red for visibility and sheathed in steel to protect them from the elements. In Holland follow Ottawa Beach Road to Holland State Park. In South Haven follow Phoenix and

Grand Haven South Pierhead Light

Water Streets to the South Beach parking area. The light can be photographed and enjoyed from a nearby public park.

■ HOLLAND HARBOR (BLACK LAKE) LIGHT ■
Holland (1872 and 1936)

When it was completed in 1936, the existing Holland Harbor Lighthouse was sheathed in steel, and no wonder. Located at the end of a long pier, the little twenty-two-foot structure takes a tremendous pounding during heavy weather. The tower rises through the slate roof of the main station building.

Travel information: In Holland turn west onto Douglas Avenue and drive approximately 6 miles to Holland State Park. For tours of this and other nearby lighthouses, contact the West Michigan Lighthouse Association at (800) 442–2084.

■ SOUTH HAVEN LIGHT ■
South Haven (1872 and 1902)

South Haven seems just the sort of place to shop for antiques, and not surprisingly, this quaint lakeside community can boast its own antique lighthouse. Located at the far end of the harbor pier, the red cast-iron tower is still an active aid to navigation. Its original fifth-order Fresnel lens remains in place, warning mariners with a flashing red light.

Travel information: From U.S. Highway 31, follow Route 196 West, then Phoenix and Water Streets to South Haven's sandy beach. The lighthouse can be reached by walking a long concrete pier, but do not chance it in rough weather.

■ ST. JOSEPH NORTH PIER LIGHTS ■
St. Joseph (1907)

Among the best known and loved of the Michigan pier lights are the St. Joseph Inner and Outer Pier Lighthouses, which function in tandem as range lights. As with all range lights, they are located some distance apart and are meant to be seen one atop the other. Mariners on the lake who see them in perpendicular alignment may rest assured that they are sailing in safe water.

A much earlier lighthouse, built on the mainland in 1832, served St. Joseph until it was discontinued during the 1920s; it was eventually demolished. The St. Joseph Pier Lights, established in 1907, still stand. The forward, or front-range light, is a cylindrical structure. The one closest to shore, or rear-range light, is octagonal. An elevated walkway links the two towers, each of which retains its original Fresnel lens.

> *Travel information:* From U.S. Highway 31 in St. Joseph, follow Marina Drive south to Tiscornia Park. The park offers an excellent view of both lights. Visitors who want a close look can walk out on the pier.

INDIANA

■ MICHIGAN CITY LIGHT ■
Michigan City (1858)

Despite its name Michigan City is in Indiana, not Michigan. Located on the Lake Michigan shore just a few miles west of South Bend, it has been an important shipping point for the better part of two centuries. A lighthouse has served its busy harbor since 1837.

The city's first lighthouse, a simple brick-and-stone tower, was replaced by a more elaborate structure in 1858. Built with wood and brick at a cost of $8,000, it had a large central gable with a squat tower and lantern perched on the roof. At present the old lighthouse looks more like a schoolhouse or library building than a navigational aid. Out of service since 1904, when it was replaced by a nearby pier light, it was eventually handed over to the Michigan City Historical Society for use as a museum.

> *Travel information:* In Michigan City take Heisman Harbor Road to Washington Park and the Michigan City Lighthouse Museum. Among many other fascinating exhibits, visitors will find the station's original fifth-order Fresnel lens. Call (219) 872-6133.

■ MICHIGAN CITY EAST PIER LIGHT ■
Michigan City (1904)

The Michigan City East Pier Lighthouse has guided vessels since the early twentieth century. Built on a square concrete platform, the structure has a pyramidal roof. An octagonal tower thrusts through the roof, raising the focal plane of the light more than fifty feet above the lake waters. Like many similar pier lighthouses, this one is encased in steel to protect it from storms.

It is said that, during the 1920s, keeper Ralph Moore hurried his three daughters indoors whenever he saw a certain speedboat roaring through the channel. "Get in the house!" he shouted. "That damn fool is coming." The particular "damn fool" the keeper had in mind was none other than Al Capone, the Chicago gangster. Capone had a house on nearby Long Beach and reached it by boat rather than drive and chance an ambush by rival bad guys.

> *Travel information:* In Michigan City take Heisman Harbor Road to

Washington Park. The pier and its lighthouse can be reached from the parking area. The nearby Michigan City Lighthouse Museum contains exhibits and information on the pier light. Call (219) 872–6133.

ILLINOIS

■ CHICAGO HARBOR LIGHT ■
Chicago (1832 and 1893)

One of the earliest lighthouses on the Great Lakes was built at the mouth of the Chicago River in 1832. Even then, the city sprouting along the lakefront was showing signs of the unrestrained growth and spirit that would turn it into one of the world's great metropolises. As the city grew, a series of lighthouses, built both on the mainland and on piers out in the harbor, guided a tremendous volume of shipping to its wharves. Because the St. Lawrence Seaway makes Chicago a seaport, ships from every nation have docked here.

The Harbor Lighthouse seen here today originally stood on the mainland near the mouth of the river and the site of the city's first light tower—long since demolished. Built in 1893, the Harbor Lighthouse was given an especially fine third-order Fresnel lens, which had been intended for the **Point Loma Lighthouse** in Southern California. The lens had been a popular attraction of the Chicago Columbian Exposition. As a public-relations gesture at the end of the big show, lighthouse officials placed the lens in the recently completed Chicago tower instead. In 1917, just before the United States entered World War I, the forty-eight-foot brick-and-steel tower was moved to the end of a harbor breakwater.

Travel information: The lighthouse is closed to the public but can be seen from many points along the Chicago waterfront. Perhaps the best viewpoint is from the far end of the Navy Pier, which can be reached easily from Lakeshore Drive. The pier is also a good place to view the thirty-foot steel tower of the **Chicago Harbor Southeast Guidewall Lighthouse** (1938).

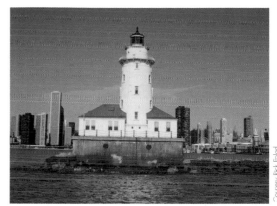

Chicago Harbor LIght

■ GROSSE POINT LIGHT ■
Evanston (1873)

Among the most beautiful buildings on the Great Lakes, the Grosse Point Lighthouse is in many ways a superlative structure. Its 113-foot tower is among the tallest on the lakes, and its second-order Fresnel lens is more powerful than that of any other lake lighthouse. The conical brick tower, painted light yellow and trimmed in dark red, is exceptionally graceful.

Although decommissioned by the Coast Guard in 1935, the Grosse Point Light continues to serve lake sailors as a private aid to navigation. Built during the 1870s for approximately $50,000, the station was meant to serve primarily as a coastal light. It was given a double-sized keeper's dwelling and several outbuildings to house the fog signal and other equipment. The tower bricks deteriorated over the years, and in 1914 the walls received a protective layer of concrete.

Travel information: Operated by the Evanston Parks Department as the key attraction of that city's lovely Lighthouse Park, the Grosse Point Lighthouse can be reached via Sheridan Road. The lighthouse and park are located near Central Avenue and the Evanston Art Museum. The grounds are open to the public daily. Call (847) 864–5181.

■ OLD SOUTHPORT (KENOSHA) LIGHT ■
Kenosha (1866)

Kenosha's Simmons Island Park is home to "Old" Southport Lighthouse, so desig-nated because it has been out of service for nearly a century. Built in 1866, just after the Civil War, the fifty-five-foot brick tower marked Kenosha Harbor for more than forty years. It was decommissioned in 1906 after construction of the Kenosha North Pier Lighthouse. The Kenosha County Historical Society recently restored the tower and adjacent dwelling. The light has been restored and now functions as a private aid to navigation.

> ***Travel information:*** In Kenosha follow Fiftieth Street to Simmons Island Park and then take Fourth Avenue and Simmons Island Road to the light-house. Just down the beach from the Old Southport Lighthouse is the **Kenosha North Pier Lighthouse** (1906), now used as part of a range light system. Accessible by foot, the pier lighthouse retains its original fourth-order Fresnel lens.

■ WIND POINT LIGHT ■
Racine (1866 and 1880)

Immediately after the Civil War, a pier light was built to guide ships into Racine Harbor. The beacon was never totally satisfactory, however, since Wind Point blocked the light from the view of mariners on vessels approaching from the north. To correct this problem, Congress appropriated $100,000 for construction of a true lighthouse on the point.

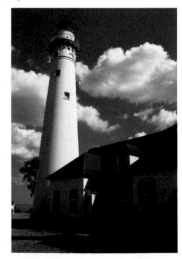

Begun in 1877 and completed three years later, the Wind Point Lighthouse was fitted with a pair of lenses. Its third-order Fresnel lens dis-played a flashing white light, while a smaller fifth-order lens marked the dangerous Racine Shoals with a red light. The station is now auto-mated, and its lenses have been replaced by an aeromarine beacon. The brick tower is 108 feet tall and attached by a passageway to its two-story dwelling.

> ***Travel information:*** From Route 32 south of Milwaukee, follow Three Mile Road and Lighthouse Drive to the station. The grounds are open to the public, but not the tower. The

town of Wind Point uses the lighthouse for offices.

From Racine's Lake Festival Park, visitors can see the forty-foot tower of the old **Racine North Breakwater Light** (1903) and the more recently constructed skeleton tower of the **Racine South Breakwater Light.** From Route 32 turn toward the lake on Fourth Street.

■ NORTH POINT LIGHT ■
Milwaukee (1855, 1888, and 1913)

Milwaukee's first lighthouse, built several years before the Civil War, served for more than thirty years before erosion undercut the structure. A second tower, erected alongside the first, was ready for service in 1888. These early towers were similar in design—octagonal and made of cast iron or steel.

The 1888 tower was only thirty-five feet tall, and within two decades, spreading tree limbs began to obscure its beacon. In 1912 lighthouse engineers came up with a novel way to solve this problem. Rather than build an entirely new tower, they constructed a broad octagonal base, about forty feet high, and then placed the original tower on top of it. In this way the overall height was raised to seventy-four feet.

The beacon helps mark the entrance to the Milwaukee River. The flashing light has a range of about twenty-one miles. The spacious keeper's dwelling, adjacent to the tower, is the original, dating from about 1855.

Travel information: The lighthouse is located in Lake Park, just off Wahl Avenue in Milwaukee. Follow Lincoln Memorial Drive to McKinley Park, then North Terrace to North Wahl.

Near downtown Milwaukee are the **Milwaukee Breakwater Lighthouse** (1926) and **Milwaukee Pierhead Lighthouse** (1906), which still employs a fifth-order Fresnel lens. The Pierhead Light can be reached by walking along the harbor pier reached via North Harbor, Polk, and East Erie Streets. The blocky Breakwater Lighthouse cannot be reached from land, but can be seen from the pier.

■ PORT WASHINGTON LIGHT ■
Port Washington (1860 and 1935)

Established shortly before the Civil War, the Old Port Washington Lighthouse dates from a time when the western shore of Lake Michigan was still partly wilderness. Shining from a bluff overlooking the lake, the light marked a busy little harbor a few miles north of Milwaukee. After nearly seventy-five years of service, the light was removed from the rooftop lantern at the original station and placed in a concrete tower at the end of a harbor breakwater. The wishbone-shaped breakwater tower remains an active aid to navigation, while the earlier lighthouse on the bluff now serves as a museum. The Port Washington Historical Society hopes to restore the old lighthouse to its original appearance.

Travel information: The first Port Washington Lighthouse—now a museum—is located at Johnson and Power Streets; call (262) 284-5305. The breakwater light can be seen from the Port Washington waterfront, but is best viewed from a boat. About 30 miles north of Port Washington is the **Sheboygan Breakwater Light** (1915), a conical, cast-iron tower that can be seen from Deland Park in downtown Sheboygan.

■ MANITOWOC BREAKWATER ■
Manitowoc (1840 and 1918)

Still an active port today, Manitowoc had its own lighthouse as early as 1840. The present breakwater lighthouse—a steel tower at the end of a long concrete pier—dates from 1918. For many years this light guided the hefty steamers that ferried railroad cars back and forth across Lake Michigan. Nowadays, it guides the automobile and passenger ferries that link the lake's Wisconsin shores with the Michigan port of Ludington.

Travel information: For a close-up view of the lighthouse, walk to the end of the breakwater on the north side of the Manitowoc Harbor. A more romantic view of the old tower can be had from the decks of the Lake Michigan ferry; call (800) 841-4243. While in Manitowoc, don't miss the Wisconsin Maritime Museum, where you'll find the fifth-order Fresnel lens that once graced the lantern room of the Manitowoc tower.

▪ RAWLEY POINT LIGHT ▪
Two Rivers (1854 and 1894)

A deadly shoal reaches nearly a mile from Rawley Point into Lake Michigan. After several tragic wrecks a light was finally placed on the point to warn ships of the danger.

Beaming from a small tower perched on the roof of the keeper's dwelling, it served well until 1894, when the current, soaring tower was completed. More than 110 feet tall, the present tower is a steel-skeleton structure with a central cylinder braced by eight legs. At the top is a three-level lantern complex equipped with an unusually powerful aeromarine beacon. Its light can be seen from twenty-eight miles away.

Travel information: The tower and adjacent two-and-one-half-story dwelling, now a Coast Guard residence, are closed to the public, but respectful visitors are welcome to walk the grounds. The station is surrounded by lush and beautiful Point Beach State Park, which offers camping, picnicking, hiking, and a wonderful opportunity to view the lighthouse. From Two Rivers follow County Road O and Sandy Bay Road to the park. For park information call (414) 794-7480.

Off Twenty-second and Jackson Streets in Two Rivers is the upper portion of the old **Two Rivers Pierhead Lighthouse** (1883). It stands adjacent to the Rogers Street Fishing Village Museum; call (920) 793–5905.

▪ KEWAUNEE PIERHEAD LIGHT ▪
Kewaunee (1891 and 1931)

A forty-three-foot square tower attached to a breakwater fog-signal building, the existing Kewaunee Pierhead Lighthouse has stood since 1931, near the height of

the Great Depression. An earlier tower had guided vessels in and out of Kewaunee's harbor since 1891. Still in use, the beacon is focused by the station's original fifth-order Fresnel lens.

Travel information: Located at the end of the pier on the north side of the Kewaunee River entrance, the lighthouse is difficult to reach from land and is best seen from a boat. A few miles to the north is the **Algoma Pierhead Light** (1932), a red conical steel tower at the end of a breakwater defining the Ahnapee River entrance near Algoma. The light, produced by a fifth-order Fresnel lens, remains in operation.

■ STURGEON BAY SHIP CANAL LIGHT ■
Sturgeon Bay (1899 and 1903)

Lighthouse Service engineers designed an experimental tower for the Sturgeon Bay Lighthouse, completed in 1899. Held erect by latticework buttresses, it proved unequal to the strong winds howling in off Lake Michigan and lasted only a few years into the new century. A new, ninety-eight-foot steel-cylinder tower replaced it in 1903. The station's third-order Fresnel lens remains in operation.

> *Travel information:* Located on an active Coast Guard station, the lighthouse is closed to the public. It can be photographed and enjoyed, however, from a nearby pier. The same pier offers a view of

the **Sturgeon Bay Ship Canal North Pierhead Lighthouse** (1882) with its metal catwalk, octagonal lantern, and striking red roof. In Sturgeon Bay follow Canal Drive to Lake Forest Park Road and park near the station entrance.

■ BAILEYS HARBOR REAR RANGE LIGHT ■
Baileys Harbor (1870)

To guide vessels into Baileys Harbor, near the far end of the peninsula that forms Door County, Wisconsin, the government established a pair of range lights in 1870. These lights replaced an older, single-lens lighthouse located on a small island far out in the harbor. The front-range light was housed in a squat, twenty-one-foot wooden tower down beside the lake. The rear-range light shone from a gablelike extension on the roof of a clapboard dwelling about one thousand feet from the

water. Automated in 1930, the station was afterward cared for by Lutheran ministers, who used the dwelling as a parsonage right up until the lights were discontinued in the 1960s.

> *Travel information:* Although out of service for many years, the Baileys Harbor Range Lighthouses remain in excellent condition. From Highway 57 in Baileys Harbor, take Ridge Drive. The schoolhouselike rear-range lighthouse stands on the right. The **Baileys Harbor Front Range Lighthouse** (1870), which looks much like

a big chess pawn, is located about one-fifth of a mile away. The ruins of **Old Baileys Harbor Lighthouse** (1851) are located on a privately owned island out in the harbor. The old tower, with its tall birdcage-style lantern, can be seen from the shore near the far end of Ridge Drive.

■ CANA ISLAND LIGHT ■
Baileys Harbor (1870)

On a clear night the impressive Cana Island Lighthouse throws its beam seventeen

miles out into Lake Michigan. Established in 1870, the light marks the northern approaches to Baileys Harbor. To help the eighty-six-foot tower and adjacent one-and-a-half-story dwelling withstand the lake's prodigious storms, construction crews built them with brick. The light yellow bricks, however, weathered more rapidly than had been expected, and after a few decades, the tower had begun to crumble. To protect it lighthouse officials had it encased in a protective cocoon made of individual iron plates riveted together. The station's original third-order Fresnel lens remains in operation.

> *Travel information:* With its pristine island setting, the Cana Island station is among the most beautiful lighthouses in America. Take County Road Q north from Baileys Harbor, then follow Cana Island Road and Cana Cove Road to the lighthouse. The Door County Maritime Museum leases the station from the U.S. Coast Guard and it is open to the public until 5:00 P.M. daily during warm weather months. Call (920) 743-5958.

■ POTOWATOMI LIGHT ■
Gills Rock (1836 and 1858)

A chain of rock-strewn islands forms a lakeward extension of the long, daggerlike peninsula of Door County. The jagged shores of these islands and the shoals that lie between them have claimed countless vessels. To guide ships safely around these formidable obstacles, the government established on Rock Island, at the end of the chain, one of the first light stations in the western Great Lakes. Completed in 1836, the original Potowatomi Lighthouse—named for an Indian tribe—served until 1858, when a hurricanelike storm swept it into the lake. Given massive walls of stone, the combination keeper's residence and light tower that replaced it still stands. Unfortunately, the lantern was removed after the station was discontinued during the 1920s. The Wisconsin Historical Society plans to restore the structure.

Travel information: The lighthouse is located in Wisconsin's Rock Island State Park. Visitors must take a ferry from Northport, at the northern end of Highway 42, to Washington Island and then a second ferry to Rock Island. Contact Washington Island Ferry, Washington Island, WI 54246; (920) 847–2546 or (800) 223–2094. The ferry provides excellent views of the **Plum Island Range Lighthouse** (1897), a white skeleton tower, and the **Pilot Island Lighthouse** (1858), a historic brick combination tower and dwelling. Occasional tours of the Potowatomi Lighthouse are offered by the Friends of Rock Island; (715) 823–6873.

▪ EAGLE BLUFF LIGHT ▪
Ephraim (1868)

Marking a safe channel from Lake Michigan into Green Bay, the Eagle Bluff Light first shone in 1868, the same year that U. S. Grant was elected president. Its square, forty-three-foot brick tower was set at a diagonal into the side of the one-and-a-half-story dwelling. This made it easier for keepers to reach the tower when cold winds blew in off the lake. Ironically, there has been no full-time keeper here since 1909, as this was among the first American lighthouses to be automated. Still active, the lighthouse has done its work alone now for almost nine decades.

The old keeper's residence, which has been attractively restored, is used as a museum by the Door County Historical Society. The lighthouse and museum are among the many attractions of Peninsula State Park, which also offers hiking, fishing, swimming, and golf.

Travel information: Follow Highway 42 to Fish Creek and the entrance to Peninsula State Park. Once inside the park, follow Shore Drive for about 4 miles to the lighthouse; call the Door County Historical Society at (920) 743–5958. Several miles to the west is the boarded-up **Chambers Island Lighthouse** (1868). Replaced by a steel tower in 1961, the octagonal brick tower and attached gabled dwelling have been boarded up and abandoned. This historic lighthouse can be seen only from the water.

▪ SHERWOOD POINT LIGHT ▪
Sturgeon Bay (1883)

Completed in 1883, the square, thirty-five-foot brick tower is attached to its residence. Although the Coast Guard still uses the handsome, though small, keeper's dwelling as a residence, the light is automated. This was the last lighthouse on the

Great Lakes with a full-time staff, and it was not automated until 1983. The station retains its fourth-order Fresnel lens, which produces a light seen from up to eighteen miles away. A small, pyramidal fog-signal building stands near the tower.

Travel information: As part of an active Coast Guard station, the lighthouse is off-limits to the public. It is best viewed from the water. Built on a caisson in open water across the bay is the **Pestigo Reef Lighthouse** (1934).

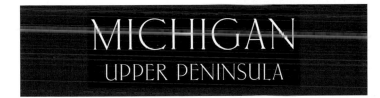

MICHIGAN
UPPER PENINSULA

■ SAND POINT LIGHT ■
Escanaba (1868)

Vessels approaching Escanaba must take care to avoid Sand Point and a cluster of nearby shoals. To warn mariners away from these dangers, the government established a lighthouse on Sand Point in 1868. A fixed red light shone from the square brick tower, beaming toward the lake from just over forty feet above the water.

The Coast Guard discontinued the light in 1939, after channel dredging rendered it obsolete. Coast Guard personnel used the building as a residence until 1985, when it was turned over to the Delta County Historical Society. Since then, the society has restored the Sand Point Lighthouse to its original appearance. The beacon, focused by a fourth-order Fresnel lens, is once again operational.

Travel information: Located in Ludington Park, just off U.S. Highways 2 and 41, the lighthouse is now a museum; call (906) 786-3763.

■ SEUL CHOIX POINT LIGHT ■
Gulliver (1895)

One of only a few safe harbors on the north shore of Lake Michigan, Seul Choix was given its name, meaning "only choice," by early French explorers. Seul Choix Point stands guard over this inviting harbor. Even so, it did not receive a lighthouse until late in the nine-teenth century. Congress finally appropriated money for the project in 1886, but partly because of its remote location, the lighthouse was not completed and operational until 1895.

The conical brick tower, seventy feet tall, was topped by a ten-sided, cast-iron lantern, giving its third-order Fresnel lens a focal plane just over eighty feet above the lake. When the Coast Guard automated the lighthouse, the Fresnel lens was removed and replaced by an airport-style beacon, visible from about seven-teen miles out in the lake.

The two-story brick keeper's dwelling still stands and is attached to the tower by an enclosed brick passageway. Although the structure and the grounds are now the property of the state of Michigan, this is still an operating light station.

Travel information: Turn off U.S. Highway 2 at Gulliver and follow Port Inland Road and then CR–431 to the lighthouse. The tower and dwelling are closed to the public, but visitors are welcome to walk the grounds. There is a small, but worthy, museum in the old fog-signal building. Contact the Gulliver Historical Society at R.R. 1, Box 79, Gulliver, MI 49840; (906) 283–3183.

■ POINT IROQUOIS LIGHT ■
Brimley (1855 and 1871)

Point Iroquois gets its name from a massacre that took place here in 1662. A war party sent westward by the Iroquois Confederation was set upon and slaughtered on this point by an army of Ojibwas.

Ships passing by the point are also in danger of ambush. On their port side are the reefs near Gros Cap in Canada, while on their starboard side are the ship-killing rocks near Point Iroquois. The St. Marys River became a heavily trafficked thor-oughfare after the Soo Locks connected Superior to the other lakes in 1855, and since that time many vessels have been lost while approaching the river. Often, an otherwise minor navigational error can be fatal here.

To help captains enter the river safely, a small lighthouse was built on Point Iroquois not long after the locks opened. Fitted with a sixth-order Fresnel lens, this modest wooden structure served until 1871, when it was replaced by an impressive sixty-five-foot brick tower and dwelling that still stand today.

Its beacon discontinued in 1965, the lighthouse is now part of the Hiawatha National Forest. The handsome structures are maintained by the Bay Mills–Brimley Historical Research Society, which operates a museum and gift shop here.

Travel information:
From I-75 take Highway 28 for about 8 miles to the town of Brimley. Then follow Six Mile Road and Lakeshore Drive to the lighthouse. Original Lighthouse Service fixtures and nineteenth-century furnishings are on display. Contact the Point Iroquois Lighthouse and Maritime Museum, Sault Ste. Marie Ranger Office, 4000 I-75 Business Spur, Sault Ste. Marie, MI 49783; (906) 437-5272.

■ WHITEFISH POINT LIGHT ■
Whitefish Point (1848 and 1861)

On the evening of November 16, 1975, the huge iron-ore freighter *Edmund Fitzgerald* plowed through a powerful storm, heading for the relatively safe waters just beyond Whitefish Point. She never made it. The enormous ship, longer than two football fields, disappeared, along with twenty-nine crewmen, a few miles north of the point. The sinking of the *Edmund Fitzgerald* gave rise to a legend and a popular ballad by Gordon Lightfoot.

Ironically, on the night the "Big Fitz" met her end, the lighthouse on Whitefish Point was out of service. The storm had cut the power supply to the station. On thousands of other nights, however—almost continuously since 1848—mariners have been able to rely on the guidance of the station's beacon.

Recognizing the strategic nature of the point and its importance to shipping, the government established a light station here in 1848. Its masonry tower gave way to an iron-skeleton structure shortly before the Civil War.

Braced by a network of iron supports, the tower's central steel cylinder is more than eighty feet tall and topped by a metal lantern. The open design was intended to take stress off the building during high winds and storms like the one that sank the *Fitzgerald*.

Automated in 1970, the station now serves as home to the Great Lakes Shipwreck Museum. Here imaginative visitors can relive the last moments of the *Fitz* and many other ill-fated ships claimed forever by the lakes.

> *Travel information:* The lighthouse and museum, housed in the former keeper's residence, can be reached from the Mackinac Bridge by taking I-75 north to M-123 and the town of Paradise. From Paradise follow Whitefish Point Road to Whitefish Point. Call (888) 397-3747 or (800) 635-1742. The museum maintains an informative Web site: www. shipwreckmuseum.com.

■ CRISP POINT LIGHT ■
West of Paradise (1904)

Veteran of nearly a century of service to mariners, the Crisp Point Lighthouse on Michigan's sparsely settled Upper Peninsula very nearly succumbed to the fate of far too many historic light towers. More or less abandoned by the government in 1989, it was all but destroyed by weather and erosion. Over the last decade, however, an idealistic couple, Don and Nellie Ross, have made saving the tower a personal crusade, and they have attained notable

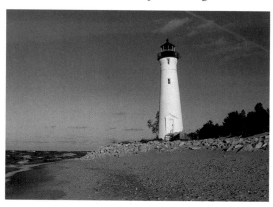

success. The advance of Lake Superior has been checked by a stone breakwater, and the lighthouse is slowly but surely being restored.

> *Travel information:* Located 18 miles from the main road, a trip to Crisp Point is something of an adventure, but, for those prepared to make the effort, a worthwhile one. Contact the Crisp Point Lighthouse Society, P.O. Box 229, Paradise, MI 49768; (906) 492-3206.

■ AU SABLE POINT LIGHT ■
Grand Marais (1874)

For many years sailors dreaded the eighty miles of dark shoreline that stretched westward from Whitefish Point. Unmarked by any navigational light, these dangerous shores claimed dozens of ships. To fill the gap and save lives, a lighthouse was placed on Au Sable Point in 1874.

The eighty-seven-foot brick tower was built on a rise, placing the beacon 107 feet above the surface of the lake. Its third-order Fresnel lens displayed a fixed white light. The attached, two-story dwelling was spacious, but the keepers who lived in it knew theirs was one of the most remote light stations in America. The nearest town, Grand Marais, lay more than twelve miles away, and there was no road. Keepers either hiked in or came by boat.

Perhaps because of its isolation, the Coast Guard automated the station in 1958, turning the property and buildings over to the National Park Service for inclusion in Pictured Rocks National Lakeshore.

Travel Information: Just as keepers once did, visitors today must walk to this lighthouse, located in Pictured Rocks National Lakeshore on the Michigan Upper Peninsula. From Highway 28 take Highway 77 north for about 25 miles to Grand Marais. Then follow the gravel-surfaced Alger County Road H–58 for another 12 miles to the Hurricane Campground. There a trail provides access to the shore and the lighthouse. Write to Pictured Rocks National Lakeshore, P.O. Box 40, Munising, MI 49862 or call (906) 387–3700.

■ MUNISING RANGE LIGHTS ■
Munising (1908)

For nearly a century the narrow, safe channel through Munising Bay has been marked by two extraordinary lighthouses. Unlike most range light structures, where the the rear tower is taller, here the forward tower is by far the taller and more impressive of the two. The fifty-foot steel front-range tower stands near the lakeshore, while the squat rear-range tower is located on a hillside some distance away. At night, both make their presence known with locomotive-style headlamps.

Travel information: The Munising Front Range tower can be found just west of town off Route 28. The rear-range tower is a few blocks away at the end of Hemlock Street.

Munising Rear Range

■ MARQUETTE HARBOR LIGHT ■
(1853 and 1866)

With the discovery of copper and iron in the mountains of the Michigan Upper Peninsula, Marquette became an important port. A lighthouse built here in 1853 guided ships into the city's harbor. Of poor construction quality, however, it lasted only a few years. The square masonry tower that replaced it in 1866 proved very much more durable and still serves to this day. A fourth-order classic lens at one time shone from atop the forty-foot tower, but an automated aeromarine beacon has taken its place.

Travel information: From U.S. Highway 41 in Marquette, follow Lake Street to the lighthouse. The tower is located on an active Coast Guard station. The nearby Marquette Maritime Museum offers occasional guided tours of the lighthouse; call (906) 226-2006.

■ BIG BAY LIGHT ■
Big Bay (1896)

Many ships have foundered in the treacherous waters just to the north of the famed Huron Mountains. To help mariners find their way safely, the government established a major light at Big Bay in 1896. It shone from a square brick tower attached to a two-story dwelling. The light was automated shortly before World War II, and in 1961 it was moved to a nearby steel-skeleton tower. The old lighthouse was then converted for use as a private residence and later as a bed-and-breakfast inn.

Travel information: The inn is located on Lighthouse Road, about 3 miles north of Big Bay. Write to Big Bay Point Lighthouse, 3 Lighthouse Road, Big Bay, MI 49808 or call (906) 345-9957.

■ SAND HILLS LIGHT ■
Near Eagle River (1919)

An imposing brick edifice with a square tower, the Sand Hills Lighthouse reflects the modernist style prevalent during the early twentieth century. The design is similar to

that of Alaska's Scotch Cap Lighthouse, which was destroyed by a tsunami during the 1940s (see page 221). Decommissioned by the Coast Guard during the 1950s, the building stood empty for decades, its interior all but gutted by time. Its walls remained solid, however, and a local lighthouse lover eventually bought the property. Handsomely restored, it is now an attractive lakeside inn.

> **Travel information:** Located off Five Mile Point Road to the west of Highway 41, the Sand Hills Lighthouse Inn has eight delightful guest rooms. Reservations should be made far in advance; call (906) 337–1744.

■ COPPER HARBOR LIGHT ■
(1849 and 1869)

Winters on Michigan's Upper Peninsula are notoriously severe, but the weather did not deter the rapid development of mining when deposits of copper were found during the 1840s. The richest copper veins were located on the Keweenaw Peninsula, which thrusts to the northeast toward the center of Lake Superior. Ship

traffic in and out of Copper Harbor expanded rapidly to carry the ore to markets in the east. Shippers and government officials soon saw the need for a lighthouse to guide the big freighters in and out of the harbor.

A stone tower with detached dwelling, it was

located on a point near the harbor entrance. Upgraded and given a Fresnel lens in 1856, it was replaced with an entirely new structure shortly after the Civil War. A square stone tower with a small attached dwelling, this second Copper Harbor Light-house still stands, although its duties have been taken over by a beacon displayed from a nearby skeleton tower.

Travel information: The town of Copper Harbor is located at the far northern end of Route 26. The lighthouse is now part of Fort Wilkins State Park. It is best reached by water from Copper Harbor Municipal Marina; call (906) 289-4215. Also in the area is the wooden **Copper Harbor Rear Range Lighthouse** (1869). Far to the east of Copper Harbor, off the tip of the Keweenaw Peninsula, is the **Manitou Island Lighthouse** (1861). Its light, produced by a third-order Fresnel lens, remains active.

■ EAGLE HARBOR LIGHT ■
Eagle Harbor (1851 and 1871)

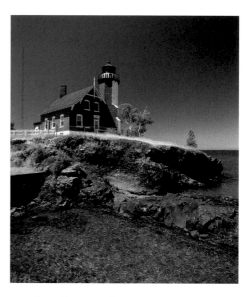

Like Copper Harbor to the east, Eagle Harbor became a bustling ore-shipping point during the copper-and-iron boom years of the nineteenth and early twentieth centuries. From 1851 onward this important Keweenaw Peninsula port was marked by a key navigational light. During its first few years of service, the station was equipped with an outmoded lamp and reflector optic but received a Fresnel lens in 1857.

Lake Superior's notorious weather took a heavy toll on the lighthouse, and it lasted less than twenty years. The forty-foot octagonal tower and attached dwelling seen here today date from 1871. For many years the tower had a fourth-order Fresnel lens, but it was replaced by a modern aerobeacon in 1968, shortly before the station was automated.

Travel information: Follow Route 26 down the Keweenaw Peninsula and turn left toward the lake just before entering Eagle Harbor. The Keweenaw Historical Society, which has restored the station to its early-twentieth-century appearance, maintains a nautical museum in one of the outer buildings. Call (906) 289-4990.

WISCONSIN
LAKE SUPERIOR

■ APOSTLE ISLANDS LIGHTS
APOSTLE ISLANDS NATIONAL LAKESHORE ■

Michigan Island Light (1857 and 1930); Raspberry Island Light
(1863); Outer Island Light (1874); Sand Island Light (1881);
Devils Island Light (1891); La Pointe Light (1858 and 1895)

Built in 1857, Michigan Island Lighthouse is the oldest of the six light stations in the Apostle Islands. Like many other lights in the upper Midwest, this one went into operation not long after the Soo Locks opened Lake Superior to shipping from the other lakes. The whitewashed tower and dwelling, with pitched roof and dormers, give this station the look of a New

England lighthouse.

The Michigan Island Light guided vessels along the eastern side of the Apostles for more than seventy years before its duties were taken over in 1930 by a skeleton-style tower moved here from Schooner Ledge in Maine. The 102-foot tower consists of a central steel cylinder braced by six legs. The light remains active and can be seen from up to sixteen miles out in Lake Superior.

Originally, the Michigan Island Light station had been intended for nearby Long Island. Once the mistake became apparent, officials commissioned a lighthouse for the correct location. Completed in 1858, the wood-frame **La Pointe Lighthouse** on Long Island served until 1895, when it was replaced by a steel-skeleton tower similar to the one on Michigan Island.

In addition to the Michigan Island and La Pointe Lighthouses, the Apostle Islands National Lakeshore in Wisconsin can boast five other historic light towers including the **Raspberry Island Lighthouse** (1863), **Outer Island Lighthouse** (1874), **Sand Island Lighthouse** (1881), and **Devils Island Lighthouse** (1891). Together, these excellently maintained structures comprise one of the nation's finest collections of lighthouses and form what is, in effect, an outdoor nautical/lighthouse museum.

Travel information: Visitors should stop first at the lakeshore headquarters, located in the Old Courthouse in Bayfield, Wisconsin. Write to Apostle Islands Lakeshore, Chief of Interpretation, Route 1, P.O. Box 4, Bayfield, WI 54814; (715) 779-3398. Island cruises are available during warm-weather months; call (715) 779-3925 or (800) 323-7619.

Sand Island Lighthouse

Raspberry Island Lighthouse

(left) Devils Island Lighthouse, (above) Outer Island Lighthouse

MINNESOTA

■ DULUTH BREAKWATER LIGHTS ■
Duluth (1901)

Built just after the turn of the twentieth century, these two lighthouses mark the breakwaters that define the channel connecting the Duluth Inner Harbor with Lake Superior. The **South Breakwater Outer Lighthouse** consists of a thirty-five-foot tower rising from the corner of a squat brick fog-signal building. Its fourth-order Fresnel lens remains in service.

Erected at the same time was the **South Breakwater Inner Lighthouse,** a steel-cylinder tower with supporting skeleton framework. This lighthouse, somewhat shorter than its neighbor, displays a flashing light produced by a fourth-order bull's-eye lens.

The **Duluth North Breakwater Lighthouse** entered service during the spring of 1910. Its metal frame is enclosed by riveted steel plates. The lantern atop its thirty-seven-foot tower contains a fifth-order Fresnel lens.

Travel information: From I-35 take the Highway 61 exit and follow signs to the Duluth waterfront area and Canal Park. The park is located beside the famous Aerial Bridge, only a few blocks from downtown Duluth. The lighthouses are on piers beside the ship canal. Adjacent to the canal and near the bridge is Canal Park Maritime Museum, which contains many fascinating exhibits on the history of Lake Superior and its lighthouses; call (218) 727-2497.

▪ TWO HARBORS LIGHT ▪

Two Harbors (1892)

Built in 1892 to guide iron-ore freighters and other vessels to the busy loading docks nearby, the Two Harbors Lighthouse remains an active aid to navigation. The light emanates from a fifty-foot square tower set into the southwest corner of a two-story brick dwelling. Situated on a grassy knoll, the tower places the focal plane of its light almost eighty feet above the lake surface.

The lantern room once contained a fourth-order Fresnel lens, but it was replaced with a matched pair of aeromarine beacons in 1970. The Coast Guard automated the station in 1981 and later turned it over to the Lake County Historical Society for use as a museum.

Travel information: From Highway 61 turn toward the lake on First Street, then right onto First Avenue and left onto Third Street. A parking area at the end of Third Street provides access to the lighthouse and its excellent museum. Visitors will find a broad array of maritime and lighthouse exhibits; call (218) 834-4898. Several guest rooms are available at the Lighthouse; call (888) 832-5606. Nearby is the **Two Harbors East Breakwater Lighthouse,** a spindly metal structure with a small lantern room only twenty-five feet above the water.

▪ SPLIT ROCK LIGHT ▪

Two Harbors (1910)

An octagonal, yellow-brick structure, the Split Rock tower is only fifty-four feet tall, but the cliff beneath it soars more than 120 feet above the lake. This makes Split Rock, with its focal plane nearly 170 feet above the water, one of the loftiest lighthouses on the Great Lakes. It also makes this one of the most spectacular and frequently photographed lighthouses in America—or the world. Ironically, Split Rock is no longer an active aid to navigation, but rather a highly popular maritime museum.

Built in 1910, the lighthouse owes its existence to a hurricanelike blizzard that struck the Great Lakes in November 1905. This mighty storm drove more than thirty sizable ore boats and freighters onto Lake Superior's rocky shores. The calamity

(Facing page) Split Rock Lighthouse

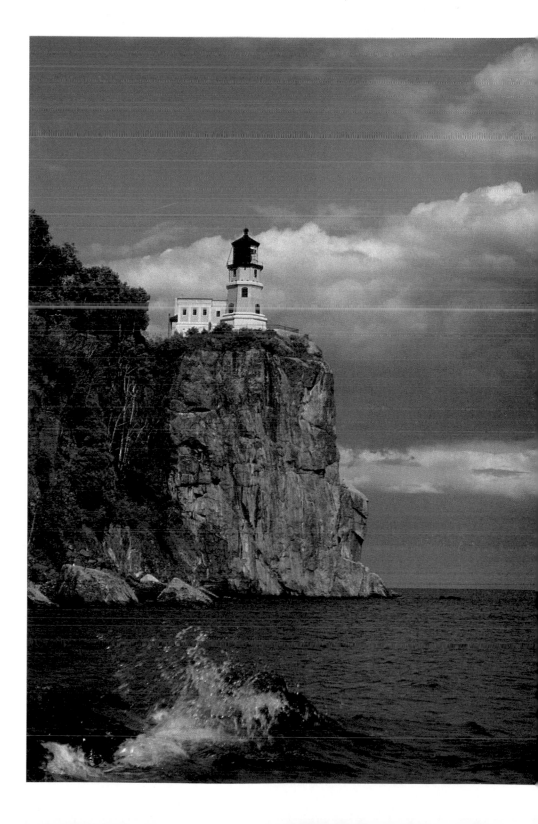

convinced officials that the system of navigation aids on Lake Superior must be improved. The most important improvement undertaken was construction of a lighthouse on Split Rock near where the freighter *William Edenborn* had met its end during the storm. In all, the project cost taxpayers some $72,000.

The station's flashing light, seen from up to twenty-two miles out in the lake, was produced by a bivalve-style Fresnel lens—still in place—that looks something like a huge clamshell. It served until 1969, when the Coast Guard decommissioned the lighthouse and handed it over to the state of Minnesota for use as a park and museum.

> *Travel information:* The Split Rock Park and Lighthouse are located about 20 miles northeast of Two Harbors on Highway 61. Open year-round, the park offers a fascinating history center as well as camping facilities, hiking trails, and picnicking areas. The lighthouse is open mid-May through mid-September. Contact Split Rock Lighthouse Park at 3755 Split Rock Lighthouse Road, Two Harbors, MN 55616; (218) 226–6372.

■ GRAND MARAIS LIGHT ■
Grand Marais (1885 and 1922)

This four-legged steel structure, which stands thirty-five feet above the lake, marks the end of the Grand Marais breakwater. In addition to warning mariners away from the low breakwater, it guides vessels into the town's harbor. Built in 1922, the relatively diminutive existing light replaced the larger tower that had stood on the shore since 1885. The light, produced by a classic lens, can be seen from up to sixteen miles away.

Travel information: Follow Highway 61 to Grand Marais, near the far northeastern corner of Minnesota. The lighthouse stands at the end of the town's primary breakwater. Contact the Cook County Historical at (218) 387-9131.

MICHIGAN
ISLE ROYALE

■ ROCK OF AGES LIGHT ■
Near Isle Royale (1908)

Built in 1908 on an open water caisson atop a notoriously dangerous shoal, the Rock of Ages Lighthouse was one of the most isolated manned light stations in America, if not the world. Keepers had to sail more than fifty miles across the often stormy waters of Lake Superior to spend a day in town, see a doctor, visit friends, or pick up food and supplies. For much of the year, the five-level, 130-foot-tall steel tower was their entire world.

In 1933 keepers had unexpected company when the freighter *George Cox* slammed into a nearby reef and sank. Rescued by the keeper and his assistant from the frigid waters of the lake, 125 survivors huddled in the lighthouse. They sat one atop the other on the tower's staircase until a ship arrived to take them to shore.

Anyone stranded on the rock nowadays would find nobody at home. The lighthouse has been automated since 1978, much to the relief, no doubt, of the lonely keepers. Following automation, the station lost its second-order classic lens—at one time the most powerful optic on the Great Lakes. A modern, 700,000-candlepower beacon shines here today.

Travel information: The Rock of Ages Lighthouse is, of course, closed to the public. It can sometimes be seen from the decks of ferries approaching Isle Royale (see page 284).

■ ROCK HARBOR LIGHT ■
Isle Royale (1855)

Now a pristine wilderness visited primarily by backpackers and outdoor enthusiasts, Isle Royale was, in the past, a thriving mining center. The discovery of copper here during the late 1840s led to construction of the Rock Harbor Lighthouse in 1855 to guide ore freighters to the island. The station consisted of a fifty-foot brick tower with attached stone dwelling.

The Isle Royale copper veins played out within a few years, and by the late 1870s, mining ceased altogether. This made the Rock Harbor Light unnecessary, and it was closed permanently in 1878. The tower and dwelling still stand.

The work of guiding vessels and visitors to Isle Royale is handled nowadays by **Isle Royale Lighthouse,** located on a barren rock near the entrance to Siskit Bay. The stone tower, com-

Passage Island Lighthouse

pleted in 1875, still displays its white light, produced by a fourth-order Fresnel lens. Also still in operation is the **Passage Island Lighthouse** (1882), which marks the channel just off the northeastern tip of Isle Royale.

Travel information: For nature lovers—and lighthouse aficionados as well—a visit to Isle Royale National Park can be the experience of a lifetime. As many travelers can attest, however, reaching Isle Royale is no easy task. Usually, it requires a lengthy ferry ride from Copper Harbor or other departure points on the Michigan Upper Peninsula, and visitors must have prior reservations for camping or accommodations on the island. Contact Isle Royale National Park, 87 North Ripley Street, Houghton, MI 49931; (906) 482-0984 or (906) 487-7153.

Isle Royale Lighthouse

Rock Harbor Lighthouse

INDEX

ABOUT THE AUTHORS

BRUCE ROBERTS and his wife, Cheryl, who helped with the research for this book, live on North Carolina's Outer Banks, not far from the Cape Lookout Lighthouse. He and Cheryl founded the Outer Banks Lighthouse Society in 1994. In 2000 they received the "Keeper of the Light" award from the American Lighthouse Foundation for their work in lighthouse preservation on the Outer Banks. For many years Bruce was Senior Travel Photographer for *Southern Living* magazine. He is the recipient of many photography awards, and some of his photos are in the permanent collection of the Smithsonian Institution.

RAY JONES is a freelance writer and publishing consultant living in Monterey, California. He began his writing career working as a reporter for weekly newspapers in Texas. He has served as an editor for Time-Life Books, as founding editor of *Albuquerque Living* magazine, as a senior editor and writing coach at *Southern Living* magazine, and as founder and publisher of Country Roads Press. Ray grew up in Macon, Georgia, where he was inspired by the writing of Ernest Hemingway and William Faulkner.